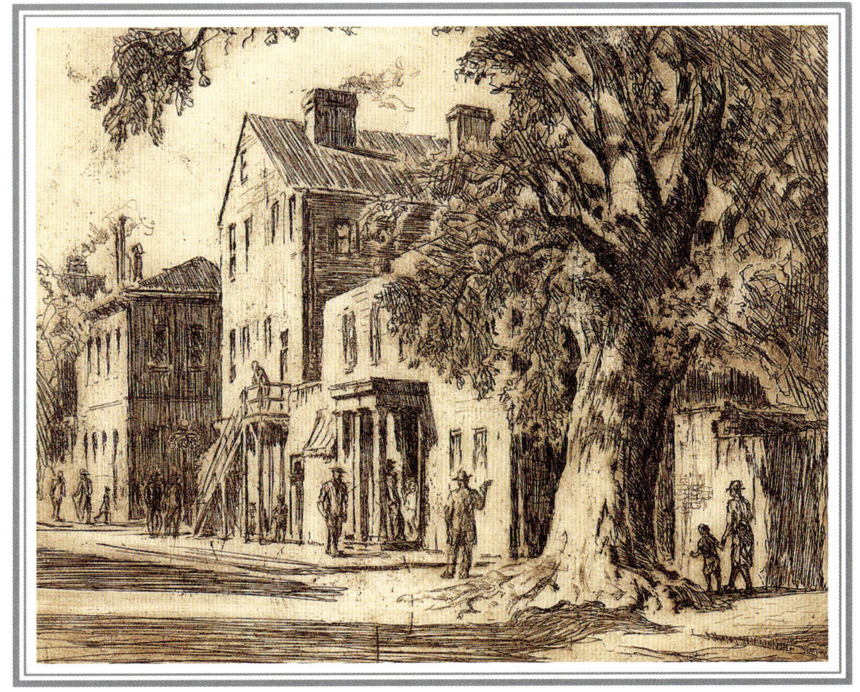

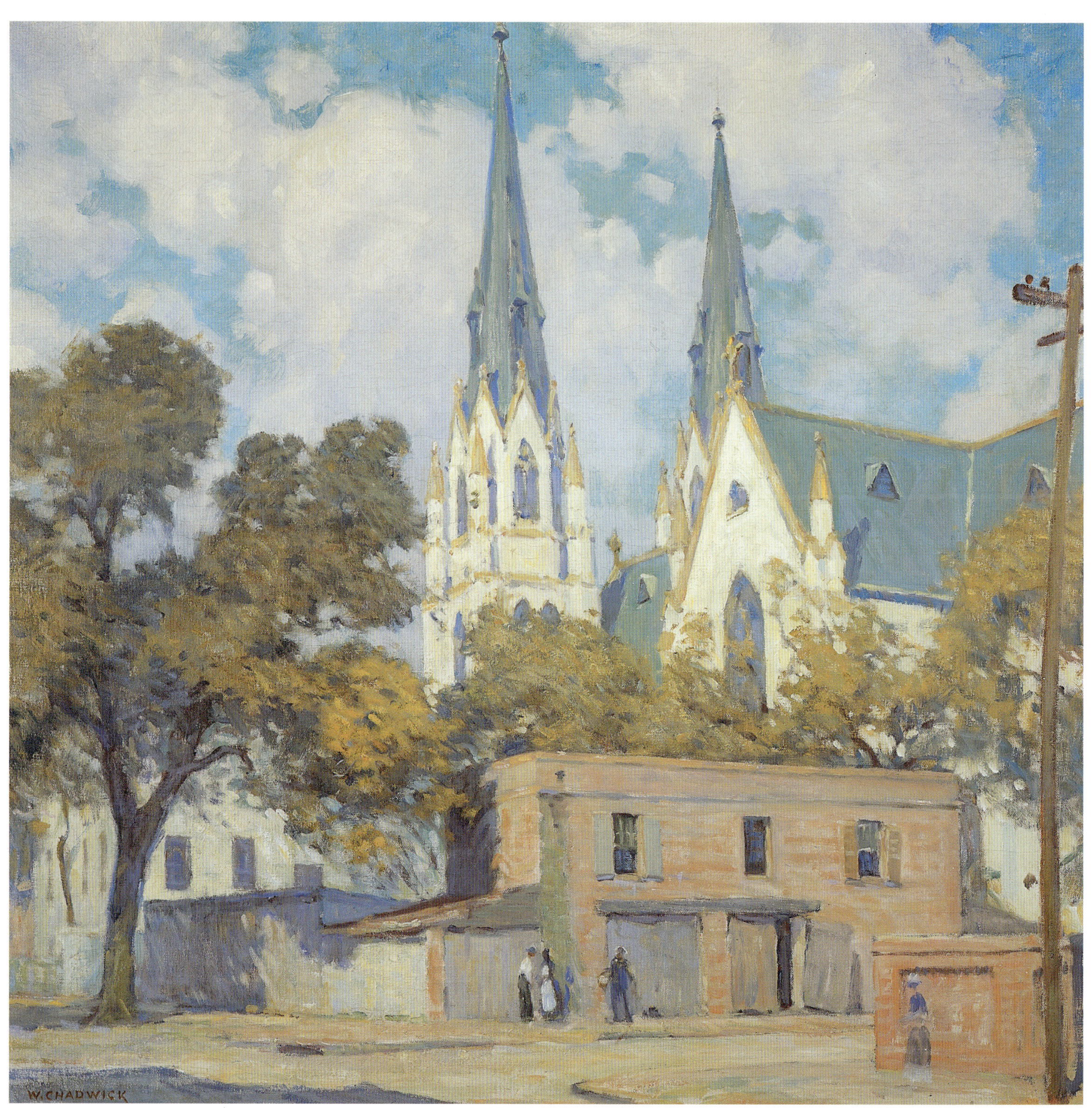
W. CHADWICK

Looking Back

Art in Savannah 1900–1960

Pamela D. King

Harry H. DeLorme, Jr.

Telfair Museum of Art

Savannah, Georgia

Exhibition dates: July 16-September 15, 1996

Editor: Norma J. Roberts

Authors:
J.A. Jennifer Ackerman
D.B. Deanne Beausoleil
C.L.B. Cynda L. Benson
F.S.C. Feay Shellman Coleman
H.H.D. Harry H. DeLorme, Jr.
K.L.H. Kristine L. Holzbach
P.D.K. Pamela D. King
D.L. Diane Lesko
S.P.M. Steven P. Mosch
C.S. Craig Stevens

Designed by Van Jones Martin.
Production assistance and type setting by Savannah Color Separations,
David Kaminsky and Jo Morrell.
Printed in Hong Kong through PrintNet, San Francisco, California.

Dimensions are given in inches (and centimeters); height precedes width, precedes depth.

Partial support of the Telfair's annual operating fund has been provided by the Georgia Council for the Arts through the appropriations of the Georgia General Assembly; and by Chatham County.

Front cover and frontispiece: William Chadwick, Church in Summer, c. 1925–26
Oil on canvas, Private Collection

Back cover: Ulysses Davis, Mary on Donkey, n.d.
Wood, Beach Institute African American Cultural Center

Half-title page: Christopher A. D. Murphy, Gnarled Oak, c. 1925–35
Etching on paper, Collection of Mr. and Mrs. Leopold Adler II

Library of Congress Catalog Card Number: 96-61004
ISBN 0-933075-02-2

Looking Back: Art in Savannah 1900–1960
Lenders to the Exhibition

The Acacia Collection of African-Americana
Ben N. Adams
Mr. and Mrs. Leopold Adler II
Beach Institute African American Cultural Center
H. Paul Blatner
Mrs. Grace Silva Cabaniss
Mr. and Mrs. John E. Cay III
Center for Creative Photography, The University of Arizona
Cheekwood Museum of Art
The Columbus Museum, Columbus, Georgia
Comer House Collection
Virginia and John Duncan
Margaret Dodd Funderburk
Reuben Gambrell
Mr. and Mrs. Robert S. Glenn
Mr. and Mrs. Harvey Granger, Jr.
Greenville County Museum of Art
William Halsey
Steven and Susan Hirsch; Courtesy of Conner-Rosenkranz, New York
Hunter, Maclean, Exley and Dunn
Mr. and Mrs. Robert S. Jepson, Jr.
Myrtle Jones
Joslyn Art Museum, Omaha, Nebraska
Arthur B. Kouwenhoven, Jr.
Thomas H. Lee and Ann Tenenbaum Collection
Library of Congress, Prints and Photographs Division
Milton Mazo, M.D.
Corrie McCallum
Ms. Fran McDonald
Francis D. McNairy
Mrs. Martha A. McNeil
Barbara Belcher Mericle
Mr. and Mrs. Richard Meyer III
Mr. and Mrs. David E. Miller, Jr.
The Montclair Art Museum
Morris Museum of Art, Augusta, Georgia
The Family of Mary Lane Morrison
Museum of Arts and Sciences, Macon, Georgia
The Nelson-Atkins Museum of Art, Kansas City, Missouri
Augusta Oelschig
Dr. and Mrs. C. Lamont Osteen
Mrs. Louise Lautier Owens
The Phillips Collection, Washington, D.C.
Private Collection
Mary Barron Saunders, Joanna, South Carolina
City of Savannah
Savannah State College
The Schoen Collection, New Orleans, Louisiana
Mr. Vince Sikorski
Mr. and Mrs. W. Lucas Simons
Ronald J. Strahan
Richard and Kay Tarr, Greenwood, South Carolina
Estate of John W. Taylor; Courtesy of Conner-Rosenkranz, New York
Rita Trotz
Unitarian Universalist Church, Savannah, Georgia
Catharine and Gordon Varnedoe
Wichita Art Museum, Wichita, Kansas

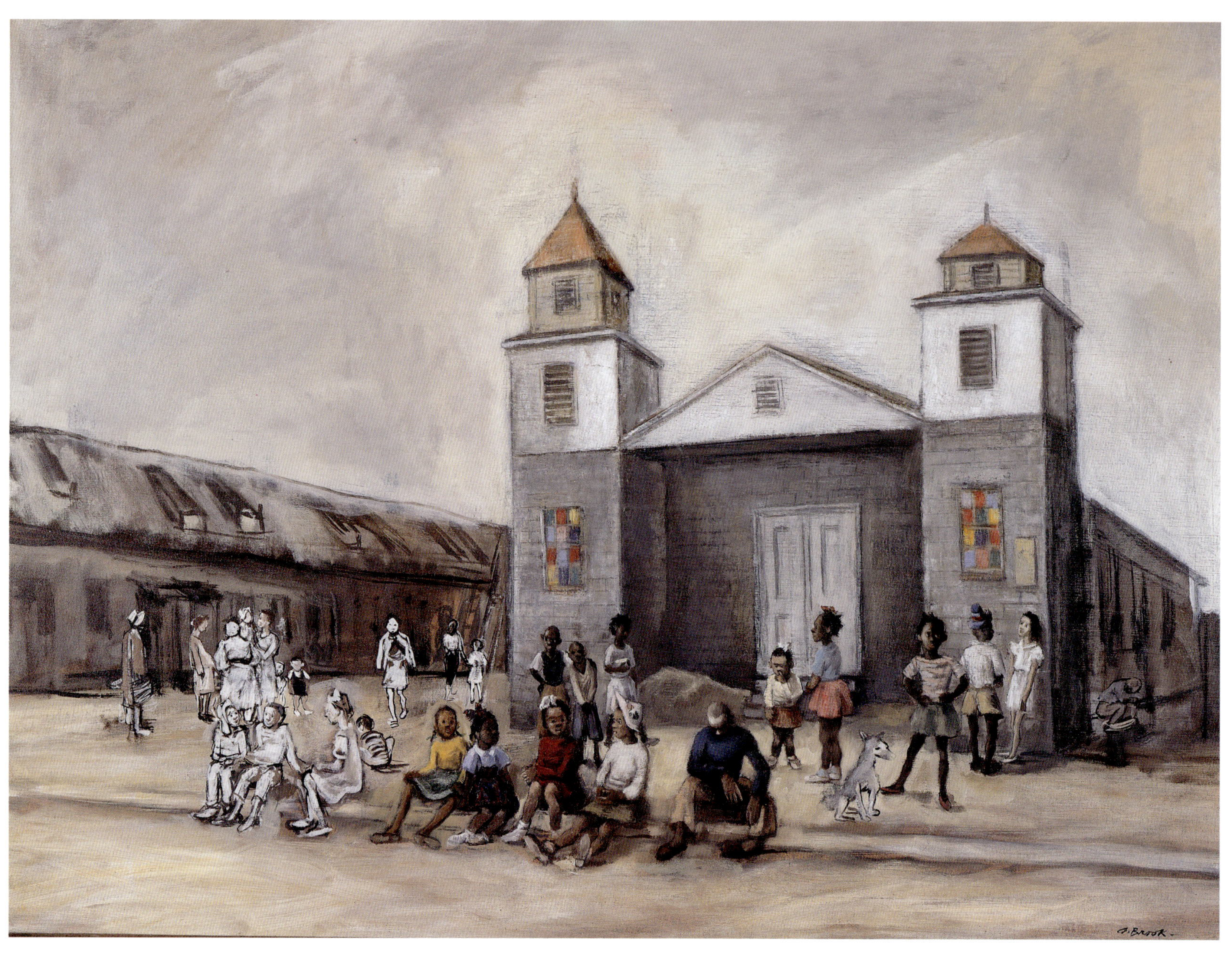

Alexander Brook, Savannah Street Corner, *n.d.*
Telfair Museum of Art, Gift of the Artist, 1972

Contents

Director's Statement

FOR A NUMBER OF YEARS the staff at the Telfair Museum of Art has kept alive the idea that an exhibition about art in Savannah would be an exciting and worthwhile project. Given that the museum is the oldest art museum in the South, with a long history of involvement in art instruction and collecting, such an exhibition is long overdue. Now that the city of Savannah is the site of the 1996 Olympics yachting events, and is well established as a magnet for international and national tourism, it is particularly appropriate and timely to present this exhibition and catalogue.

Countless visitors have succumbed to Savannah's charms, from the Marquis de Lafayette and General William Tecumseh Sherman to official dignitaries and casual tourists. Almost without exception visitors have delighted in the city's distinct and dignified, yet sensuous southern ambiance. Magnificent moss-draped oaks line the streets and shade city squares; beautiful architecture of a bygone era, replete with a myriad of unusual and delightful details, has been preserved. Savannah's busy port; the shops and cotton warehouses lining Bay and River Streets; cemeteries filled with fascinating monuments; and the city's proximity to the Atlantic Ocean are all well-known attractions. Some landmarks are gone: the plantation house of The Hermitage was razed in 1935 and the venerable Old City Market was demolished for a parking garage in 1954 (a costly error that has promoted strict preservation guidelines).

The Old City Market lives on, however, through paintings, drawings, prints, and photographs, as does The Hermitage. Fortunately, most of Savannah's heritage remains, and in the art works selected for this exhibition can be experienced—through the artist's vision and firsthand from a contemporary viewpoint. For local residents with strong generational ties, nostalgia will be a key ingredient; for visitors, this southern city and six decades of its history will come to life through its art, as lively, charming, and enticing as ever.

To organize *Looking Back: Art in Savannah 1900–1960* and to produce a worthy catalogue was a significant undertaking, accomplished in a relatively short time. We are proud of the results and recognize that success was predicated upon the help and goodwill of a large number of individuals. The Telfair's curator of fine arts and exhibitions, Pamela King, and curator of education, Harry DeLorme, have worked diligently to assure that Savannah's art world would be given its due. They deserve our recognition and appreciation for an important contribution to the history of Savannah and the Telfair. They conferred with many artists, collectors, and connoisseurs, and enlisted the aid of art history professors and graduate students for research and catalogue entries. Within this context, special thanks are due to Cynda Benson of the faculty of the Savannah College of Art and Design for her willingness to organize graduate students, to serve as preliminary editor of their entries, and to contribute her own catalogue entries. We are grateful to all the entry authors; Feay Shellman Coleman deserves special thanks for her willingness to take on entries late in the project. The entire Telfair staff participated in various capacities, and they deserve our recognition for their hard work: in particular, assistant curator Beth Moore, registrar Tania Sammons, and designer/preparator Milutin Pavlovic.

The Telfair Museum of Art is very fortunate to have had the interest, expertise, and commitment of Van Jones Martin, who designed and produced this fine catalogue. Van Martin, who is perhaps best known for his beautiful book, *Classic Savannah*, recognized the importance of *Art in Savannah* and undertook the project at close to the "eleventh hour." In addition to his duties as designer and producer, he photographed, with painstaking perfectionism, a large percentage of the works included here. It is no exaggeration to state that the production of this wonderful catalogue would not have been possible without him. The catalogue's editor, Norma Roberts, also made a very significant contribution. She accepted the challenge within its restricted time frame and devoted herself to the project, as she does with every text she edits. Her thoughtful attention to detail and wise counsel have refined and perfected the catalogue's prose.

On behalf of the Board of Trustees of the Telfair Museum of Art, we gratefully acknowledge the lenders to the exhibition, who are listed separately, and the individuals whose assistance and advice concerning artists, art works, collectors, and Savannah's history as an art community have made this exhibition a reality.

Diane Lesko
Director

Acknowledgments

The many individuals whose names appear below have provided information and other assistance and deserve our special recognition.

Ben N. Adams, Antique Alley; The Honorable Floyd Adams, Mayor of Savannah; Lee and Emma Adler; Nancy Anderson, Museum of Arts and Sciences, Macon, Georgia; Clara Augero, Savannah State College

Graham W.J. Beal, Joslyn Art Museum; Stephen Patterson Belcher; Muriel and Malcolm Bell, Jr.; Randolph Black, The Montclair Museum of Art; H. Paul Blatner; Stephen Bohlin-Davis, Juliette Gordon Low Birthplace; Beverly Brannon, Library of Congress; Annette Brock, Beach Institute African American Cultural Center, Savannah; Michael Brown, City of Savannah; Tom Butler, The Columbus Museum, Columbus, Georgia

Grace Silva Cabaniss; Alex Cann; India Christman; L. Keith Claussen, Morris Museum of Art; Tim Close, Albany Museum of Art, Albany, Georgia; Floyd Coleman, Howard University; Michael Collins; Guy Craft, Savannah State College; Joanne Cubbs, High Museum of Art; Verna Curtis, Library of Congress

Robert Dinkensheets; Lamar Dodd; Dorothy Dugdale, Beach Institute African American Cultural Center, Savannah; Virginia and John Duncan

Barbara Fertig, Coastal Heritage Society and Armstrong State College; Danielle Funderburk, The Columbus Museum, Columbus, Georgia; Fred Fussell

Reuben Gambrell; Dr. William H. Gerdts, The City University of New York; A. M. Goldkrand; Hugh Golson; Howard Greenberg, Howard Greenberg Gallery; Carroll Greene, Jr., Beach Institute African American Cultural Center and The Acacia Collection of African-Americana; Sarah Greenough, National Gallery of Art; J. Richard Gruber, Morris Museum of Art

William Halsey; Phillip J. Hampton; Fran Harald, Juliette Gordon Low Birthplace; Ellen S. Harris, The Montclair Art Museum; Robert M. Hicklin, Jr., Robert M. Hicklin, Inc.; Edward D. Hill; Steven and Susan Hirsch; Mrs. William E. Hutchinson, Jr.

GeorgeAnne Inglis; Kim Iocovozzi; Mary Ison, Library of Congress

Tambra Johnson, Library of Congress; Myrtle Jones; Willis Hakim Jones

Katherine Keena, Juliette Gordon Low Birthplace; Donald Keyes, Georgia Museum of Art; Joseph Killorin; Anne King, LaGrange College; Dave Knoke, Knoke Galleries; Lee Kogan, Museum of American Folk Art, New York; Arthur B. Kouwenhoven, Jr.

Josephine Langan, Kuhlman Corporation; Judy Larson, High Museum of Art; W.W. Law, Ralph M. Gilbert Civil Rights Museum; John Lawrence, Lamar Dodd Art Center, LaGrange College; Jack Leigh; Brook Anderson Linga, Diggs Gallery, University of North Carolina, Winston-Salem; Eleanor Goldberg Longwater

Corrie McCallum; Judith McWillie, University of Georgia; Gerald Melberg, Melberg/Ritts Fine Art; David E. Miller, Jr.; Charles S. Moffett, The Phillips Collection; Bob Morris; Alvin Nealy

Barbara Odevseff, Wichita Art Museum; Augusta Oelschig; Stephen Ostrow, Library of Congress; Dean Owens

William Paul, University of Georgia; Estill Pennington, Morris Museum of Art

Doris Rabb, Fort King George Historic Site; Jeffrey Rosenheim, The Metropolitan Museum of Art; Joel Rosenkranz, Conner-Rosenkranz, New York; Andrée Ruellan

Chris Sade, Atlantic; Philip Saraf; Mr. and Mrs. David Saussy; Martha Severens, Greenville County Museum of Art, Greenville, South Carolina; Vince Sikorski; Abigail Silzer, Time/Life Syndication; Mrs. James E. Silva; Jennifer Smiga; Ann Smith, Georgia Historical Society, Savannah; Mrs. William Sprague; Edward S. Spriggs, Hammonds House, Atlanta; Gail Stavitsky, The Montclair Art Museum; Tracy Stephanski; Albert Stone; George Stone; Ronald J. Strahan

Marsha Tiede, Center for Creative Photography

Albert Ullman

Catherine Wade Wahl, Morris Museum of Art; John Wetenhall, Cheekwood Tennessee Botanical Gardens and Museum of Art; Mark Williams, Center for Creative Photography; Lucille Wright; Marc F. Wilson, The Nelson-Atkins Museum of Art; Inez S. Wolins, Wichita Art Museum

The Telfair Academy of Arts and Sciences and Art in Savannah

Pamela D. King

FROM REVOLUTIONARY TIMES, Savannah has been supportive of, and hospitable toward, the visual arts. Local artists in addition to visitors from the North have found a receptive audience for their creations in this vibrant southern port. The visual arts were officially institutionalized here with the founding of the Telfair Academy in 1875 by the will of Mary Telfair. Because of Miss Telfair's vision, Savannah was among the first cities in this country to establish cultural institutions for the general public. The last quarter of the nineteenth century also saw the creation of the Metropolitan Museum of Art and the Brooklyn Museum in New York; the Museum of Fine Arts in Boston, and the Philadelphia Museum of Art.

By 1886 the Telfair family home had been transformed into a public edifice housing a collection of contemporary art and plaster casts of Antique sculpture. The museum's first director, German American artist Carl L. Brandt (see John Walz's portrait bust of Brandt, fig.1), conferring with the board of the Academy's then-parent institution, the Georgia Historical Society, assembled a collection for the enjoyment and edification of visitors. A very early pamphlet on the Telfair proclaims that "this is the only well equipped ART GALLERY in the South. It contains a rare collection of paintingsby modern artists. . . . Strangers to the city will find a visit to the Gallery both interesting and profitable."[1] Upon request Brandt also gave art lessons to aspiring Savannahians, notably Emma Wilkins, who would figure in the later history of the Telfair and art in Savannah in general.

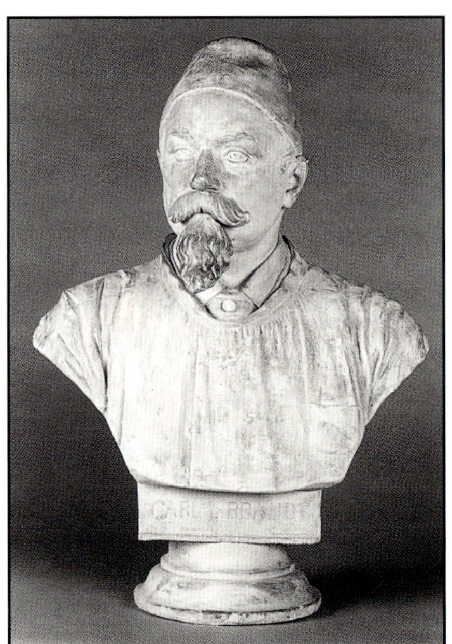

Fig. 1. John Walz (1844–1922). Carl Brandt, *1891. Plaster, 37 x 29 x 16 in. (94 x 74 x 41 cm). Telfair Museum of Art.*

Brandt's art, which became part of the collection as well as the decoration of the building, was conservative for the times. Steeped in the idealized realism of the 1860s, his technique was accomplished and photographic, as for example in his oil portrait of General Henry Rootes Jackson (fig. 2), the president of the Georgia Historical Society.

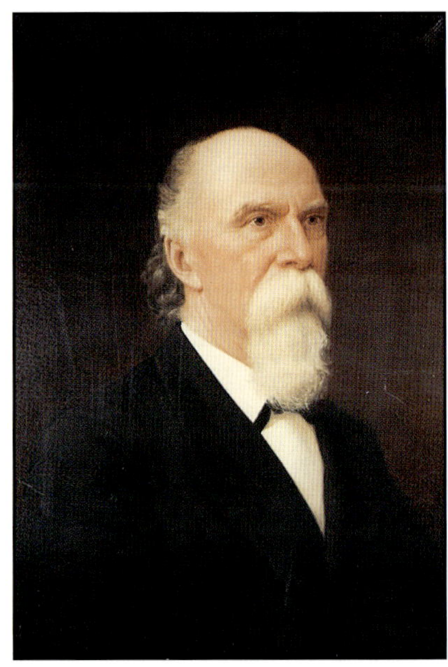

Fig. 2. Carl L. Brandt (1831–1905). General Henry Rootes Jackson, *1897. Oil on canvas, 30 x 23 in. (76.2 x 58.4 cm). Telfair Museum of Art, Gift of the artist, 1897.*

Following Brandt's death in 1905, the American painter Gari Melchers guided the growth of the collection. From 1906 until 1916, he acted as art advisor and purchasing agent for the museum. Visiting fellow artists' studios and salons and exhibitions, both in the United States and Europe, Melchers selected works for the Telfair. Many

1. *"Telfair Academy of Arts and Sciences," n.d., Telfair archives.*

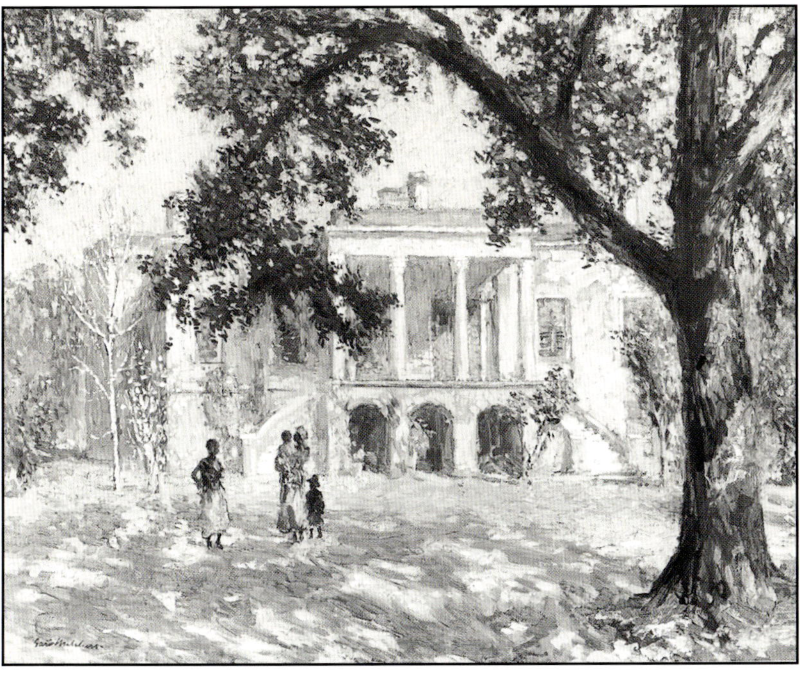

Fig. 3. Gari Melchers (1860–1932). The Plantation Home, *c.1916. Oil on canvas, 29 3/8 x 35 1/2 in. (75 x 90.2 cm). Collection of Belmont, The Gari Melchers Estate and Memorial Gallery.*

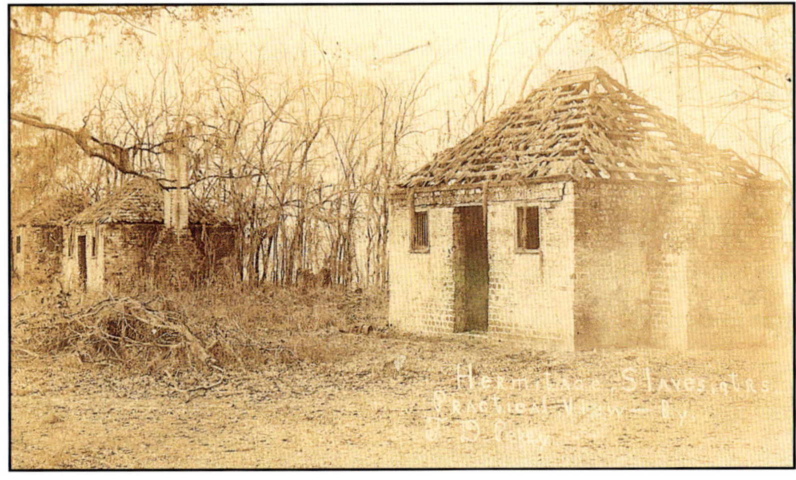

Fig. 4. J.D. Perry. Slave Quarters at The Hermitage. *4 9/16 x 7 9/16 in. (12 x 19.2 cm) Photograph. Comer House Collection, Savannah, Georgia.*

that were procured under his aegis are the most important paintings in the museum's collection. A generation younger than Brandt, Melchers brought to Savannah the newer style of Impressionism. During his association with the Telfair, Melchers traveled regularly to Savannah to rehang the collection, visit relatives (his wife was the niece of the Board's president), and oversee the artistic direction of the young museum. At times he was able to capture the local scene in his own paintings, whether in formal portraits or in depictions of earlier images of wealth and glory, such as *The Plantation Home* (fig. 3).

Perhaps attracted at first to the picturesque qualities of dilapidated slave quarters (see fig. 4, for example), artists and others began to acknowledge the contributions of African Americans to the vitality and genuineness of the community as a whole. Black culture would become the focus of attention for many academically trained artists, especially in the wake of the Harlem Renaissance and the New Deal.

Regular instruction at the Telfair began as early as the 1920s and continued until 1965.[2] The Savannah Art Club (later Art Association) was instrumental in engaging the New York Impressionist Eliot Clark to offer painting instruction in Savannah (fig. 5). Members of the art club had written to the Art Students League in New York asking for someone to come to Savannah and teach. Clark took up the challenge. His tenure here not only enhanced the skills of local artists but also resulted in numerous beautiful canvases of his own depicting Savannah's River Street, downtown, and outlying areas.

Another well-known artist who taught at the Telfair, Hilda Belcher, a painter from Vermont and New York City, established a relationship with Savannah in the 1920s. A portrait commission in the previous decade was her introduction to the city. Like Clark,

2. The Telfair held an exhibition of works by artists who had taught at the museum school through 1951. Included in the show were Hilda Belcher, Adolphe Blondheim, Carl Brandt, Clifford Carlton, Eliot Clark, William Halsey, Emil Holzbauer, Corrie McCallum, Christopher A. D. Murphy, Eliot O'Hara, Rebekah Saunders, Anna Heyward Taylor, and Walter Thompson.

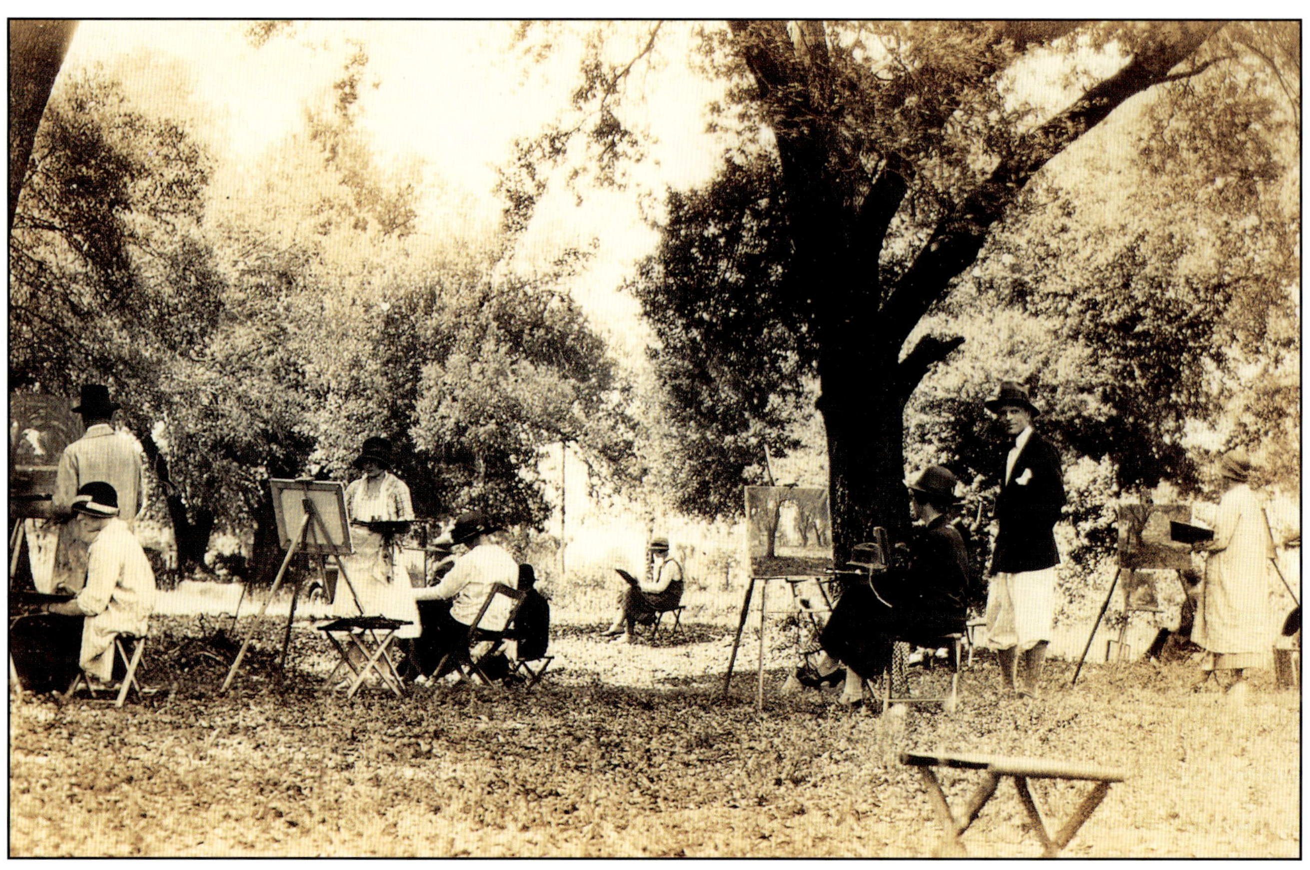

5. Unknown photographer. Eliot Clark and students in Armstrong Field, c.1924. 4 x 6 ⅜ in. (10.2 x 16.2 cm). Collection of Robert M. Hicklin, Jr.

she taught at the Telfair and created her own paintings here, both portraits and works inspired by African American church activities.

In addition to its educational program the museum exhibited its permanent collection of outstanding works of art and offered a schedule of national and regional traveling exhibitions. The Telfair was a member of, and active participant in, the American Federation of Arts (AFA), a promoter of the exhibition and appreciation of art, especially American art. The AFA enabled the Telfair to present programs such as slide presentations on art, as well as exhibitions of primarily contemporary art. A 1911 exhibition from the AFA included the paintings of leading American artists Thomas Anshutz, George Bellows, William Merritt Chase, William Glackens, Childe Hassam, Robert Henri, and Ernest Lawson. A decade later, paintings of the West were showcased, with works by Ernest Blumenshein, Irving Couse, J. Henry Sharp, and Walter Ufer, among others. Thus the museum proved to be a valuable asset to the city and region, hosting these exhibitions well into the 1950s.

Regional art exhibitions shared the schedule with the national touring shows. The museum was the regular host for the annual exhibitions (begun in 1923) organized by the Southern States Art League (SSAL), an organization founded "to encourage art and its appreciation in the South."[3] To accomplish its purpose, the SSAL encouraged artists, admirers, and purchasers alike.[4] Savannah was

3. 11th Annual Exhibition of the Southern States Art League *(exhibition checklist, Savannah, Ga.: Telfair Academy of Arts and Sciences, 1931), n.p.*
4. *Ethel Hutson, "The Southern States Art League,"* The American Magazine of Art 30 *(February 1930)*: 88.

usually represented in the SSAL exhibitions, and many of her artists were involved in the organization.

Another influential group, the Association of Georgia Artists, each year organized exhibitions that were installed at the Telfair. Prizes, often donated by local businesses and individuals, were awarded; the largest prize, however, was the Telfair Academy purchase prize. The museum acquired works from both the SSAL and the Association of Georgia Artists shows, including Anna Hunter's *Recessional* and Emma Wilkins's *Playing with Reds*, both of which are included in the present exhibition.

In addition to bringing art exhibitions to Savannah, the SSAL and the Association of Georgia Artists, provided opportunities for native Savannah artists to exhibit their work across the state and throughout the South. These exhibitions encouraged interaction between artists and provided stimulation for creativity, which often translated into the desire for further education. Savannah provided many opportunities for formal and informal instruction. One of the premier sources of art education was the Telfair school where a wide variety of opportunities for students of various ages and accomplishments had been available since the nineteenth century. No doubt William Halsey's summation of the purpose of the Telfair school has been pertinent throughout its history. Halsey, an instructor here in the early 1940s, wrote that "the primary aim of the school . . . is to give a sound technical knowledge of the use of drawing and painting materials and their possibilities, together with a broad viewpoint of art values."[5] Such "art values" were also dispensed at Savannah State College (historically a black institution), Armstrong College (a fledgling school in the 1940s), and the Savannah extension campus of the University of Georgia (begun after World War II). Works by three of the professors of these colleges—Walter Simon and Phillip Hampton, who taught at Savannah State; and Reuben Gambrell who taught at the Savannah extension campus of the University of Georgia—are included in the current exhibition. The latter school was established at Hunter Army Airfield in 1946 to accommodate the general public and the many veterans who were able to study under the G.I. Bill. According to Gambrell, it was the influence exerted by the Savannah Art Association that made art instruction part of the curriculum. He had many students who were not part of a regular degree program but enrolled solely for instruction in art.[6] Gambrell found Savannah very welcoming to the visual arts at this time. Later, in 1951, at the behest of the Savannah Art Association, he returned as an instructor at the Telfair.

The Savannah Art Association was established in 1920 as the Savannah Art Club, with the mandate "to encourage those artistically inclined to advance the 'Standards of Art' in the City of Savannah and to cultivate a desire for the highest and best in Art."[7] Many of the charter members were active in affairs of the Telfair, whether as instructors or students at the school or serving on the Board of Trustees. Included in the current exhibition are charter members Lila Cabaniss, Mary Comer Lane, Juliette Gordon Low, Christopher A. D. Murphy, and Emma Wilkins.

The Camera Club of Savannah, supported by the Telfair, was established at the turn of the century. The group found the Telfair to be a strong advocate of their chosen art form and a regular exhibitor of the members' works.

What do artists from the North find when they come to Savannah? A port city of the Old South, laid out in a handsome city plan, filled with historic architecture and beautiful parks, surrounded by a lush, verdant landscape of marshes. In a more poetic vein, a proud Savannahian described his home as

> a city of quiet charm whose architectural heritage has not been lost in the transition to modern needs, and about whose venerable squares and picturesque waterfront still lingers the serenity of a bygone era.[8]

The Telfair's first director, Carl Brandt, could be considered one of the earliest artists to visit and work in Savannah in the late nineteenth and early twentieth centuries. Brandt was followed by Walt Kuhn, whose career as a champion of modernism would blossom in the 1910s and 1920s. Famous for his melancholy depictions of circus performers, Kuhn came through Savannah in 1903, fresh from his studies in Germany.[9] Another modernist, Milton Avery, visited Savannah in the 1940s; although he did not work here, he was cer-

5. *Quoted in "Telfair Studios Humming with Activity of Artists,"* Savannah Evening Press, *May 3, 1943.*

6. *Conversation with the artist, May 9, 1996.*

7. *"Standing Rules of the Savannah Art Club," Georgia Historical Society, Savannah, Ga., 1920.*

8. *Walter Charlton Hartridge, "Savannah: Its Mercantile Tradition and Architectural Heritage,"* Savannah *(Columbia, S.C.: Bostick & Thornley, 1947), 1.*

9. *Brandt had purchased a significant painting from Kuhn's teacher in Munich, Heinrich von Zugel, for the Telfair's permanent collection not long before. Perhaps this connection prompted the younger artist's stop in Savannah.*

tainly impressed by the city and its environs.[10]

Not surprisingly, several Impressionists were captivated by the physical beauty of the city and the charm of its landscape, as well as by its colorful inhabitants. From the Old Lyme art colony in Connecticut came William Chadwick and Harry L. Hoffman, who captured on canvas not only the tangible elements of what they saw but also the light of a place near the sea and the atmosphere softened by tropical humidity. Eliot Clark, an Impressionist cum Tonalist, created many paintings inspired by his Savannah sojourn. There were Impressionists among the local artists as well, including Christopher P. H. Murphy, William Posey Silva, and Emma Wilkins.

Jules Pascin, who visited Savannah in the 1910s and 1920s proved important to the careers of several painters who are associated with the city. He was part of a group that studied and worked at the Art Students League, as had Eliot Clark, and at the colony of Woodstock, outside of New York City. In particular, Pascin influenced Alexander Brook, Andrée Ruellan, and John Taylor, who were part of a movement in the 1930s and 1940s that championed the realist tradition in American art and shunned the more esoteric advances of European modernism. Brook, Ruellan, and Taylor were American Scene painters who captured and celebrated the commonplace, much as had Hilda Belcher in the 1920s and onward; all four worked in this genre in Savannah. One of Brook's best known American Scene paintings, *Georgia Jungle* (fig. 6), which was created in Savannah, won first prize in the Carnegie International of 1939.

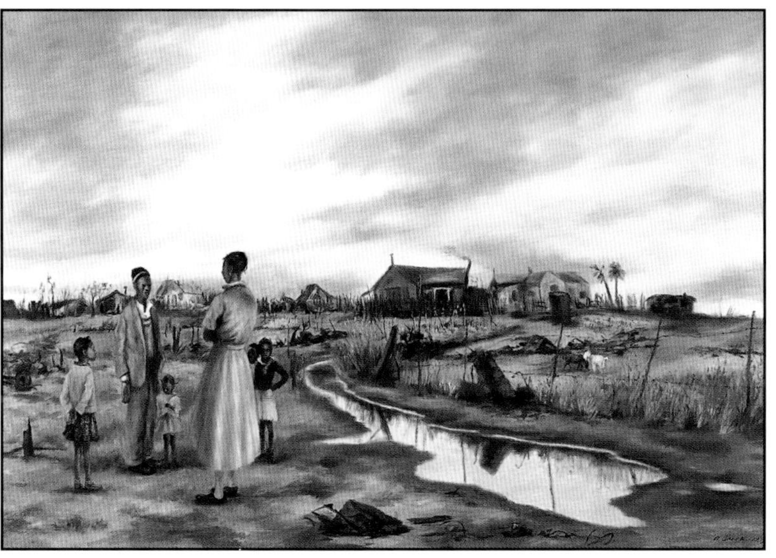

Fig. 6. Alexander Brook (1898–1980). Georgia Jungle, *1939. Oil on canvas, 35 x 50 in. (89 x 127 cm). Museum of Art, Carnegie Institute, Pittsburgh, Pennsylvania.*

Native southern artists, too, participated in the American Scene movement. Savannah's Augusta Oelschig, Telfair instructor Reuben Gambrell, and the "dean of Georgia artists," Lamar Dodd, created insightful paintings documenting their environment. The landscape, whether urban or rural, of Georgia and South Carolina provided a myriad of possible subjects for their work.

For visiting artists, their southern experiences, of whatever duration, were part of a new national focus on the South. There was a growing movement beginning in the 1920s to promote all things American, as distinct from European. Indigenous virtues were hailed as superior to the imported ones. Critics of literature and art called upon artists to produce works that would commemorate their native land. One critic remarked in the 1930s that "never before did a nation seem so hungry for news of itself."[11] Part of that self was the South. Artists ventured on their own to experience this region of the country, or visited on assignment. Frances Benjamin Johnston, for example, was sent to work on the Carnegie Survey of the Architecture of the South (1933–40); and Margaret Bourke-White documented the paper industry in Savannah for *Life* magazine in 1939. The Farm Security Administration, part of the New Deal government's attempt to document the plight of the rural poor, employed many famous photographers, including Walker Evans (his Savannah images, however, were not done for the government). The Work Projects Administration (WPA) supported artists during the Depression by commissioning murals for public buildings. In 1934 William Hoffman painted a medieval scene for the children's room of the main branch of the public library in Savannah. It is still in place today. Other artists in the current exhibition who produced WPA murals include Alexander Brook, Andrée Ruellan, and John Taylor.

Many visiting artists took an active role in Savannah's arts community and no doubt influenced local painters. Some actually taught Savannahians privately or at the Telfair or other school.

10. Conversation of Harry DeLorme with March Avery, January 1996.

11. Quoted in Nancy Heller and Julia Williams, Painters of the American Scene *(New York: Galahad Books, 1982), 136.*

Augusta Oelschig benefited from working with Henry Lee McFee; one of Myrtle Jones's greatest influences was studying with Emil Holzhauer at the Telfair. Another artist who, through his talent and gregarious nature, affected many artists here was Alexander Brook. Although he did not give standardized classes, he frequently gave demonstrations and critiques at the Telfair and for Gambrell's classes for the University of Georgia extension. Probably more important, however, was his practice of having a virtually open studio that served as a social gathering place for artists where they could converse, support each other, and even play ping-pong. Brook had his studio/home on Factor's Walk in the late 1930s and early 1940s. Several artists followed his example and moved there. In September 1940 a headline in the *Savannah Morning News* proclaimed, "NEW ART COLONY IN FACTOR'S WALK. Visiting and Local Artists Open Studios. LIFE CLASSES STARTED. Famous Cotton Row on Bay Changes Character."[12] Indeed, prior to the 1930s the area was purely commercial and had fallen into disrepair as the cotton industry floundered. With their large windows and northern exposure, the grand buildings overlooking the Savannah River (fig. 7) were perfect for studios, and no doubt they were eminently affordable.

Above: Fig. 7. Unknown photographer. Savannah Harbor, 1910. Georgia Historical Society, Savannah, Ga.
Below: Fig. 8. Unknown photographer. Old City Market, 1950s. Georgia Historical Society, Savannah, Ga.

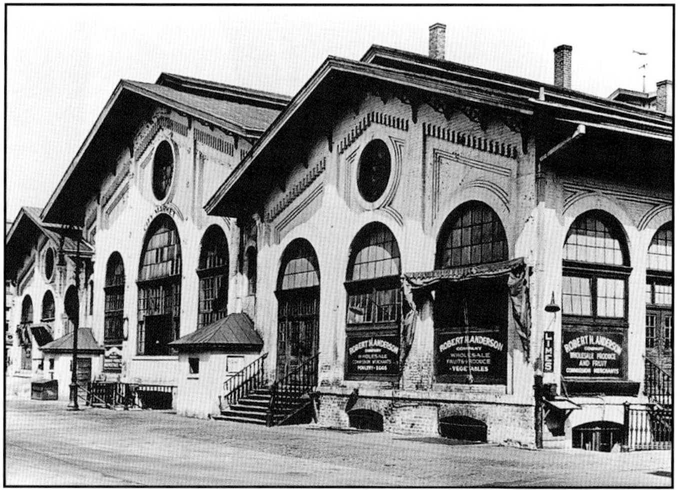

Given the location of so many studios in this vicinity, it is no wonder that the river and harbor, River Street with its ramp approaches, and Factor's Walk became the subject of many works of art. Another favorite subject of area artists was the Old City Market (fig. 8). The attraction was not solely the Victorian architecture; the pulse of life—shoppers looking for the day's fruits and vegetables and other dinner ingredients, the picturesque vendors and hucksters—proved lively subjects for painters of the city. Many of Savannah's artists found the side and back streets more attractive as subject matter than the well-groomed avenues. Still, the more lyrical subjects of the area did not escape notice. Forsyth Park's lovely fountain has been recorded many times. The live oak trees draped in Spanish moss in downtown squares and outlying locations such as Bonaventure Cemetery, Beaulieu, and Pin Point must have seemed enticing and exotic to a visitor from the North. These proved an irresistible draw, too, for those familiar with the terrain.

Art produced in and about Savannah between 1900 and 1960 is generally characterized by a conservative style, whether it is the academic realism of Carl Brandt and Valentino Molina, the Impressionist musings of Harry L. Hoffman and William Chadwick, or the unabashed realism of the American Scene painters. All of these styles represent the leading trends of their day. But this is perhaps the charm of Savannah's art. A description of Andrée Ruellan's work serves to summarize this phenomenon. Harry Salpeter writes that "Miss Ruellan publishes no revolutionary message, does not raise the temperature, but does give one the satisfaction of making art creations in the line of tradition."[13] Perhaps as elsewhere, this was the kind of art that Savannahians could unflinchingly embrace, for Savannah is a city that welcomes and supports the visual arts. And in Savannah the center of the visual arts is the Telfair Academy.

12. *"New Art Colony in Factor's Walk,"* Savannah Morning News, *September 18, 1940, p.14.*
13. *Harry Salpeter, "About Andrée Ruellan,"* Coronet *(December 1938): 98.*

Traditionalists, Outsiders, and the Not-so-Naive

Harry H. DeLorme, Jr.

DESPITE A BUSTLING ART SCENE, for a mid-sized southern city, and the presence of numerous artists of note in search of subject matter, the Savannah of the early twentieth century is arguably best known in art and folklore circles for works by traditional and self-taught artists. Once broadly categorized as "folk art," these works include handed-down modes such as African American carving, as well as make-do art of the pre- and post-Depression era and the work of a few talented, idiosyncratic artists of little or no formal training. Notwithstanding some encouragement by academically trained artists and a brief period of attention by folklorists, until recent times most of these individuals received little or no recognition in the geographic area that spawned their work. Aside from the traditional and the idiosyncratic in Savannah, national and local artists of the American Scene and talented amateurs assimilated the look of so-called folk painting into a faux-naive style that may have provided an antidote or alternative to modernism's increasingly nonobjective bent.

A number of factors contributed to the environment that fostered the art made outside the city's small artistic loop. These factors vary with the type of art and artisans considered. For academically trained artists, Savannah's location on a major north/south thoroughfare provided the opportunity to stop and partake of local color. A strong art club brought visiting artists of national reputation to the city beginning in the 1920s. Artists who visited told other artists of their discovery of this sleepy, picturesque city with ragged edges and seemingly exotic African American culture. Classes with visiting and local professionally trained artists were available at the Telfair Academy, and at Savannah State College. Schoolchildren, black and white, visited the Telfair for tours of the art collection. Studio spaces with views of the river were available and inexpensive, and flourished in the former cotton warehouses and offices along River Street.

TRADITIONALISTS

Beneath the surface of Savannah, in African American homes and gardens, in vendors' pushcarts, and beneath mounds of produce at the city's old public market, traditional arts and folk aesthetics continued to thrive into the twentieth century. Traditional artists are broadly defined here as makers of functional and nonfunctional works that follow larger cultural patterns and currents of community use. The highly debated term "folk art" is now most closely associated with the traditional arts, but the definition of the term will likely continue to be refined. In the meantime, a broader, perhaps inaccurate, meaning persists in popular usage.[1]

During the period of this survey, 1900–1960, traditional art was particularly strong in the African American neighborhoods of Savannah and the low country of Georgia and South Carolina. European and European American crafts were present, but African American examples were more prevalent, or at the least better documented. Traditional arts by African Americans—documented and described by Robert Farris Thompson, John Michael Vlach, and others—include canes, nonfunctional carvings, quilts, baskets, furniture, and grave decorations.[2] Some of these objects bear evidence of the continuity of African influence in this region well into the twentieth century. The presence of such items may be explained by Savannah's historically large African American population, the continued illegal importation of African and Afro-Caribbean slaves until 1858, and, consequently, strong memories of African ancestors in the community. In the 1930s, the population of the Savannah area still included numerous elderly people who had once worked as slaves on plantations in Savannah and in the Sea Islands

1. *See Henry Glassie,* The Spirit of Folk Art, The Girard Collection of the Museum of International Folk Art *(New York: Harry N. Abrams, 1989). Glassie discusses the intersection of the terms "folk" and "art" in current usage.*
2. *See John Michael Vlach,* The Afro-American Tradition in Decorative Arts *(Athens, Ga.: Brown Thrasher Books, The University of Georgia Press, 1990); and Robert Farris Thompson, "African Influence on the Art of the United States," reprinted in* Afro-American Folk Arts and Crafts *(Jackson, Miss.: University Press of Mississippi, 1983).*

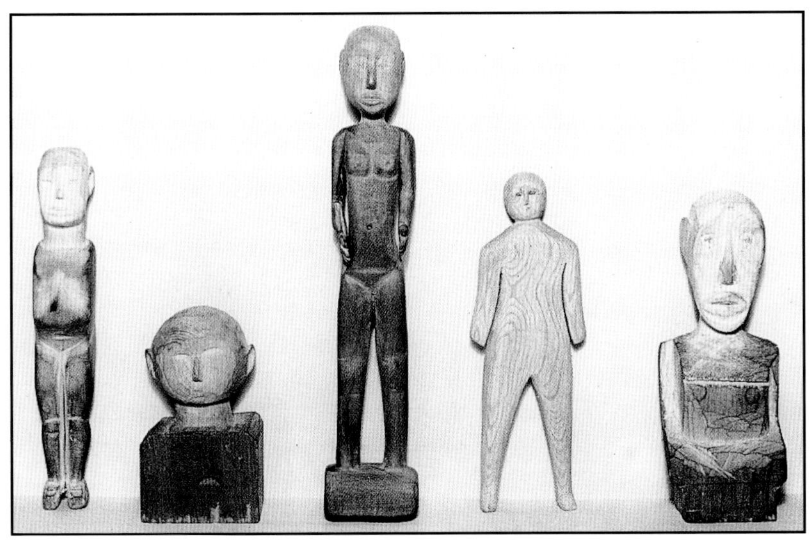

Fig. 9. Jerome Carter, Wood sculptures, Savannah, Georgia, c.1930s. (Photograph by Muriel and Malcolm Bell, Jr.)

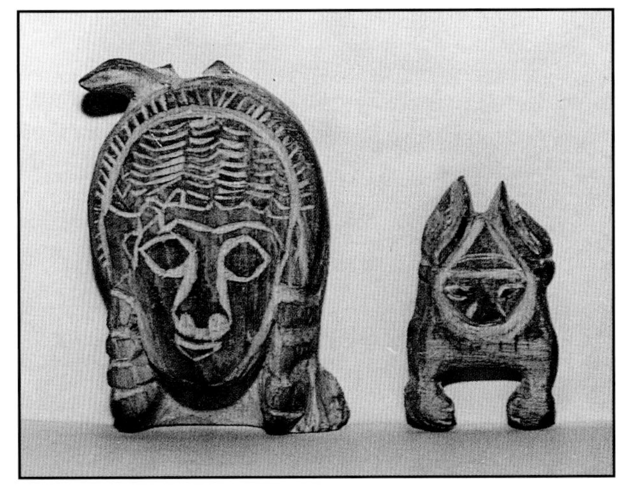

Fig. 10. Jerome Carter, Wood sculptures, Savannah, Georgia, c.1930s. (Detail of photograph by Muriel and Malcolm Bell, Jr.)

of Georgia and South Carolina. Numerous observations and recollections of African-influenced beliefs and aesthetic objects in the low country have been recorded. In 1907, Mrs. Telfair Hodgson recounted experiences on her father's plantation, "Colerain," near Savannah, which indicated the antebellum presence of African-influenced funerary practices and grave decoration:

> The slaves were not allowed to leave the fields during the daytime, so night weddings and night funerals were the custom. Negro graves were always decorated with the last article used by the departed, and broken pitchers and broken bits of colored glass were considered even more appropriate than the white shells from the beach nearby. Sometimes they carved rude figures like images of idols, and sometimes a patchwork quilt was laid upon the grave.[3]

"Rude figures," as Mrs. Hodgson described them, turn up in the astounding twentieth-century graveyard sculptures of Cyrus Bowens of Sunbury, Georgia, reproduced along with other examples of African American wood sculpture in an extraordinary book, *Drums and Shadows*, produced in 1940 by the Georgia Writers' Project.[4] For the Savannah unit of the project, three Savannahians—writer Mary Granger and photographers Muriel and Malcolm Bell, Jr.—sought to document African "survivals" in America, with the help of advisors such as Africanist Melville J. Herskovits and sociologist Guy B. Johnson. Focusing entirely upon African American communities in Savannah and coastal Georgia, they produced interviews and photographs that are still a vital resource to folklorists, historians, linguists, and others. Many of the individuals interviewed remembered African parents, grandparents, or acquaintances, and quotes from these interviews are frequently cited by scholars as oral evidence for the continuation of an African aesthetic in craft activity and folk belief. In the context of this exhibition, some of these bear repeating. Of particular interest to art historians have been photographs and descriptions of woodcarving. The comments of Robert Pinckney of Thunderbolt, Georgia, have been used in particular to make the link between African figurative sculpture and twentieth-century African American carving:

3. *Sarah Hodgson Torian, ed., "Ante-Bellum and War Memories of Mrs. Telfair Hodgson,"* Georgia Historical Quarterly *27 (1943): 352.*

4. *Georgia Writers' Project,* Drums and Shadows: Survival Studies Among Georgia Coastal Negroes *(Athens, Ga.: The University of Georgia Press, 1940; reprinted, Brown Thrasher Books, The University of Georgia Press, 1986). Discussed in Thompson, "African Influence," 48–50, and Vlach,* The Afro-American Tradition in Decorative Arts, *146–47.*

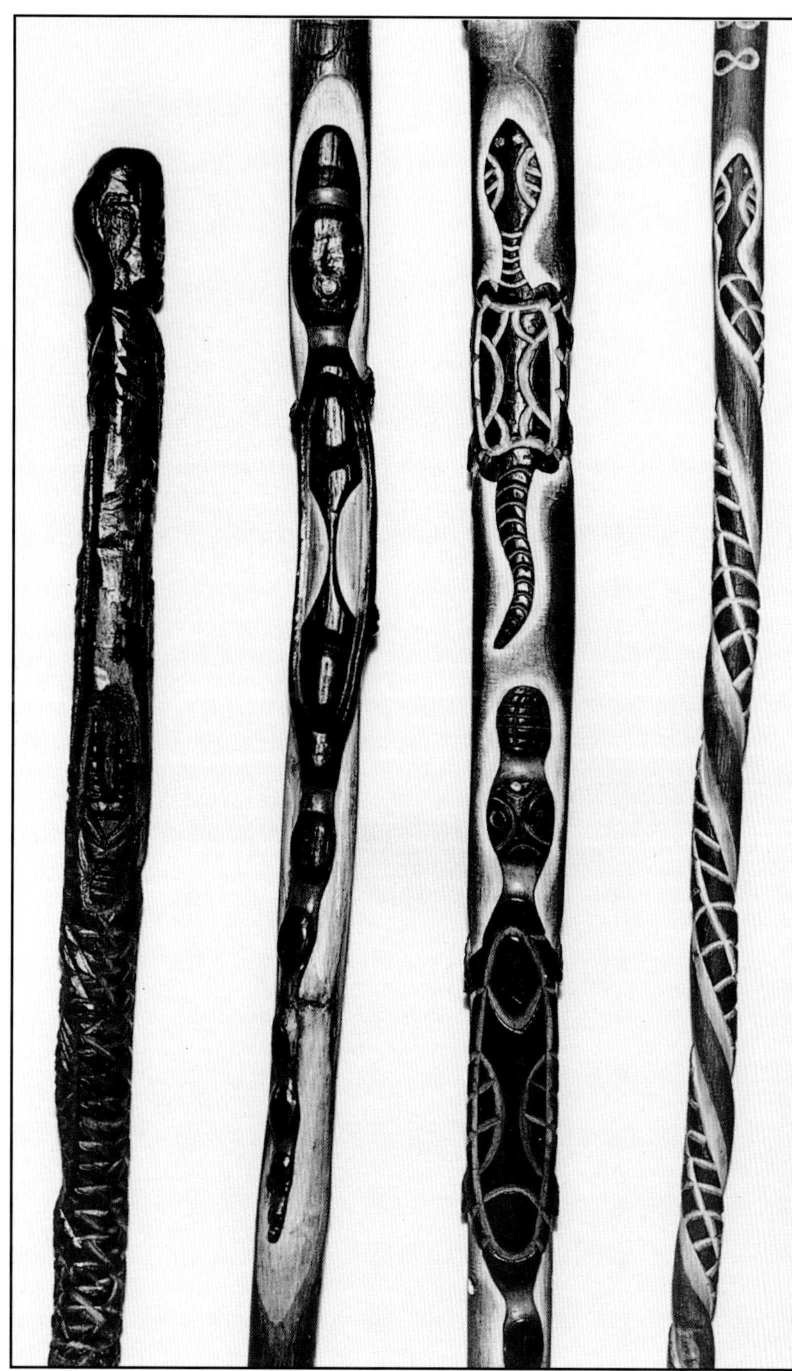

Fig. 11. Left: Unidentified artist, walking stick, Savannah, Georgia. Right (3): James "Stick Daddy" Cooper, walking sticks, Savannah, Georgia, c.1930s. (Photograph by Muriel and Malcolm Bell, Jr.)

> I remember the African mens use to all the time make little clay images. Sometimes they [were] like men and sometimes they [were] like animal. Once they made a big one. They put a spear in his hand and walk 'round him and say he was the chief. But that clay got too much river mud in it an' he ain't last long. Sometime they try to make the image out of wood, but seem like the tool ain't right, so most times they [were made] of clay.[5]

Although these African clay sculptures did not survive, numerous examples of African American woodcarving in the Savannah area did. These range from carved figures, busts, and masklike forms by Jerome Carter of Frogtown (see figs. 9, 10) to the slim, reptile-adorned canes of James "Stick Daddy" Cooper of Port Wentworth (see fig. 11), to a jointed wood figure used as a yard decoration by Lee Ross of Ogeechee Road.[6] The most frequently found carved objects are canes or walking sticks, some of which are identified with conjurers or root doctors.[7] Unfortunately, no surviving works by the previously mentioned Savannah carvers have been located at present. Much of the physical evidence for an African-influenced carving tradition resides in the work of William Rogers of Darien, Georgia. Rogers's work ranged from canes and animal carvings of frogs and alligators to figurative utensils. The artist's daughter also recalls that Rogers carved a rice mortar and pestle from a large tree trunk, and that he "made anything that was needed" around his farm.[8] The carving of utilitarian objects such as utensils is paralleled in a more figurative work by an unknown artist, a wooden spoon found in the Old Fort section of Savannah (fig. 12). Earlier figurative utensils by Africans in the Savannah area were recalled by a former slave who was interviewed for the *Drums and Shadows* project.[9] Some of Rogers's work, particularly his carved frog (p. 85) and canes (pp. 85, 86), have been described in terms of similari-

5. *Georgia Writers' Project,* Drums and Shadows, *106. Translated from phonetically spelled dialect in the original text.*
6. *Ibid., 25 (James Cooper), 33 (Jerome Carter), 54 (Lee Ross).*
7. *Ibid., 70. Although he did not make canes, Allen Parker of Tatemville, a root doctor, reportedly made utilitarian objects as well as carvings of snakes, lizards, frogs, and other animals.*
8. *Personal communication with Lucille Wright, May 1996.*
9. *Georgia Writers' Project,* Drums and Shadows, *67.*

ties to African sculpture.[10]

Often ignored in discussions of Rogers is the fact that he was an extremely important man in his community, serving as the last black representative in Georgia's state government before the disenfranchisement of blacks in 1907.[11] Perhaps it is not too great a stretch to suggest that Rogers's leadership status in his community related to his production of certain objects, particularly canes and staffs. Ramona Austin notes, with caution, that African American canes "most closely resemble the staffs of Kongo chiefs."[12] Valiantly, futilely standing up for the rights of black voters, serving for five years as a representative of MacIntosh County, Rogers was most certainly an elder of importance in his community. Additional study of Rogers's work, family history, social status, and other factors will be necessary, not only to trace his work to specific African cultural precedents but also to determine its larger meanings. As folklorist Henry Glassie notes, "we might come to think of folk art as human creativity in a social context. That is not a bad beginning."[13]

Traditional art of African influence was by no means confined to wood sculpture. Basket makers, drum makers and other artisans were noted in *Drums and Shadows*. Savannah basketry, which was inextricably tied to the tradition of black street vendors and market hucksters, virtually disappeared with the destruction of the Old City Market building in 1954. Other works once attributed to African American traditions, particularly the form known as the "memory jug," appear to have more complex cultural roots. Previously associated only with the South, and regarded as a three-dimensional manifestation of the African-influenced decoration of graves, memory vessels have now been found as far beyond the South as Switzerland.[14] Nonetheless, a Savannah example (p. 112) in the current exhibition is said to have once decorated an African American grave in the Woodville cemetery near Savannah, according to the family of the deceased.[15] This example includes cowrie shells (ubiquitous in African art and culture), as does another Savannah memory jug, salvaged from a burned house in an African American neighborhood (fig. 13). This latter piece takes on a figurative presence through the addition of a skull finial, which may underscore a funerary theme and intent. Whether African American memory jugs point to African influence or to African American modifications of a European or European American form, the mystery of this object type has only increased with time.

Nineteenth-century craft types, including perhaps memory jugs, Victorian glass "whimsies," and stick furniture, persisted and in the early years of the twentieth century joined a host of new inventive art and craft forms, such as bottle cap sculpture and matchstick and toothpick crafts. The lean years of the 1930s hit particularly hard in the South, spawning cultural productions ranging from make-do crafts to the make-do architecture of shantytowns such as Savannah's "Tin City." Cast-off scraps from a consumer-oriented society were fashioned into useful items, whimsical pastime pursuits, as well as

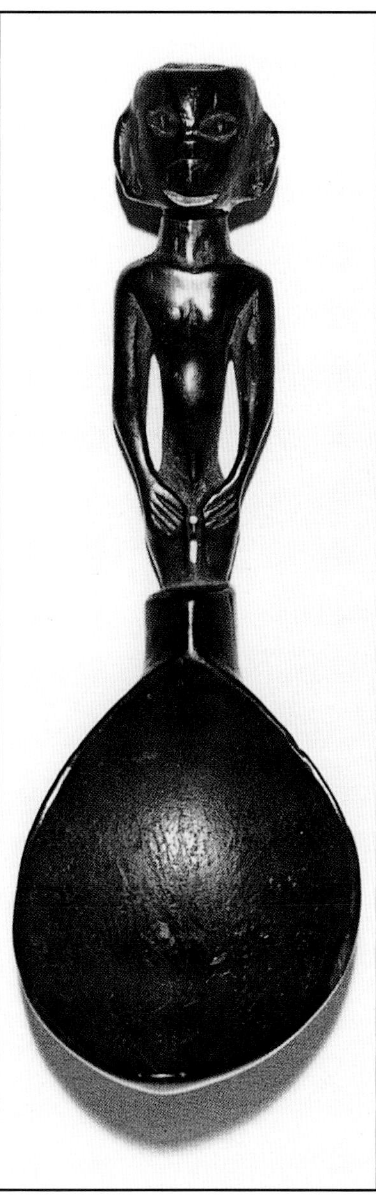

Fig. 12. Unidentified artist, Spoon, *Savannah, Georgia. (Photograph by Muriel and Malcolm Bell, Jr.)*

10. *See Thompson, "African Influences," 45; and Ramona Austin, "Defining the African American Cane," in George H. Meyer,* American Folk Art Canes: Personal Sculpture *(Bloomfield Hills, Mich.: Sandringham Press, 1992).*

11. *Donald J. Grant,* The Way It Was in the South: The Black Experience in Georgia *(New York: A Birch Lane Press Book, Carol Publishing Group,(1993),209–10.*

12. *Austin, "Defining the African-American Cane,"* 222.

13. *Glassie,* Spirit of Folk Art, *36.*

14. *Telephone interview with Brooke Anderson Linga, May 1996.*

15. *Telephone interview with H. Paul Blatner, May 10, 1996.*

objects for sale. This "culture of making do,"[16] as historian Carroll Greene calls it, encompassed traditional craft items and more popularly derived forms alike.

The post-Depression era in Savannah yielded unusual types such as sculptural memorials, which may have been known in Savannah as "Castles in the Sky." Two examples in the current exhibition (pp. 110, 111) may indicate an African American variant of precedents like the Victorian glass whimsie, or the puzzle bottles often attributed to sailors. Both inscribed "Savannah," the two works were purchased in different places and at different times, and, judging by their style, appear to be by two different artisans. One work is dedicated to a mother, the other to a deceased couple, suggesting personally commissioned or executed memorials.

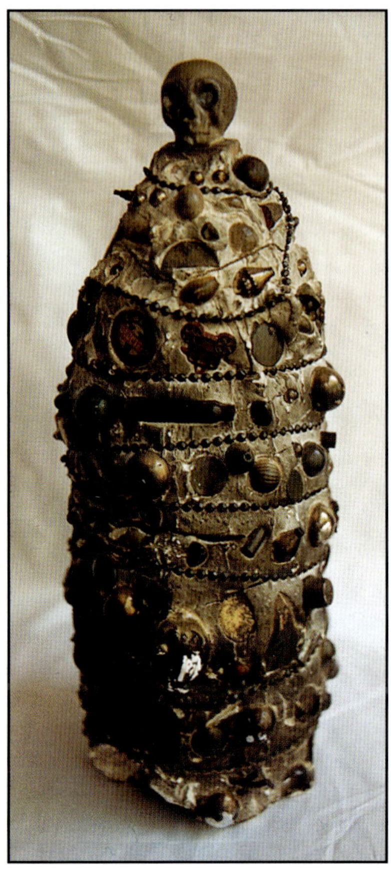

Fig. 13. Unidentified artist, Memory Vessel, c.1930s to 1940s, mixed media on ceramic jug. Acacia Collection of African-Americana

Outsiders and the Self-Taught

Outside of the Savannah Art Club, the Telfair Academy, and the city's colleges, and perhaps outside tradition or economic concern, individual artists of little or no training were known and occasionally encouraged in Savannah. Famous examples include Ulysses Davis, now Savannah's best-known sculptor of the twentieth century. Davis's work was "discovered" and first exhibited by educator and museum founder Virginia Kiah, who described his early influences as follows:

> His creative urge was probably inspired early in life as he watched an uncle doing pencil sketches of people, and his first efforts were devoted to whittling spinning tops for himself and neighborhood boys. When he was eleven years old he gave up whittling and turned to carving, using any soft wood he could find. He became interested in carving the human figure, and when he saw demonstrations at the movies of the carving of forms like people, animals and flowers, he made up his mind to pursue his new interest.[17]

Despite temptations to compare Davis with the Afro-Georgian carving traditions already discussed, no such direct link is known. In a 1978 interview with Virginia Kiah, Davis denied the influence of African art on his work, though he would later produce images of African kings based on a popular advertising campaign. Davis's repertoire includes lizards and other beasts noted in African American carving, and his inclusion of the ball-in-cage device in works such as *Tower of Babel* (p. 41) may subtly hint at his awareness of other woodcarvers. Davis's subject matter—religious images, patriotic figures, portraits, animals, and whimsical creations—mirrors that of many self-taught artists. His best carvings display a great deal of sculptural sophistication and inventiveness, culminating in opulent mature works adorned with "twinklets," the artist's term for rhinestones and other jewelry fragments.

Aside from sculptures by Ulysses Davis, relatively few examples of religious visionary art in early twentieth-century Savannah are known. For example, in the Chatham County Jail in Savannah, Ben Davis, who was serving a life sentence for murder, began to draw religious imagery. Known only through a newspaper story of 1933, Davis is said to have eventually made paintings, including large-scale works, after his transfer to a Milledgeville prison farm.[18] In addition to prisons, small churches, both black and white, were also likely locations of religious expression by the self-taught. The figuratively embellished "gospel car" of Bishop Grace (fig. 15) was a striking visual counterpart to worship services in which brass bands brought down the spirit to an impassioned congregation.[19]

Given Savannah's status as a seaport town, one might expect to find nautical images by local self-taught artists. Paintings, relief images, ship models, and marine images in general were often produced by seamen on long voyages, by those stationed in the local port, and by retired sailors in rest homes. Two Savannah practitioners of this genre, both African American seamen, are William Gray and William O. Golding. Gray, who may have worked for the Ocean Steamship Company, painted one known work (p. 53) in the tradition (a term used loosely here) of marine painting. Naive paint-

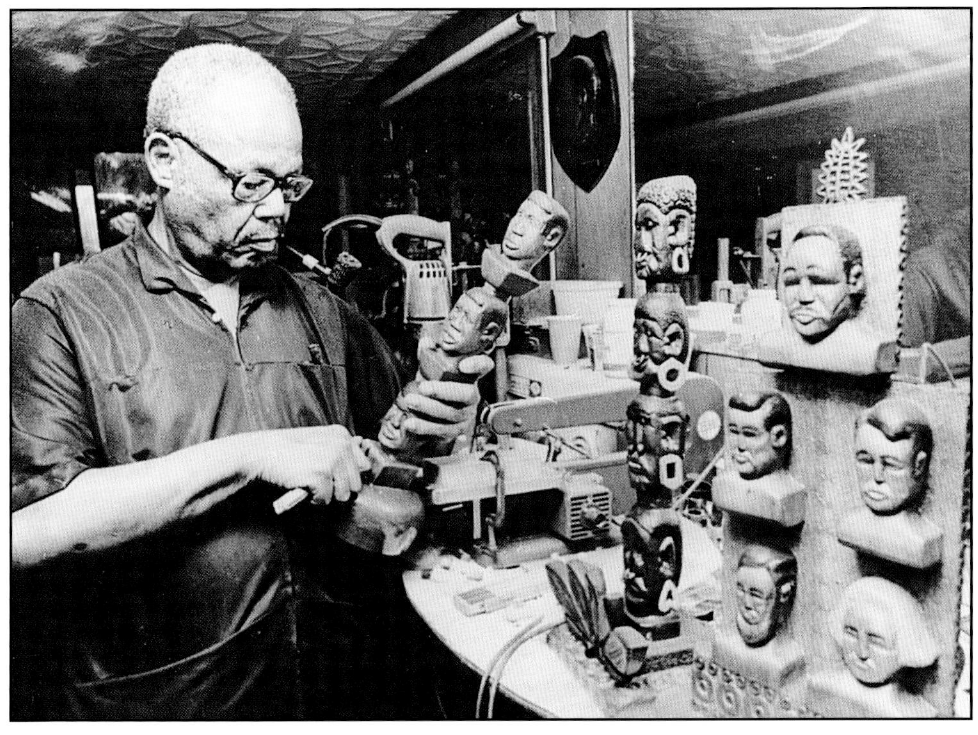

Fig. 14. Ulysses Davis with woodcarvings in his barbershop, c.1978. (Photograph courtesy Savannah News-Press*)*

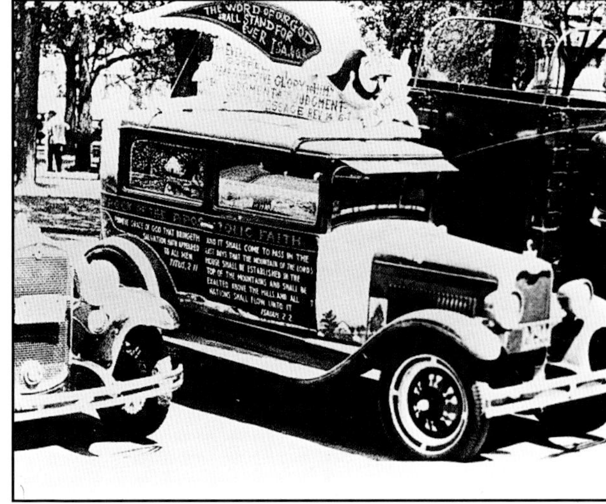

Fig. 15. Bishop Grace's Gospel Car, c.1930s. General Photograph Collection, The Georgia Historical Society

ings of ships at sea are common in American history, and Gray's engaging work does not stray far from the norm.

Nautical subjects received more personalized interpretation in the work of William O. Golding, who is said to have made about sixty color drawings during periods of treatment at the the marine hospital in Savannah during the 1930s.[20] Golding's work, which has been included since the 1970s in exhibitions of southern and self-taught art, shares commonalities with the work of other memory painters in his compositions of far-off lands and local scenes depicted according to his own sense of reality. Like other self-taught artists, Golding developed distinctive conventionalizations of forms, like the setting or rising sun, mountains, trees, lighthouses, and birds in flight (so plentiful as to function as pattern or texture), which occur throughout his work. These animated compositions bustle with rhythmic repetitions of lines and shapes, resulting in something like a visual sea chantey.

Golding was encouraged to draw by Margaret Stiles, an academically trained artist and member of the Savannah Art Club who volunteered at the hospital where Golding was being treated. Golding's colorful life story is known through letters sent to Stiles during her stays out of town, and in them he gives some indication that she was exhibiting his work. In a letter to Stiles, dated August 10, 1933, Golding writes of his drawings, "I have took great pains with some of them for some have taken 2 to 3 days making. I think

16. *Telephone interview with Carroll Greene, May 18, 1996.*
17. *Virginia Kiah, "Ulysses Davis: Savannah Folk Sculptor,"* Southern Folklore Quarterly *42 (1978): 271.*
18. *Lillian Chaplin Bragg, "Life Term Prisoner Makes Religious Pictures,"* Savannah Morning News, *January 31, 1933.*
19. *Bishop Grace was the spiritual leader and founder of the Houses of Prayer, still strong in Savannah and the United States today. A visit by Bishop Grace to Savannah's Brownville neighborhood is described in Georgia Writers' Project,* Drums and Shadows, *46–51.*
20. *Anna Wadsworth, in* Missing Pieces: Georgia Folk Art 1776–1976 *(Atlanta: Georgia Council for the Arts and Humanities, 1976), 47.*

they are getting better and better all the time; [there] are some you can pick out for exhibition purposes."[21] Stiles's interest in Golding's work was likely as aesthetic in nature as it was humanitarian, for the decade of the 1930s was the time of America's discovery of contemporary "primitive art."

The Not-so-Naive

Interestingly, though modern art never thrived in the Savannah of the mid-twentieth century, the city's artists, both academically trained and amateur, took interest in the work of self-taught artists, who were increasingly displayed within a modern art context. Nationally and internationally, a mounting interest in so-called primitive art—including African, Oceanic, and non-Western art in general; art of the insane; and American folk art (the traditional and the idiosyncratic)—had repercussions that reached Savannah by the 1930s. In addition to local artists like Margaret Stiles, visiting artists from New York had become preoccupied with the perceived primal vision of the self-taught. Nationally prominent artist Alexander Brook, a galvanizing force in Savannah's art scene, was a collector of the work of Nashville's visionary sculptor, William Edmonson.[22] Edmonson was the first black and the first self-taught artist to have a solo exhibition at the Museum of Modern Art, New York. Other artists and collectors of folk art active in the low country were Arnold Blanch and Lucille Blanch. Arnold Blanch painted in coastal Georgia and South Carolina, and he was well known to Brook and other artists at work in the port city. Blanch's images of rural landscapes (for example, *Some Place in Georgia*, 1940, Metropolitan Museum of Art) exemplify the American scene as subject, and evidence a simplicity of form and flattening of space possibly derived from naive painting. These faux-naive stylistic features permeate a great deal of American Scene painting from the 1930s and 1940s. Yet-to-be fully explored factors contributing to this aesthetic include the previously discussed interest in primitive art, the exhibition of self-taught artists as modern artists, and the identification of naive paintings and folk art with America's history. In a conservative artistic environment like Savannah's, the appropriation of aspects of naive painting may have been an acceptable option for artists who eschewed formal abstraction but nevertheless desired their work to be perceived as "modern."

National and local artists also saw the faux-naive style as an appropriate mode for recording the African American folk culture of Savannah. The painter Anna Hunter perhaps best embodies this tendency on the local scene. Hunter had been a writer for the *Savannah News-Press* for many years when, in 1946, she enrolled in a children's art class taught by Augusta Oelschig. Oelschig's work frequently explores aspects of African American life in Savannah but is often painted realistically or expressionistically without overtly incorporating the flattened forms of naive painting. Hunter approached similar subject matter in a style that simultaneously reflects her relatively untrained status as well as a knowledge of current trends garnered during her years as a literature and art writer for the *Savannah News-Press*. Describing Hunter in a brochure for her first one-artist exhibition in 1948, modernist painter Gina Knee (wife of Alexander Brook) wrote: "what counts is that her work has the spirit of fine Folk Art particularly because she truly grasps the spirit of the things closest to her. You feel she loves to paint her subject and that she paints the subject she loves."[23] Obviously, Knee considered Hunter's "folk" style appropriate for folkloric subject matter, as in the harvesting image *Recessional* (p. 61). (As an interesting aside, Knee's exhibition brochure includes playful collages about Hunter's artistic endeavors as well as bogus reviews lampooning the verbiage of contemporary [modern] art critics.) Although some of her works actually betray a lack of skill, and others incorporate sentimental themes and racial caricature, Hunter's best works show a genuine sensitivity to her subject matter as well as a modernist sense of painterly space. The artist says of herself in a newspaper interview, "I'm not a technical person but always conscious of new trends and my lack of training."[24] Hunter sold numerous pieces in Savannah and the Southeast, and exhibited at an interior design studio in New York. Photographs of Savannah Art Club paintings from the late 1940s through the 1950s attest to the popularity of Hunter's folksy style.

Consequences and Continuations

The art production of Savannah in the early twentieth century parallels that of many other provincial centers, with a few important distinctions. The scenic nature of the old city, the coastal landscape, and the African American environment and folk culture attracted and inspired visiting artists and locals alike. Perceived exoticism aside, the size and strength of the African American community in Savannah provided a sympathetic environment for the continuation of cultural modes with some African antecedents.

What has been called an Afro-Georgian carving tradition did not die out suddenly. The civil rights era and the Black Power movement of the 1960s and 1970s sparked a renewed interest and pride in African heritage, which prompted a reclamation of traditional wood carvings and canes with African motifs. Savannah canes were produced by younger individuals such as Vernon Edwards, who learned his craft from the older Savannah cane carvers.[25] Others, like Arthur Peter Dilbert, updated traditional forms to fit economic demands and the sentiments of the 1960s. A sampling of his carved canes includes combinations of reptiles and the upraised fist of the Black Power movement, as well as shamrock-adorned canes produced to meet the needs of revelers at Savannah's large St. Patrick's Day parades. More recently, Willis Hakim Jones, a young collector of African Americana, has adopted cane carving as a reclamation of tradition.[26]

The individual self-taught artist is likewise manifested in post-1960 Savannah. Memory drawings such as those that William Golding produced in the 1930s find a later counterpart in the work of Captain William E. Jordan, who took an interest in art after losing his sight in 1957. In a systematic approach to drawing without sight, Jordan is said to have produced over six hundred works representing places he had visited. In addition he founded a gallery and art association, which were short-lived.[27] Later still, Rudolph Valentino Bostic created powerful religious paintings on discarded cardboard, utilizing a personally reinvented chiaroscuro technique. In Bostic's work, the culture of making do—still very much alive—meets Michelangelo and Georges Rouault as well as popular biblical illustration. Bostic, an "outsider" to professional training is now receiving attention "inside" the art world, with gallery representation in major cities.

Exhibitions have increased awareness and sometimes confusion regarding nonacademic art. Savannah area artists such as William Rogers and Ulysses Davis received regional exposure in the landmark exhibition *Missing Pieces: Georgia Folk Art 1776–1976* (organized for the Atlanta History Center and exhibited at the Telfair Academy, 1976), now criticized for a catch-all approach to representing folk art of the past with the self-taught art of the present. This was followed by *The Afro-American Tradition in Decorative Arts* (Cleveland Museum of Art, 1978) and *Black Folk Art in America* (Corcoran Gallery of Art, 1981), which brought national attention to traditional artists like Rogers and the self-taught Davis, respectively. Savannah's major commitment to preserving the work of a self-taught artist is exemplified by the community's successful effort to purchase and maintain over two hundred works by Ulysses Davis, now in the collection of the Beach Institute African American Cultural Center.

Material culturalists decry the folk art explosion in the realm of commercial galleries and museums for its perceived detrimental effect on the standard bearers of discernible traditions. Certainly, emphasis has been placed on self-taught and traditional art that looks like "fine art," as John Michael Vlach has pointed out,[28] but this is certainly not radically different from the relative marginalism of contemporary craft in general to painting, drawing, and sculpture. In any case, the debate over the nature of folk art and the separation of folk culture (and craft in general) from high art is likely to continue long into the future. Distinctions will be made as new information comes to light through rigorous investigation by scholars of different disciplines. Looking beyond gallery promotion, the art market, labels, etc., to larger patterns and detailed information regarding the artist and his or her community, the Davises and Bostics of the world may even prove to be as much traditionalists as visionary loners. Art is rarely, if ever, created in a vacuum. Savannah's old and complex social and physical landscape has provided a wellspring for the city's artists throughout the twentieth century. Lumped together until recent times, the tradition bearers, idiosyncratic creators, and those in between will surely find an increasingly conducive environment in one old city's future.

21. *Ibid.*

22. *Edmund L.Fuller,* Visions in Stone: The Sculpture of William Edmonson *(Pittsburgh, Pa.: University of Pittsburgh Press, 1973), 27.*

23. *Exhibition brochure, printed by* Savannah Morning News *(1948), Telfair Academy artist file.*

24. *Mardelle Musk, "Newspaperwoman Turns Artist,"* Charleston Evening Post, *October 13, 1950.*

25. *Telephone interview with H. Paul Blatner.*

26. *Personal communication with Willis Hakim Jones, May 1996. Self-taught as a cane carver, Jones is a second-generation craftsman whose father produced stick furniture in Savannah as a young man.*

27. *Brochure for Jordan Art Gallery (1960), Telfair Academy artist files.*

28. *See John Michael Vlach,* Plain Painters: Making Sense of American Folk Art *(Washington, D.C.: Smithsonian Institution Press, 1988).*

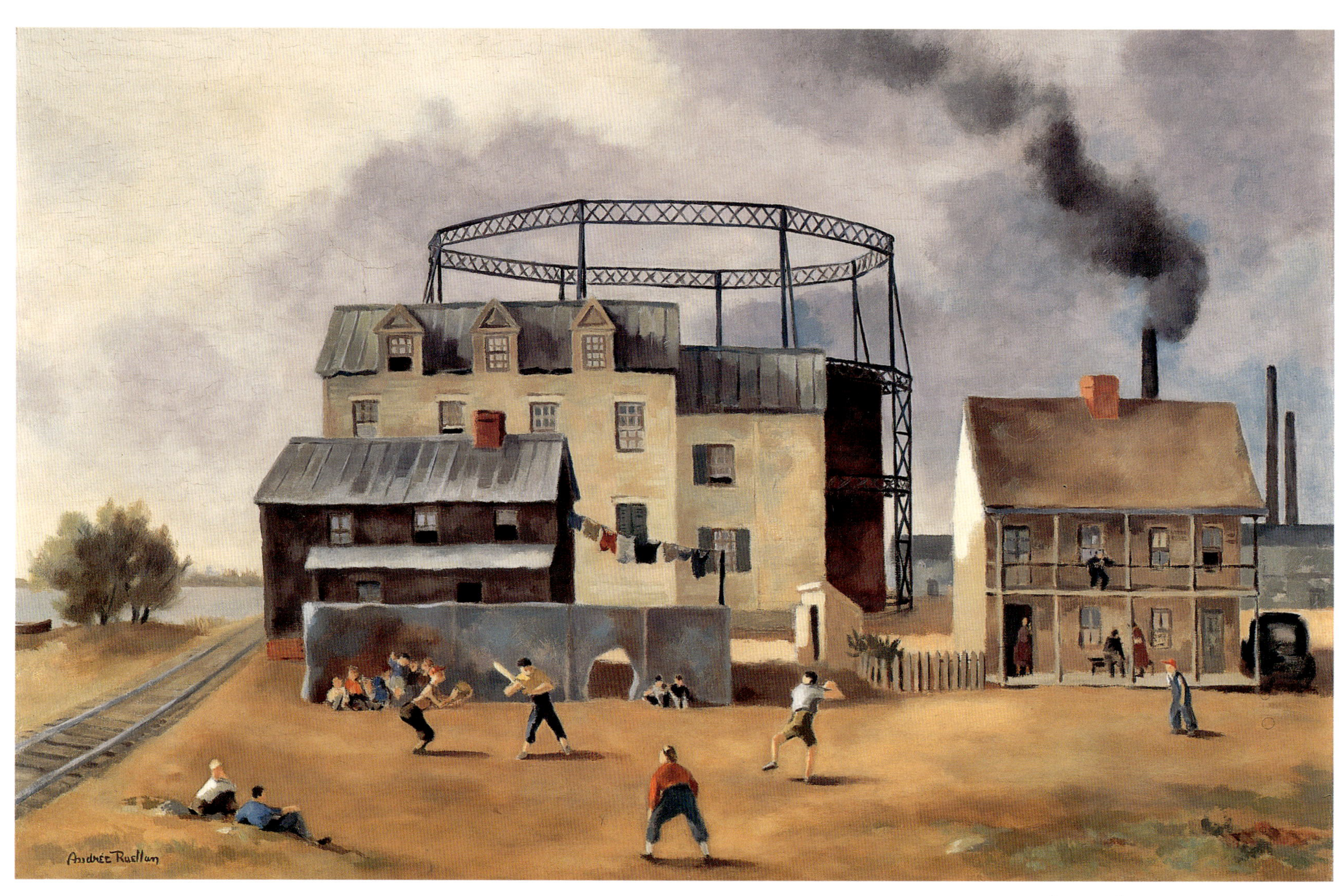

Andrée Ruellan, The Wind-Up, *1941*
The Phillips Collection, Washington, D.C.

Catalogue of the Exhibition

Hilda Belcher

(1881–1963)

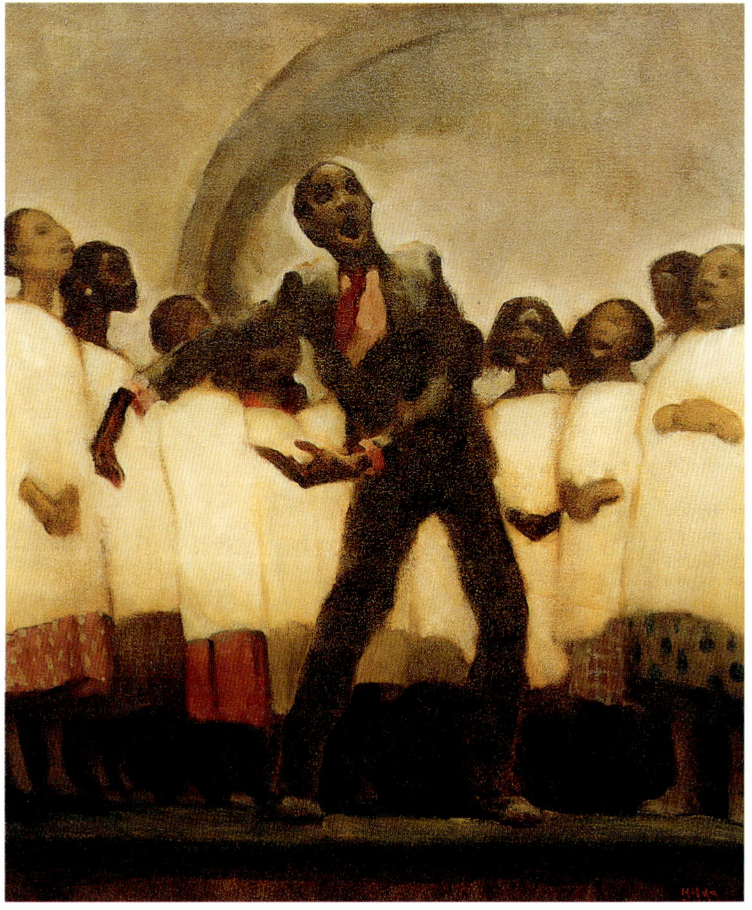

GO DOWN MOSES, 1936
Oil on canvas
36 x 30 in. (91.4 x 76.2 cm)
Collection of Barbara Belcher Mericle

HILDA BELCHER OF PITTSFORD, VERMONT, was one of the many extraordinary artists who visited Savannah. Although not well known today, she was an outstanding figure in American art in the 1920s and 1930s. In 1926 she became the second woman ever to be elected to the National Academy of Design. She won numerous awards for her painting from 1908 through the 1940s. Belcher was the only woman participant among 693 who entered the prestigious Strathmore watercolor contest in 1908; she won first prize. In 1935 a reviewer for the *New York Times* proclaimed her "one of the most distinguished women artists in America."[1]

Belcher came to art naturally. Her mother, Martha Wood Belcher, was a gifted painter in her own right and encouraged her daughter's innate talents at a young age. After graduating from high school in New Jersey, where the family had moved to establish her father's stained-glass business, Belcher went to New York City in 1900 to study painting at the Chase School. She worked under George Bellows and George Luks, but her most influential instructors were Kenneth Hayes Miller and, especially, Robert Henri. All of these artists were of the school that promoted painting the everyday world in a direct manner. Belcher took these lessons to heart, but after graduating in 1904, had to make her living designing stained-glass windows and selling illustrations and cartoons to publishing companies and to magazines such as *Harper's*, *Century*, *Woman's Home Companion*, and *St. Nicholas*. In 1910 she received an invitation from her earlier mentor, Henri, to participate with a "rebellious" group of artists in the *Exhibition of Independent Artists*. She submitted three works.

Belcher was able to support herself through sales of her work, portrait commissions, prize money, and by teaching art both privately and, in 1911–12, at the Art Students League in New York. She maintained studios in New York and Pittsford along with her mother; both painted and sketched in the Northeast and, in 1913–14, on a grand tour of western Europe.

Belcher achieved success as a portraitist early in her career; she was especially noted for her likenesses of children painted in watercolor. Even though all of her art training was in oil, she preferred the watercolor medium. In 1948 she recalled, "I'd never studied watercolor in school, probably that's why, having to find my own way in it, I enjoyed it more."[2]

The artist's first contact with Savannah came in 1913 with a portrait commission from the Waring family. This began a relationship with the city and its inhabitants that would last from the 1920s through the 1930s. She would visit for months at a time, painting, teaching, and exhibiting at the Telfair. Typical of her formal portraits of Savannahians is *Mary Comer Lane*. Wearing an elegant dress and holding a red feather fan, the subject is seated before a neutral, but enlivened, background with only a few props to indicate her gentility. Light softly streams in from the left.

Stately, yet unaffected, the sitter is preserved in a genuine way. The rich brushwork and the immediacy of her personality recall Henri's influence on Belcher.

Society patrons were not the only subjects that caught the eye of the artist. She recorded the streets of the city and the surrounding landscape, including Bonaventure Cemetery, Wormsloe, Bradley's Point, and Tybee Island. Figure studies, as opposed to formal portraits, also occupied her brush. Belcher was very interested in depicting Savannah's African American community. This interest, along with her specialty of depicting children in watercolor, is combined in *Choir Girls, Savannah*. Belcher focuses here on three young girls who seriously and solemnly sing praises to God. By contrast, a livelier chorus is seen in *Go Down Moses*. The entire choir, in white robes, forms a crescent behind the preacher. The viewer can almost feel the vibrancy of the music in the air and the sound of true conviction in the singers' voices.

Go Down Moses, an oil painting, is the culmination of Belcher's studies, usually in watercolor, depicting African Americans worshiping and singing in church. She exhibited these works widely in the South and Northeast to enthusiastic acclaim. They were painted at a time when "negro spirituals" enjoyed great interest among urban whites, especially in New York. Choreographers created dances to this music, and the Federal Theatre Negro Chorus held performances in New York, where the impact of the Harlem Renaissance was still felt.[3] Thus it was that African Americans in southern settings had become an important subject for artists.

Belcher's genre scenes can be linked to the art movement that was at its height in this country in the 1930s—Regionalism, or American Scene painting, led by, among others, Thomas Hart Benton. Regionalism was the culmination of an insistent American iconography that had been called for by critics over many years. The South became a subject of interest to many. Benton, himself, traveled through the region in 1926 and produced several images based on what he saw.

To convey their message, the Regionalists chose realism as their vehicle, ignoring the growing presence and influence of modernism. Hilda Belcher, during her forty-some-year painting career, witnessed the development of Cubism, Precisionism, and Abstract Expressionism. She, too, chose to render her subjects in a realist style.

P.D.K.

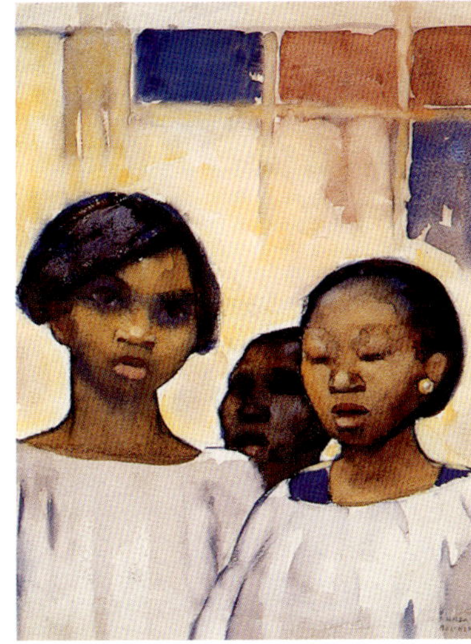

Choir Girls, Savannah,
1934
Watercolor on paper
22 x 15 in.
(56 x 38.1 cm)
Collection of
Barbara Belcher Mericle

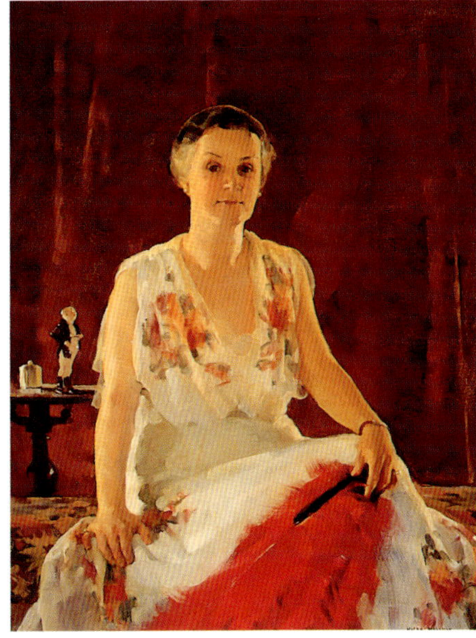

Mary Comer Lane,
1934
Oil on canvas
40 x 30 ½ in.
(102 x 77.2 cm)
Collection of the
Family of Mary Comer Lane

1. *Anne Miller Downs,* Savannah Morning News, *April 9, 1935; quoted in Janie Cohen, "Hilda Belcher: A Realist Rediscovered,"* American Art Review. *6, no. 4 (1994): 90.*

2. *Letter from H. Belcher to Mrs. Snare, August 2, 1948. Quoted in Cohen, "Hilda Belcher," 91.*

3. *Cohen, "Hilda Belcher," 95.*

Muriel Barrow Bell
(b.1913)
Malcolm Bell, Jr.
(b.1913)

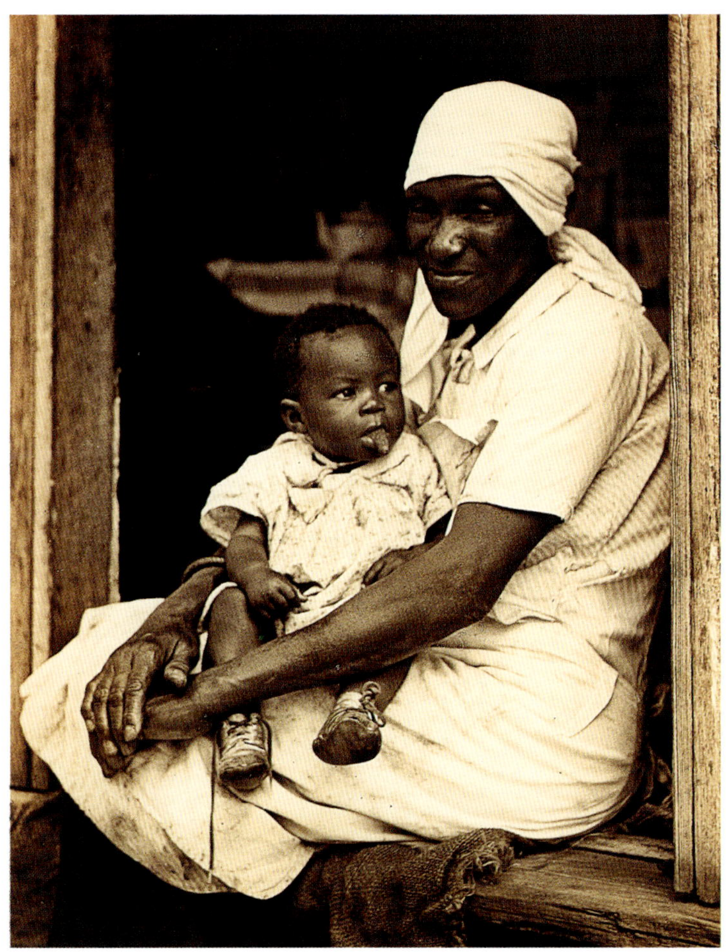

WOMAN AND BABY AT PIN POINT,
c.1939
Photograph
13 3/16 x 10 1/4 in. (33.5 x 26 cm)
Beach Institute
African American Cultural Center

OF ALL NATIVE SAVANNAHIANS active in photography, the husband and wife team of Muriel and Malcolm Bell, Jr., has found perhaps the largest audience beyond their home city. This is due largely to a single, stunning photo essay that accompanied the Georgia Writers' Project publication *Drums and Shadows* in 1940.[1] The Bells were not professionally trained photographers in the 1930s, when they linked up with their "older and interesting family friend,"[2] Mary Granger, supervisor of the *Drums and Shadows* project. Granger enlisted the Bells to assist in the documentation of African American folklife in Savannah and coastal Georgia. The Bell's work for this landmark study consists of photographs of artifacts (see figs. 9–12) and penetrating character studies.

In their photographers' note to the 1986 edition of *Drums and Shadows*, the Bells describe their working methods:

> We used a German-made Eastman Kodak, a 2 1/4 x 3 1/4-inch ground glass camera called a Recomar. A sturdy tripod and a large black cloth enabled us to stop the lens down to its limit of f/32 and to bring forth a sharp image on the inverted glass screen. The stationary subject permitted ample time to compose our picture; first one of us, then the other made the necessary adjustments from under the black cloth.[3]

The Bells displayed their photographs in the 1940s in exhibitions at the Telfair Academy and at the New York Stock Exchange, where they won several awards. For many years, their work was visible on the local scene, illustrating the literary page of the *Savannah News-Press*. The couple remained active in the cultural life of the community, supporting organizations including the Georgia Historical Society and the Telfair Academy. Muriel Bell served as a trustee of the latter institution. Malcolm Bell, Jr., also made his name as a successful banker, and has published several books on Savannah history.

H.H.D.

1. *Georgia Writer's Project,* Drums and Shadows: Survival Studies Among The Georgia Coastal Negroes *(Athens, Ga.: The University of Georgia Press, 1940; reprinted, Brown Thrasher Books, The University of Georgia Press, 1986).*
2. *Ibid., xxix*
3. *Ibid., xxx.*

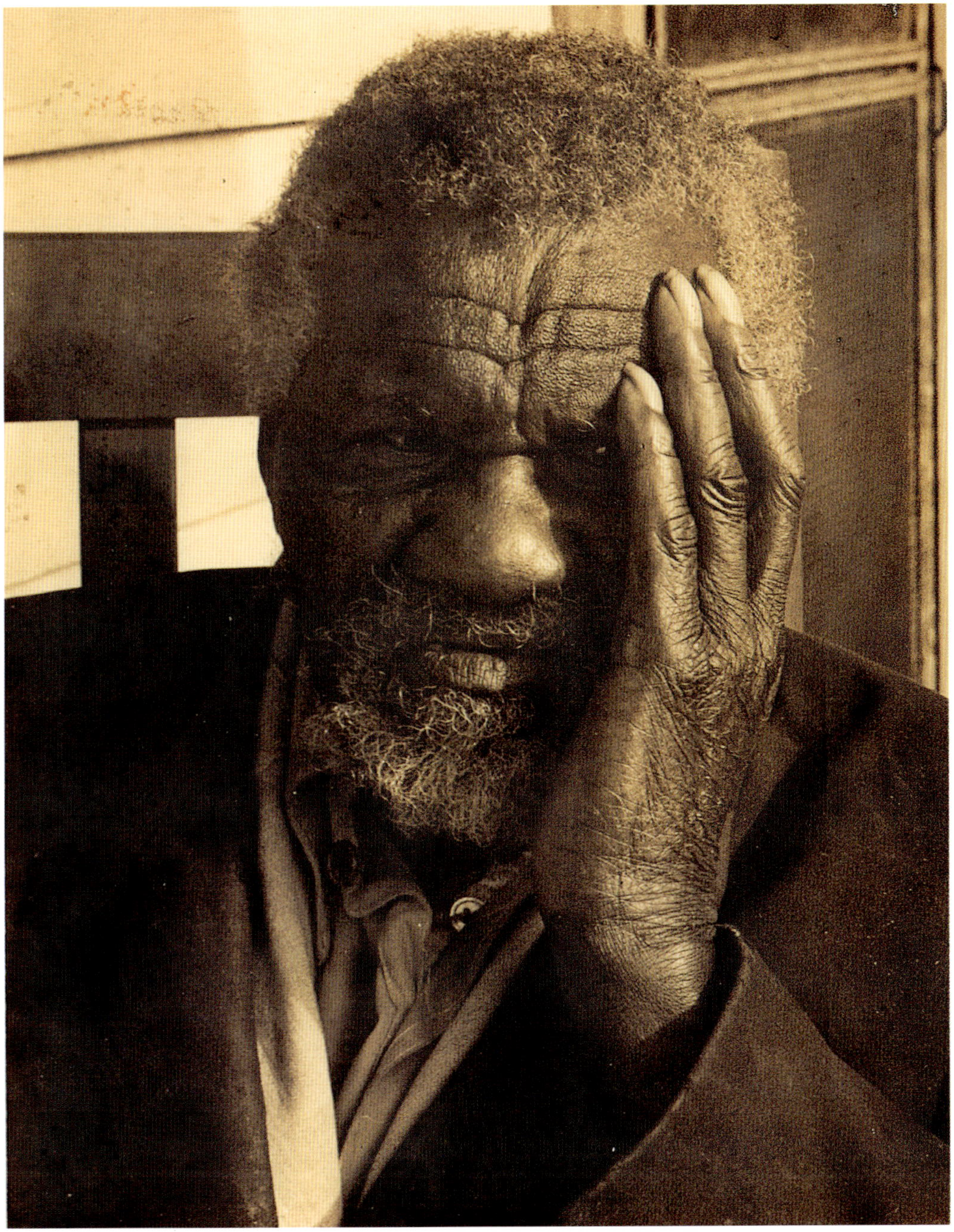

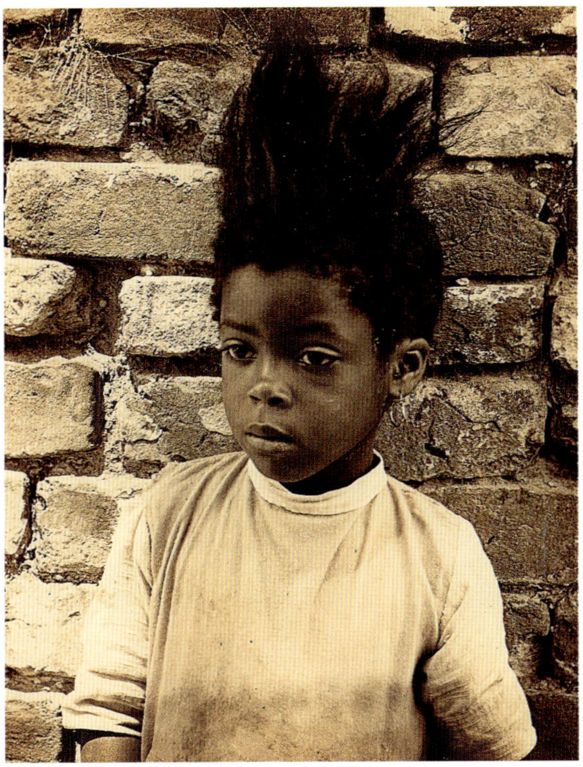

Girl at Pin Point, c.1939
Photograph
13 ½ x 10 ⅜ in. (33.5 x 26 cm)
Beach Institute
African American Cultural Center

Tony Delegal at Ogeechee Town, c.1939,
Photograph
13 ¼ x 10 ⅛ in. (34 x 26 cm)
Collection of Ronald J. Strahan

Louis Bouché

(1896–1969)

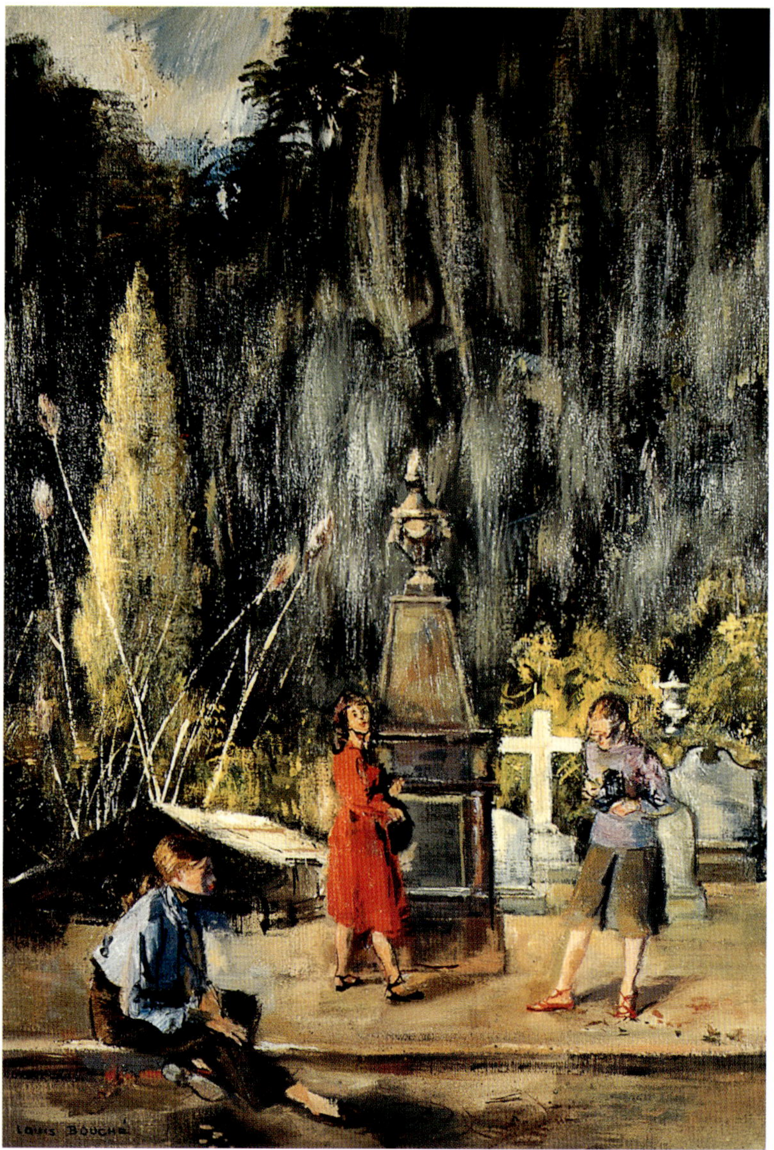

BONAVENTURE, n.d.
Oil on canvas
31 ⅜ x 21 ¼ in. (80 x 54 cm)
Telfair Museum of Art,
Gift of Marian Bouché, 1969

A TREMENDOUSLY VERSATILE ARTIST, Louis Bouché was born into an artistic family in New York City. In 1910, at age fourteen, Bouché traveled to Paris to study at the Ecole des Beaux-Arts. He returned to New York in 1915, where he studied at the Art Students League for a year under Frank Vincent DuMond and Luis Mora. During this period, Bouché's painting style reflected the main influence at the time, French Impressionism. Soon, however, Bouché became interested in "Victorianism," which he defined as bad taste and sentimentality in art.[1] Until the early 1920s he created deliberately sentimental paintings, glorifying and exaggerating the subjects with humorous intent. Critic Carl Van Vechten describes this as Bouché's "Nottingham Lace" period.[2]

Bouché had turned away from easel painting by the early 1930s to focus on mural painting and interior decoration. His work from this period includes a mural for the Department of Justice building in Washington, D.C., and interior decoration for Radio City Music Hall. He also painted huge glass panels.

In the early 1940s, Bouché returned to painting on canvas. For about two years, he explored Cubism and abstraction, and experimented with geometric patterning. Following this brief period, he turned to a style he termed "realistic Impressionism," characterized by a greater attention to detail, a lighter, airier palette, and loose brush work. He continued in this style for the rest of his career.[3]

Bonaventure is an example of Bouché's so-called realistic Impressionism; it depicts three women posing before a memorial at Bonaventure Cemetery in Savannah. The three models are curiously unconnected to one another, and appear more like tourists than mourners. Despite the setting, *Bonaventure* is quite light, both in its mood and in its bright color. The Spanish moss that dominates the top half of the canvas is especially loosely painted, though Bouché must have spent a great deal of time on the effect. Bouché himself considered *Bonaventure* among his finest works.[4]

In addition to painting, Bouché taught at the National Academy of Design and the National Institute of Arts and Letters in New York. He also served as the associate director of the New York School of Interior Decoration, and was an artist in residence at the American Academy in Rome.

J.A.

1. *Letter from Marian Bouché to a Miss Geffen, February 4, 1953.*
2. *Ibid.*
3. *Ibid.*
4. *Letter from Marian Bouché to the Telfair Academy, December 9, 1969.*

Margaret Bourke-White

(1904–1971)

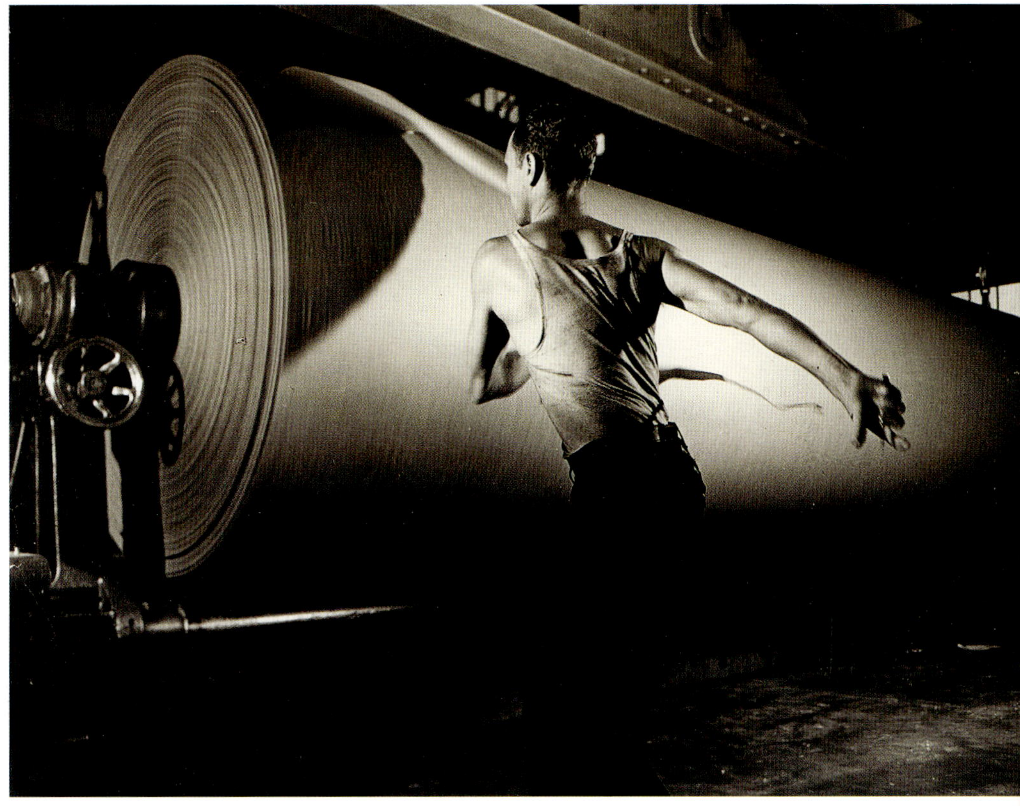

Worker Tears Off a Sample from a Roll of Paper to Test Its Quality, Savannah, Georgia, c.1939
Photograph
11 x 14 in. (28 x 36 cm)
Margaret Bourke-White, *Life* Magazine, © Time, Inc.

A STUDENT OF THE PICTORIALIST PHOTOGRAPHER Clarence H. White at Columbia University in New York, Margaret Bourke-White rejected the soft, tonal aesthetic of her teacher and became a photojournalist specializing in sharp-focus industrial images. She worked for Henry Luce's *Fortune* and *Life* magazines; her photograph of Fort Peck Dam appeared on the cover of the first issue of *Life* in 1936. She rapidly became America's most famous female photographer of the 1930s and 1940s, not only for her work but also for her daring feats, such as hanging out of an airplane to get the perfect aerial photograph.

In the late 1930s *Life* magazine sent Bourke-White to Savannah to document a celebration of the southern pine-pulp paper industry. The resultant photo-essay was published in the May 15, 1939, issue under the title "Life Goes to a Paper Festival at Savannah."[1] The twelve photographs published in the essay include images of Savannah high-school girls in paper dresses and swimming suits, the Paper Masque ball at the DeSoto Hotel, and the paper-making industry (photographed at the Union Bag & Paper Corporation).

One of these images was published with the caption "Tester Earl Young tears off sample from roll of paper to test its quality. Southern-pine paper will soon invade newsprint field with $6,000,000 plant at Lufkin, Tex." This photograph was also chosen to represent Bourke-White and *Life* in the 1979 exhibition and catalogue, *Life: The First Decade*, where it was published under the current title *Worker Tears Off a Sample from a Roll of Paper to Test Its Quality, Savannah, Georgia*.[2] This photograph shows Bourke-White's consummate skill in capturing industrial images. The static simplicity of the massive paper roll contrasts with the swift movement of the worker's arms as he rips off the paper sample. Bourke-White's spotlighting intensifies the focus on the worker's arms, which parallel the paper roll, creating a dynamic image of a mundane aspect of paper manufacture.

Also in the exhibition are other photographs of Savannah that were not published in the *Life* essay. These include two more images of the paper industry: stevedores loading paper pulp for shipping, and a barking machine. *Barking Machine* varies only slightly from an image that was included in the *Life* photo-essay. Bourke-White shot the published photograph from a somewhat closer vantage point at a moment when the logs were beginning to spill out of the open end of the drum.

Bourke-White also photographed some of the poverty-stricken areas of Savannah, as in *Negro Section, Savannah, Georgia*. This image attests to her continuing interest in the plight of the southern poor during the Depression, a topic she explored in the book *You Have Seen Their Faces*, which she coauthored with her future husband, Erskine Caldwell.[3] In 1936 Bourke-White and Caldwell met in Augusta, Georgia, where his parents lived, and traveled by automobile from Georgia to Arkansas photographing the sharecroppers and others who were struggling desperately to survive the Depression.

Just a few months after her trip to Savannah, World War II broke out, initiating a new phase in Margaret Bourke-White's career. She became the United States' first female war correspondent. After the war she continued to find subjects around the globe until Parkinson's disease forced her into early retirement in 1957.

C.L.B.

1. *"Life Goes to a Paper Festival at Savannah,"* Life, *v. 6, no. 20 (May 15, 1939): 82–85.*

2. Life: The First Decade *(New York: Time, Inc., 1979), 31–32.*

3. *Margaret Bourke-White and Erskine Caldwell,* You Have Seen Their Faces *(New York: The Viking Press, 1937).*

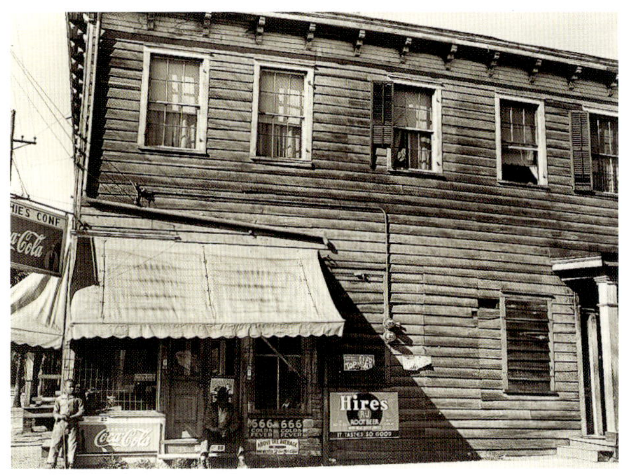

Above: NEGRO SECTION, SAVANNAH, GEORGIA, c.1939
Photograph
11 x 14 in. (28 x 36 cm)
Margaret Bourke-White, *Life* Magazine, © Time, Inc.

Right: STEVEDORES LOADING PULP WHICH IS MANUFACTURED IN THIS PLANT AND THEN SHIPPED TO OTHER PLANTS WHERE PAPER IS COMPLETED. SAVANNAH, GEORGIA, c.1939
Photograph
11 x 14 in. (28 x 36 cm)
Margaret Bourke-White, *Life* Magazine, © Time, Inc.

Below: BARKING MACHINE, SAVANNAH, GEORGIA, c.1939
Photograph
11 x 14 in. (28 x 36 cm)
Margaret Bourke-White, *Life* Magazine, © Time, Inc.

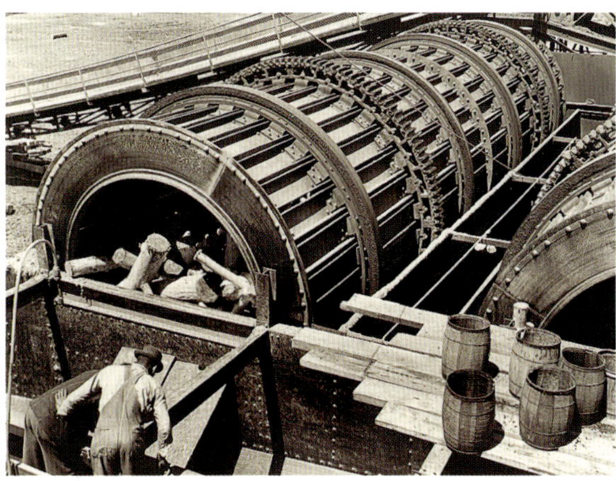

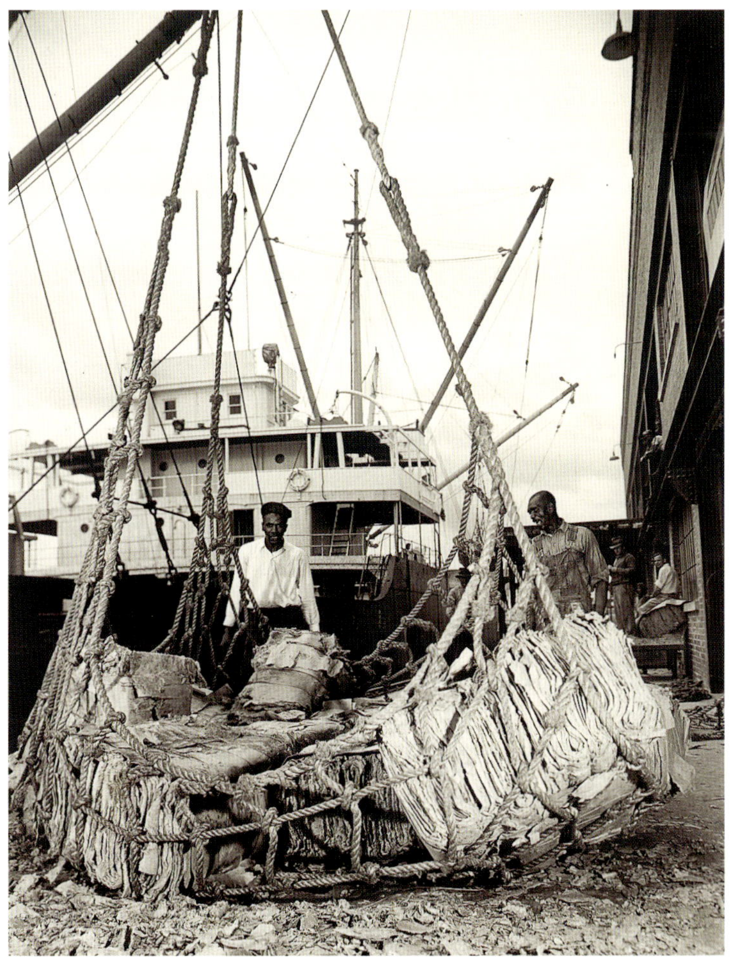

Alexander Brook

(1898–1980)

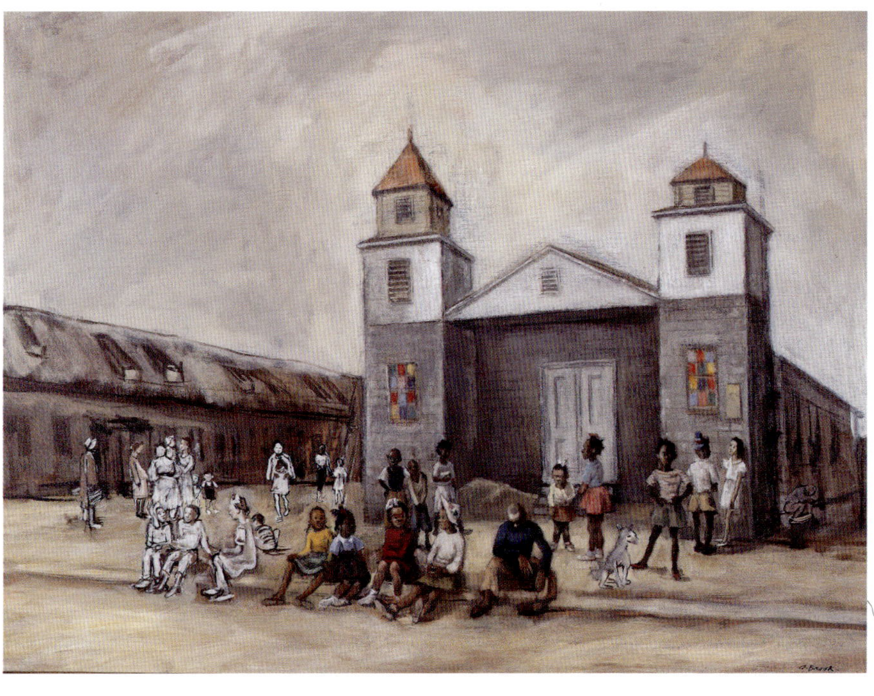

SAVANNAH STREET CORNER, n.d.
Oil on canvas
28 ¼ x 35 ¼ in.
(72 x 90 cm)
Telfair Museum of Art,
Gift of the Artist, 1972

DURING THE LATE 1930S and 1940s, Alexander Brook figured largely in the art scene of Savannah, judging by the many articles about him in the local newspaper. A celebrity in Savannah, Brook also enjoyed recognition on a national level.

Born in Brooklyn of Russian immigrant parents, Brook started painting and drawing at age twelve while at home recovering from an illness. He pursued his art career at the Art Students League, studying with, among others, Kenneth Hayes Miller, an artist known for his robust depictions of contemporary life. In 1915 Brook taught at the Art Students League, and in 1919 participated in the league's first summer school, held at Woodstock, New York. The Woodstock art colony supported several artists who later worked in Savannah; for example, Henry Lee McFee, an instructor at the colony at the time of Brook's residency there. Brook eventually moved to Woodstock in 1921 and stayed for two years.

Returning to New York City, Brook took on the job of assistant director of the Whitney Studio Club, an organization newly founded by Gertrude Vanderbilt Whitney to foster young American artists. (The Whitney Studio Club later became the Whitney Museum of American Art.) Gertrude Whitney and her Studio Club director, Julianna Force, favored art works of the realist tradition, shunning the abstractions of European modernism that had recently come to America. Their taste and Alexander Brook's—as well as the country's—was perfectly in tune.

From the late 1920s through the Depression era, America saw the triumph of realism and American Scene painting, the not-always objective recording of everyday life. Everything from poor or abundant farms in the South and Midwest to scenes of Coney Island became subject matter for artists. At this time Brook's preference of subjects (landscape and genre scenes, portraits, and still lifes) was becoming clear, and his painting style had matured. Using a somber palette and fluid brushwork, he created paintings that have a sentimental edge no matter how dismal the scene. "I find," he said,

> that I am more concerned, both sympathetically and aesthetically, with the simpler and sadder things about me. It is purely a personal thing that I find more beauty in the forlorn, the wretched and the humble than I have found in the conventionally beautiful.[1]

But he contended that there was no social message in his work as was the case with other artists painting similar subjects. One of Brook's best-known paintings reflecting his unconventional philosophy concerning what is beautiful is *Georgia Jungle* (p. 14), a Savannah subject that received first prize at the 1939 Carnegie International. This was both a triumph for the artist and a victory for the realist tradition.[2]

Brook came to Savannah in 1937 an established artist . He took up residence in an old cotton warehouse overlooking the Savannah River, converting parts of the apartment into studios for himself and his wife, Gina Knee, who was also a painter. No doubt *Winter Raiment* embodies the casual air of the artists' studio. A prodigious number of local children were frequent guests in the studio; many had their portraits painted by Brook.[3]

Portraiture was a large part of Brook's oeuvre. A very effective example is *Clifford Tallulah Mattox*, a sensitive, compassionate pic-

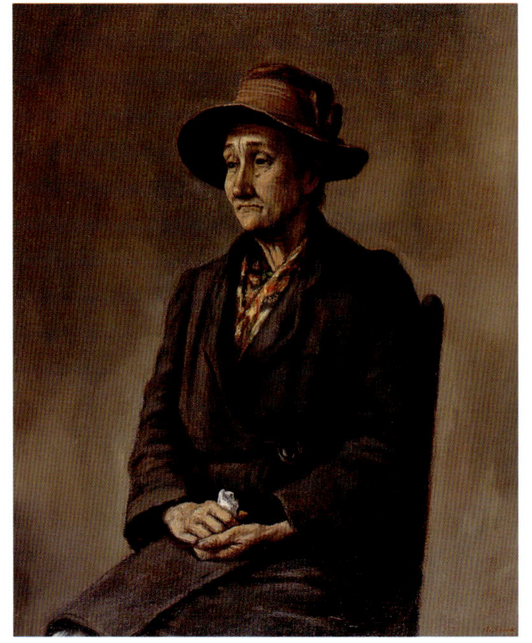

Clifford Tallulah Mattox, 1947
Oil on canvas
36 ½ x 29 ⅛ in. (93 x 74 cm)
Telfair Museum of Art,
Gift of the Artist, 1972

Winter Raiment, n.d.
Oil on canvas
14 ¼ x 7 in. (36.2 x 18 cm)
Telfair Museum of Art,
Gift of the Artist, 1972

ture of a woman who has seen better times. The subject is an old woman who sold newspapers on the street; she is pictured sitting in a high-back chair, wearing her hat and coat, and looking careworn. A couple of years before this painting was completed, Brook explained his attitude toward portraiture:

> If I plan to do a portrait, whether it is one of my own choice or a requested commission of someone I hardly know or do not know at all, I find that my first impression of the proposed sitter is usually the one I strive to paint. . . . I find myself always attempting to recapture that first impression, to hold and bring it to fruition. Whenever I hold closely to my original, instantaneous observation or try to emphasize even more the qualities I saw in my first conception I paint with greater ease and the result is more satisfactory to me.[4]

Brook's aesthetic suited Savannah's taste. Over the years, he became involved in the art community and in several projects of civic interest, including the renovation of River Street and retaining the public library downtown. Although Brook left Savannah for Long Island in the late 1940s, he remembered his adopted city and the Savannahians who loved him. In 1972 he donated ten of his paintings of Savannah subjects to the Telfair.

P.D.K.

1. *"Alexander Brook Talks About Art,"* Savannah Morning News, *March 23, 1941, p.18.*
2. *A.W. Kelly in* A Retrospective Exhibition of Paintings by Alexander Brook *(New York:: Salander-O'Reilly Galleries, 1980), 2.*
3. *One Savannah girl, Barbara Ann Sharpe, became known nationwide when her portrait by Brook was used on the cover of the* Saturday Evening Post, *September 13, 1947 (see "Savannah Girl, Artist Win Praise by Post Cover,"* Atlanta Constitution, *Sept. 11, 1947).*
4. *Alexander Brook,* Alexander Brook *(New York: American Artists Group 1945), n.p. Brook's portraits range in subject from Savannah children to Hollywood movie stars.*

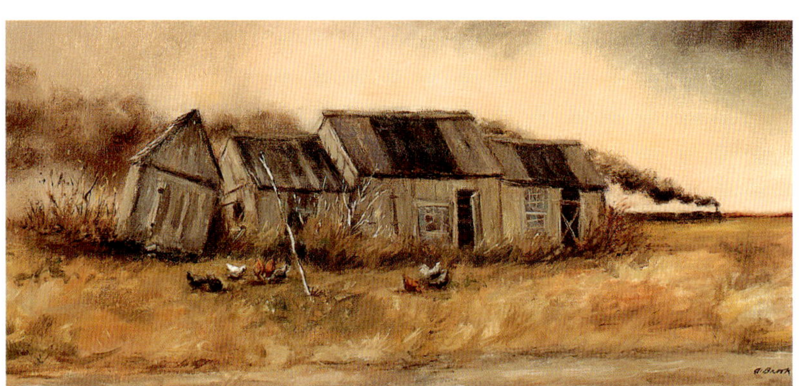

Savannah Chickens and Shacks, n.d.
Oil on canvas
12 x 26 in. (31 x 66 cm)
Collection of the Morris Museum of Art, Augusta, Georgia

Lila Cabaniss

(1885–1969)

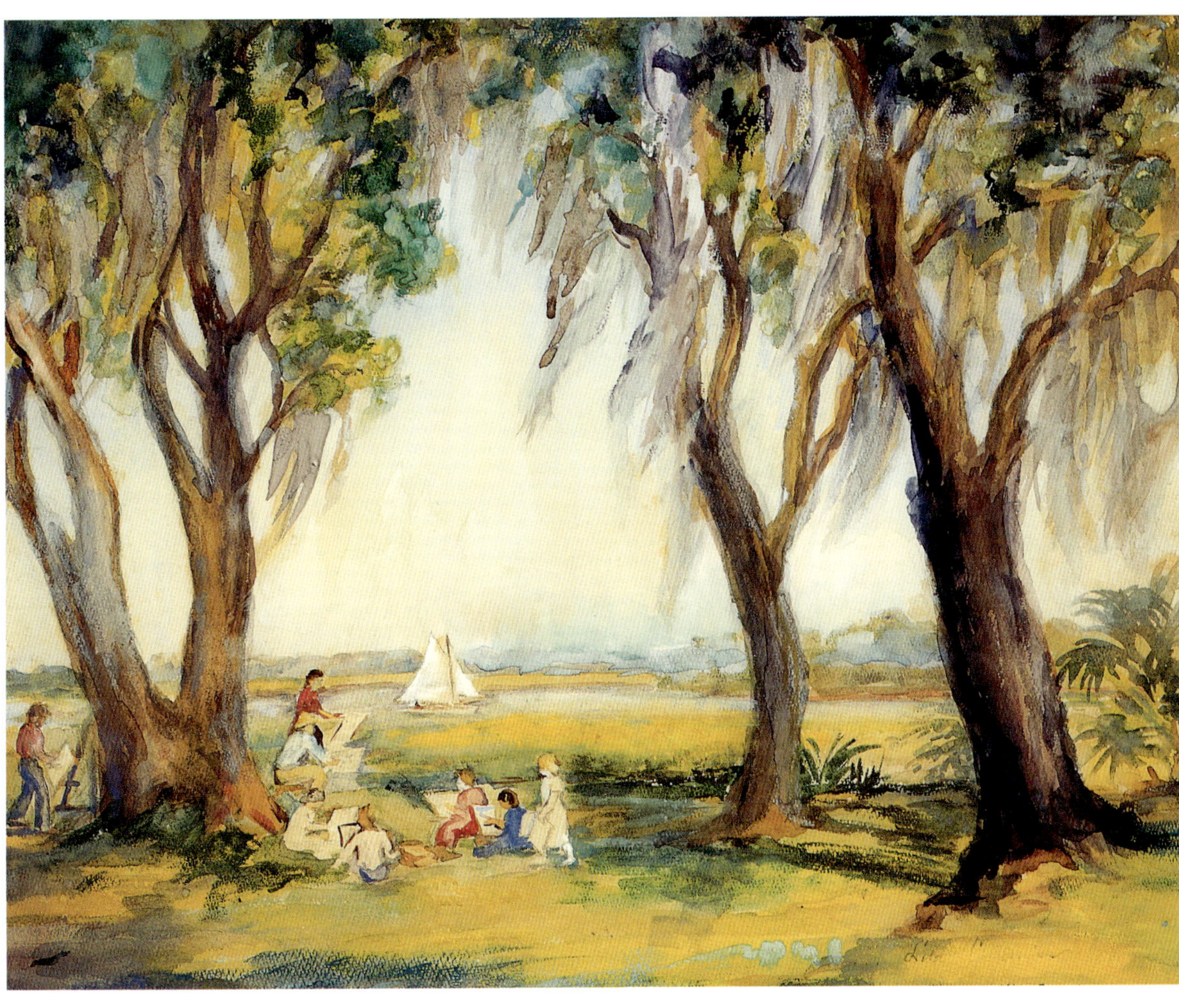

Landscape with Students Sketching, n.d.
Watercolor on paper
17 ⅛ x 20 ¾ in. (sight) (44 x 53 cm)
Collection of H. Paul Blatner

THE MOST NOTABLE ACHIEVEMENT of Lila Marguerite Cabaniss—"Miss Lila"—was to bring the art world to the Chatham County school system. A native of Savannah, Cabaniss began teaching at the age of seventeen and continued until her retirement in 1947. In 1915 she instituted an art curriculum in the school system and developed a program of field trips for younger children to the Telfair Academy of Arts and Sciences. A cofounder of the Savannah Art Club and a member of the Association of Georgia Artists, Cabaniss painted landscapes and floral still lifes.

A soft palette of color and fluid brush strokes capture the serenity of a southern view in *Landscape with Students Sketching*. The composition—a group of artists painting beside a river—may be a representation of one of Cabiniss's own classes. Here she draws attention to the minuscule figures within a monumental landscape through downward brush strokes and a strong foreground composition. A dry brush stroke over a wash base creates a translucent ground for the dense layering of watercolor. The carefully modeled foreground opens up to an atmospheric background, giving the entire painting an airy feeling.

Cabaniss exhibited extensively with the Southern States Art League, most notably in the 1924 exhibit at Telfair Academy. She studied at Columbia University, the University of Georgia, the University of Virginia, the New York School of Normal Arts, and the Art Students League of New York. In addition to her Telfair exhibitions, she participated in Philadelphia's sesquicentennial celebration. To honor her achievements in art, the Savannah College of Art and Design, along with her family, developed a scholarship in her name.

K.L.H.

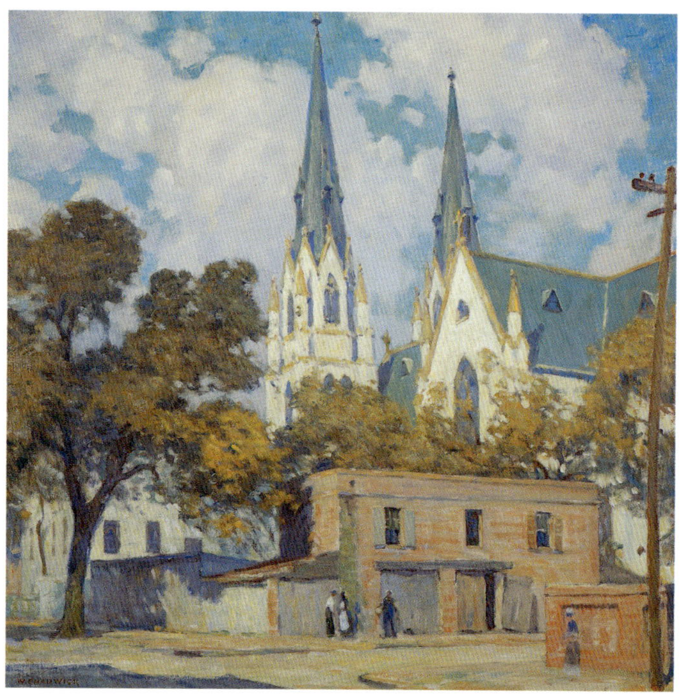

Church in Summer, c. 1925–26
Oil on canvas
30 ¼ x 30 ¼ in. (77 x 77 cm)
Private Collection

William Chadwick

(1879–1962)

A native of Yorkshire, England, William Chadwick grew up in Holyoke, Massachusetts, and spent most of his adult life in the Old Lyme, Connecticut, art colony. Chadwick first became aware of Old Lyme while attending the Art Students League in New York, where influential teachers such as J. Alden Weir and William Merritt Chase were introducing many students to the Impressionist style. The proximity of rural Connecticut to the art world of New York made it a favored locale for many landscape painters, such as the well-known American Impressionist Childe Hassam, who summered at Old Lyme between 1903 and about 1907. William Chadwick spent the summers of 1902–10 in Old Lyme, and settled there permanently in 1915. His work combines the painterly style of Hassam and Weir with the somewhat tighter style of his mentor at the Art Students League, Boston painter Joseph DeCamp.

Chadwick taught at the Telfair Academy between 1925 and 1926. During this time he painted views of Savannah and its environs, such as *Church in Summer* and *Towering Palms, Savannah*. *Church in Summer* depicts a three-quarter view of the Cathedral of St. John the Baptist from the corner of Lincoln and Macon Streets. Here the church spires can be seen towering above and behind the south transept. The low brick buildings in the foreground no longer exist, but otherwise the view is the same today.

Towering Palms, Savannah shows Chadwick's sensitivity to the effects of light and shadow in the landscape. The loose, painterly style is characteristic of paintings created out-of-doors, in which rapid execution is necessary to capture fleeting atmospheric effects. Visual and compositional similarities indicate that this view was painted from the same location seen in Chadwick's *At Bradley's Point* (location unknown), which shows what appear to be the same buildings and trees but from a slightly different vantage point.

The Telfair Academy gave Chadwick his first one-artist show in 1927. Most of the works in the exhibition traveled to the Society of Fine Arts in Wilmington, Delaware, later the same year. There would not be another major exhibition of his work until after his death in 1962, when the Old Lyme Art Association mounted a memorial exhibition. His work finally achieved national recognition in 1978 with an exhibition that was organized by Love Galleries of Chicago and traveled to several museums in the United States.

C.L.B.

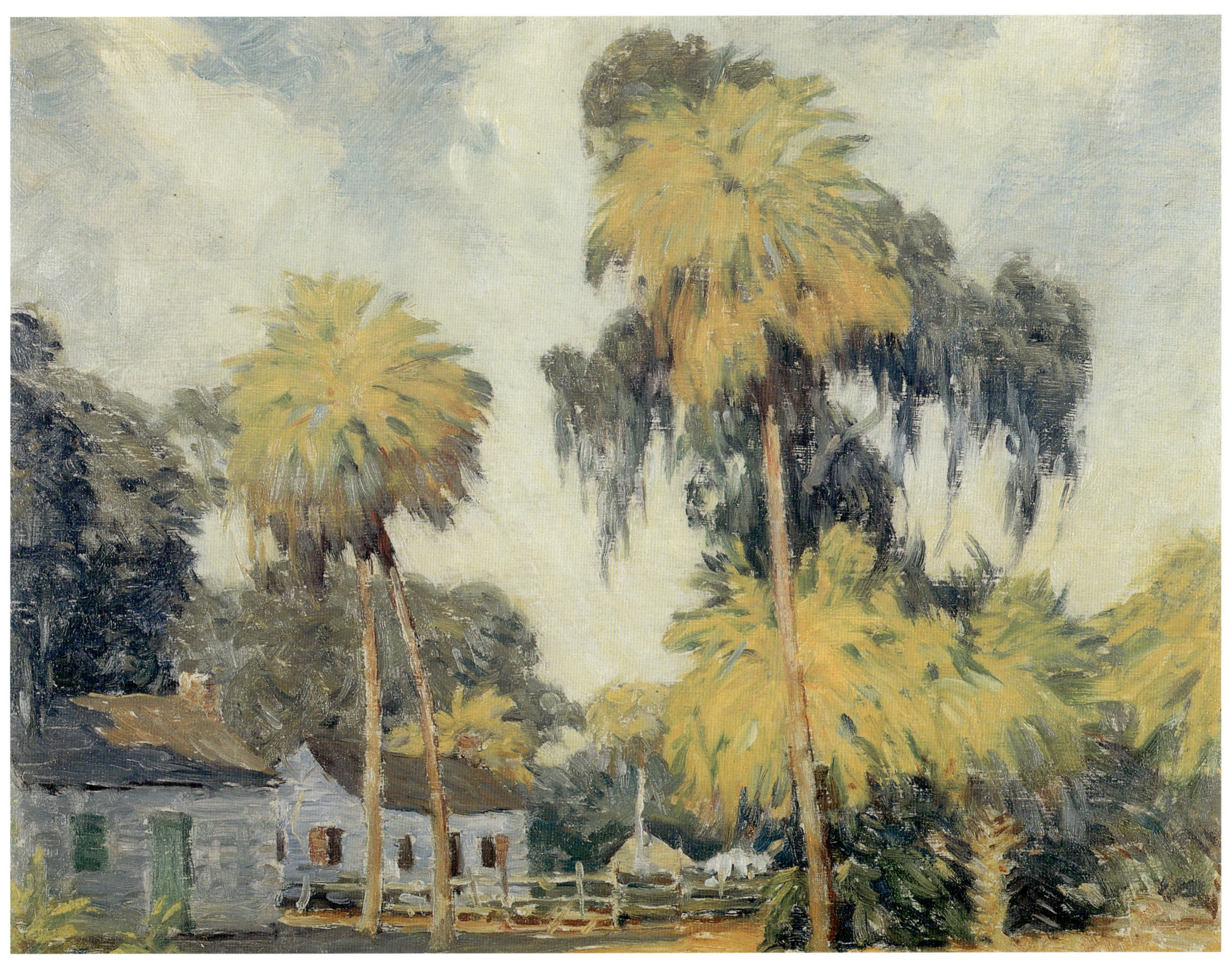

Towering Palms, Savannah, 1926
Oil on canvas
14 ¼ x 18 ¼ in. (36.2 x 46.4 cm)
Collection of Mr. and Mrs. W. Lucas Simons

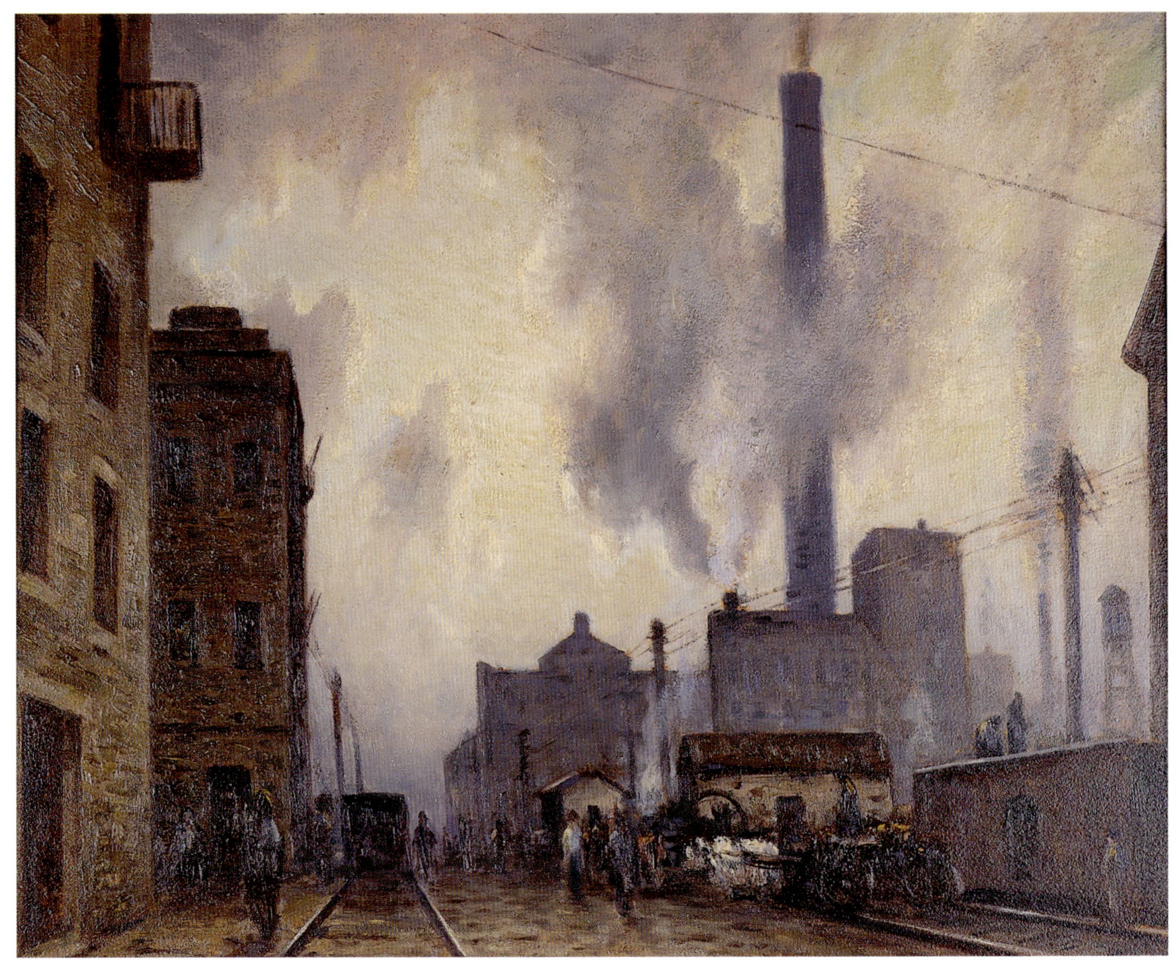

Smoking Plumes of Savannah, 1924
Oil on academy board
23 7⁄16 x 28 ½ in. (60 x 72.4 cm)
Telfair Museum of Art, Gift of
Mary Lane Morrison, 1985

Eliot Clark

(1883–1980)

A NATIVE NEW YORKER, Eliot Clark was one of many northeastern artists to work in Savannah. His father, Tonalist painter Walter Clark, was the younger Clark's primary influence. As the son of an esteemed painter, Clark grew up among artists, and was afforded opportunities to tour America and Europe and to spend his summers at an artists' colony in Gloucester, Massachusetts. As an adult, Clark taught at the Art Students League and was active in many art organizations, serving as president of the National Academy of Design, the American Water Color Society, and Allied Artists of America.

Clark's painting style was a blending of the two art movements he most admired, Tonalism and Impressionism. In addition to his painting career, Clark was a prolific author whose works include biographies of fellow artists John Twachtman, Alexander Wyant, Childe Hassam, Theodore Robinson, and J. Francis Murphy, as well as *The History of the National Academy of Design, 1825–1953*. Among Clark's more famous admirers was President Woodrow Wilson, who wrote to Clark from the White House in 1915: "I have hung your picture . . . in the study here, and derive a great deal of pleasure from it daily. It seems to be a particularly delightful piece of painting."[1]

Clark first came to Savannah at the request of the Savannah Art Club, for which he taught in the winters of 1922 and 1923. Clark considered the atmospheric, monochrome scenes of waterfronts, buildings, and landscapes he produced in Savannah among the best works of his career.[2] *Barnard Street Ramp* is typical of Clark's Savannah work. This depiction of the hazy Savannah riverfront at dusk reveals his interest in capturing subtle tonal variations. As in most of his waterfront paintings, the principal colors here are mauve and gray. Clark's use of harmonious color strongly suggests that he was influenced by James A. M. Whistler,[3] whereas his loose, thick application of paint may indicate an interest in the technique of Camille Pissarro.

Throughout his career, Clark most enjoyed painting scenes of nature; he felt that an artist's creations "must contain the truth of nature."[4] With this understanding, it is possible to view paintings like *Barnard Street Ramp*, *The Old and the New*, *Savannah Waterfront*,

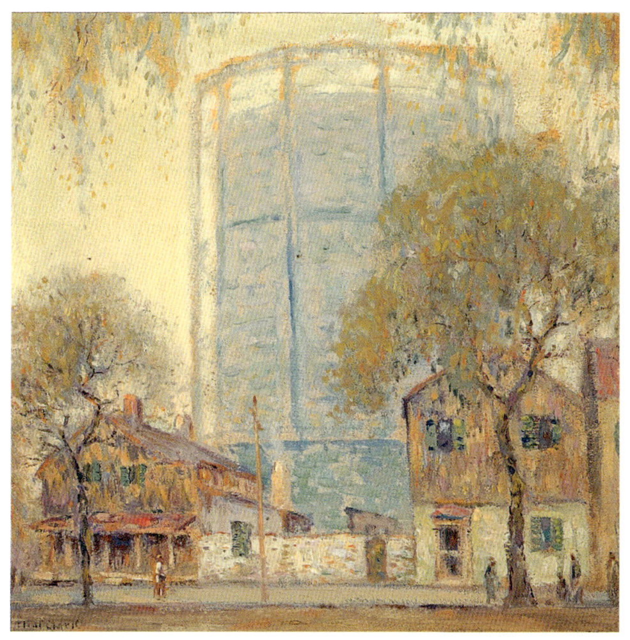

The Old and the New, c.1924–25
Oil on academy board
14 x 14 in. (36 x 36 cm)
Collection of Mr. and Mrs. Robert S. Glenn

and *Smoking Plumes of Savannah* as comments on the rapid growth and industrialization of the small, southern city. However, the artist's widow, Margaret Fowler Clark, writes that all of Clark's work in Savannah grew solely out of a genuine affection for the town: "The picturesque city with its silvery southern light, its many gardens, and ancient oaks hung with gray Moss, enchanted Eliot. During those Savannah winters he painted many of his finest works."[5]

After leaving Savannah, Clark settled in Virginia, where he lived and worked the rest of his life. Clark's connection to Savannah was renewed in 1979—one year prior to his death at age ninety-seven when the Telfair Museum hosted an exhibition of his Georgia works.

J.A.

1. *Telfair Museum archives.*
2. *Estill Curtis Pennington,* A Southern Collection *(Augusta, Ga.: Morris Communications Corporation, 1992), 106.*
3. *Ibid.*
4. *Telfair Museum archives.*
5. *Pennington,* Southern Collection, *106.*

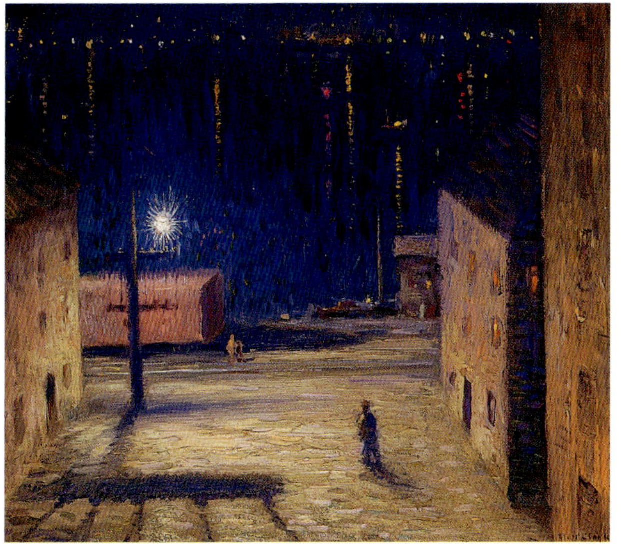

Savannah Waterfront, c.1924–25
Oil on academy board
18 x 20 in. (46 x 51 cm)
Collection of Mr. and Mrs. Robert S. Glenn

Barnard Street Ramp, c.1922–24
Oil on canvas
20 ⅛ x 27 ⅛ in. (51.1 x 69 cm)
Collection of Dr. and Mrs. C. Lamont Osteen

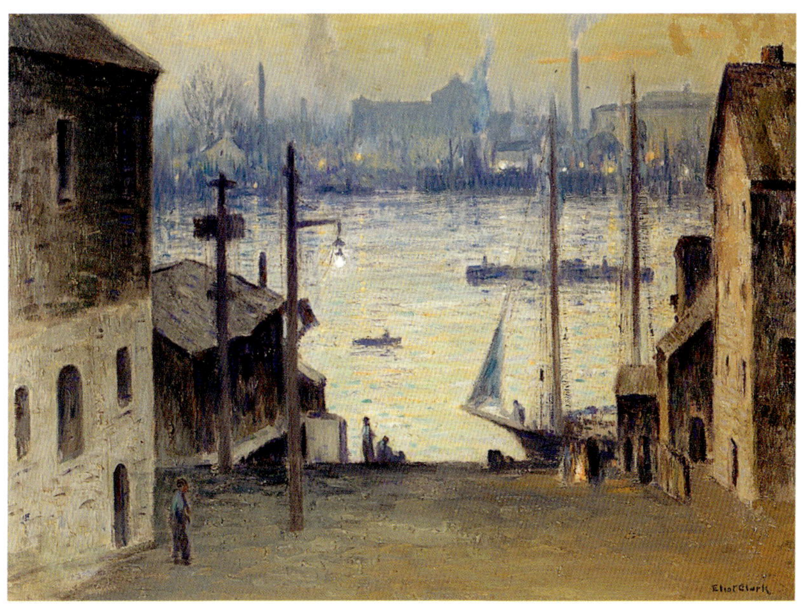

Ulysses Davis

(1913–1990)

"DISCOVERED" IN 1953 by educator and museum founder Virginia Kiah, Ulysses Davis is now widely recognized as a master of highly individual and expressive wood sculpture. Born in Fitzgerald, Georgia, Davis made his first carving, a figure of a man with movable arms, at the age of twelve. In 1942, Davis moved to Savannah to take a new job with the railroad office. He lost his job in the layoffs of railroad employees in the early 1950s, and turned to barbering, a skill he had learned as a young man. He built a barbershop behind his home, allowing space for the creation and display of his woodcarvings, which he worked on primarily at night. The barbershop itself was an artistic environment of ever-increasing density, embellished with carved elements and hundreds of small sculptures lining shelves and filling glass cases. Much of Davis's production falls into categories or types that he continued to develop until his death in 1990. These include powerful religious works, patriotic and historical pieces, fantastic beasts, whimsies, and portraits—all of which are present in Davis's early work from Fitzgerald and Savannah.

The examples in the current exhibition give some indication of Davis's range. *Farmhouse with Airplanes* provides a link with earlier rural images carved while Davis was living in Fitzgerald. Davis's later reliefs are often more densely textured and stylized. Another early piece, *Lizard*, echoes other African American carvings of reptiles made in Savannah and elsewhere at the time. Davis would continue to carve reptilian creatures in ever-evolving fantastic forms throughout his career.

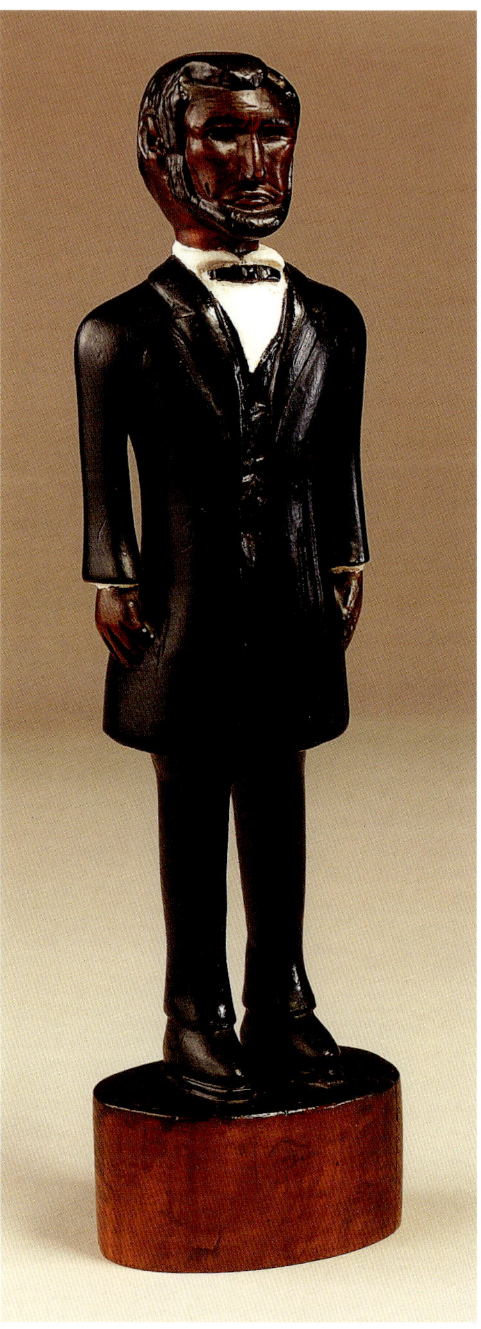

A deeply religious man, Davis asserted his Christian faith in powerful works such as his masterpiece, *Jesus on the Cross*, of 1946 (High Museum of Art, Atlanta). Less overtly religious is the enigmatic early work, *Mary on Donkey*, in which the Virgin apparently holds forth a loaf of sliced bread. The base of this work is an open piece resembling a carved temple. Also biblical in title more than in content is *Tower of Babel*, which includes an open chamber with a female head in the top section, and the ball-in-cage in the center. The ball-in-cage carved from a single block of wood is an internationally popular type of woodcarving puzzle, which Davis used in several sculptures. Another important aspect of Davis's work is patriotic imagery, exemplified by his standing figure, *Abe Lincoln*, of 1944. This work presages his well-known series of carved busts of U.S. presidents, from George Washington to George Bush.

Davis's mature work of the 1970s and 1980s is characterized by an increased use of chip-carving techniques, more densely textured surfaces, and greater use of gold paint and "twinklets"—Davis's term for small glass beads and jewelry fragments.

H.H.D.

ABE LINCOLN, 1944
Wood, with black and white paint
15 x 4 x 3 in. (38.1 x 10.2 x 8 cm)
Collection of
Mr. and Mrs. David E. Miller, Jr.

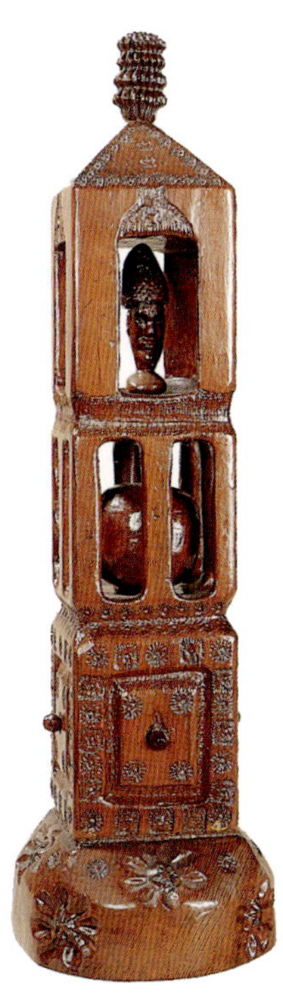

Tower of Babel, n.d.
Wood
20 x 5 ½ x 5 ½ in. (51 x 14 x 14 cm)
Collection of Beach Institute African American Cultural Center

Mary on Donkey, n.d.
Wood
17 ¼ x 11 ½ x 3 ½ in. (44 x 29.2 x 9 cm)
Collection of Beach Institute African American Cultural Center

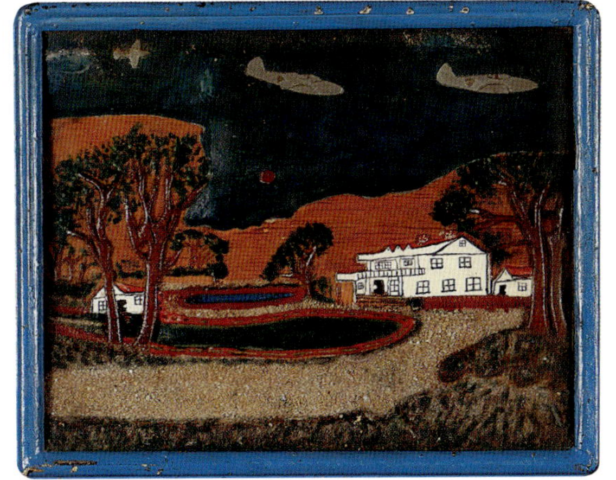

Farmhouse with Airplanes, 1943
Carved and painted wood relief
13 x 15 ⅝ in. (33 x 40 cm)
Collection of Mr. and Mrs. David E. Miller, Jr.

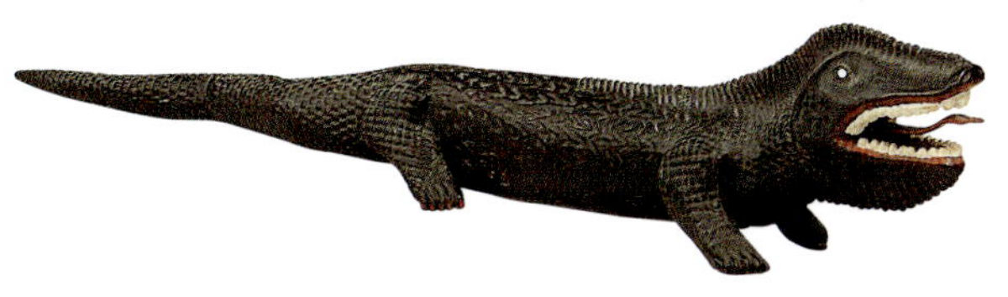

Lizard, c.1930s to 1940s
Wood, with black, red, and white paint
3 x 25 x 3 in. (8 x 64 x 8 cm)
Collection of Mr. and Mrs. David E. Miller, Jr.

Lamar Dodd
(b.1909)

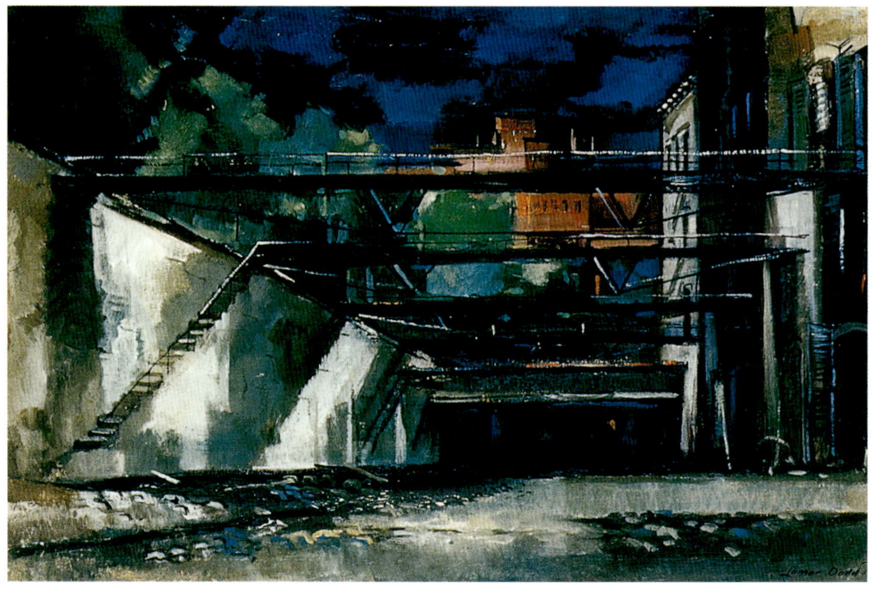

Factor's Walk, 1950
Oil on canvas
24 x 36 in. (61 x 91.4 cm)
Collection of Margaret
Dodd Funderburk

Lamar Dodd is known for his range and diversity of style and subject matter. Born in Fairburn, Georgia, he studied architecture at the Georgia Institute of Technology from 1926 to 1927. In 1930 Dodd moved to New York to pursue a career as a painter. He studied at the Art Students League with other notable artists such as Boardman Robinson, George Bridgeman, Jean Charlot, and John Steuart Curry. Dodd exhibited in a one-artist show at the Feragill Gallery in New York City before returning to the South. He moved first to Birmingham, Alabama, to immerse himself in the study of local southern scenes and the American industrial landscape. In 1937 he joined the faculty of the University of Georgia and became head of the art department. At this time, his study of architecture influenced his choice to focus on industrial realism in his paintings. In the 1950s, Dodd traveled to Europe, the Near East, Russia, and India for the State Department's Advisory Committee on Art. He was exposed to abstraction of line and pure design that he found in the art of other cultures. These replaced the idealized naturalism that had been characteristic of his work until this time.

Savannah, an image of the city rooftops, demonstrates Dodd's transition from purely pictorial landscapes to a linear, Cubist style. In this dark composition he concentrates on the planar relationships of the surface and the effects of light and dark. Sharp strokes of color applied in thick layers accent the buildings. Because of its high perspective and layered application of paint, this urban cityscape has a luminous, mysterious quality. Dodd shows us industrial Savannah with its dark side and in so doing captures the development of contemporary America.

Concentrating on color rather than line, Dodd continued his study of urban landscapes with the 1950 representation of Factor's Walk. Here the artist has used deep patches of intense color and shadow to depict an intriguing underworld along the Savannah River. The muted tones of the foreground train the viewer's attention on the play of light and shadow in the underground tunnels formed by the catwalks. The walkway leads the viewer into the dark abyss of the shadows. The low, below ground, perspective creates the sensation of looking upward. The deep blues, reds, and greens of the cityscape above add to the malevolent feeling of the painting.

In addition to creating independent works of art, in 1951 Dodd illustrated a book on the Savannah River, called *The Savannah*, by Thomas Stokes.[1] Lamar Dodd continues to work today on contemporary issues in his art.

K.L.H.

1. *Thomas Lunsford Stokes,* The Savannah *(New York: Rinehart, 1951).*

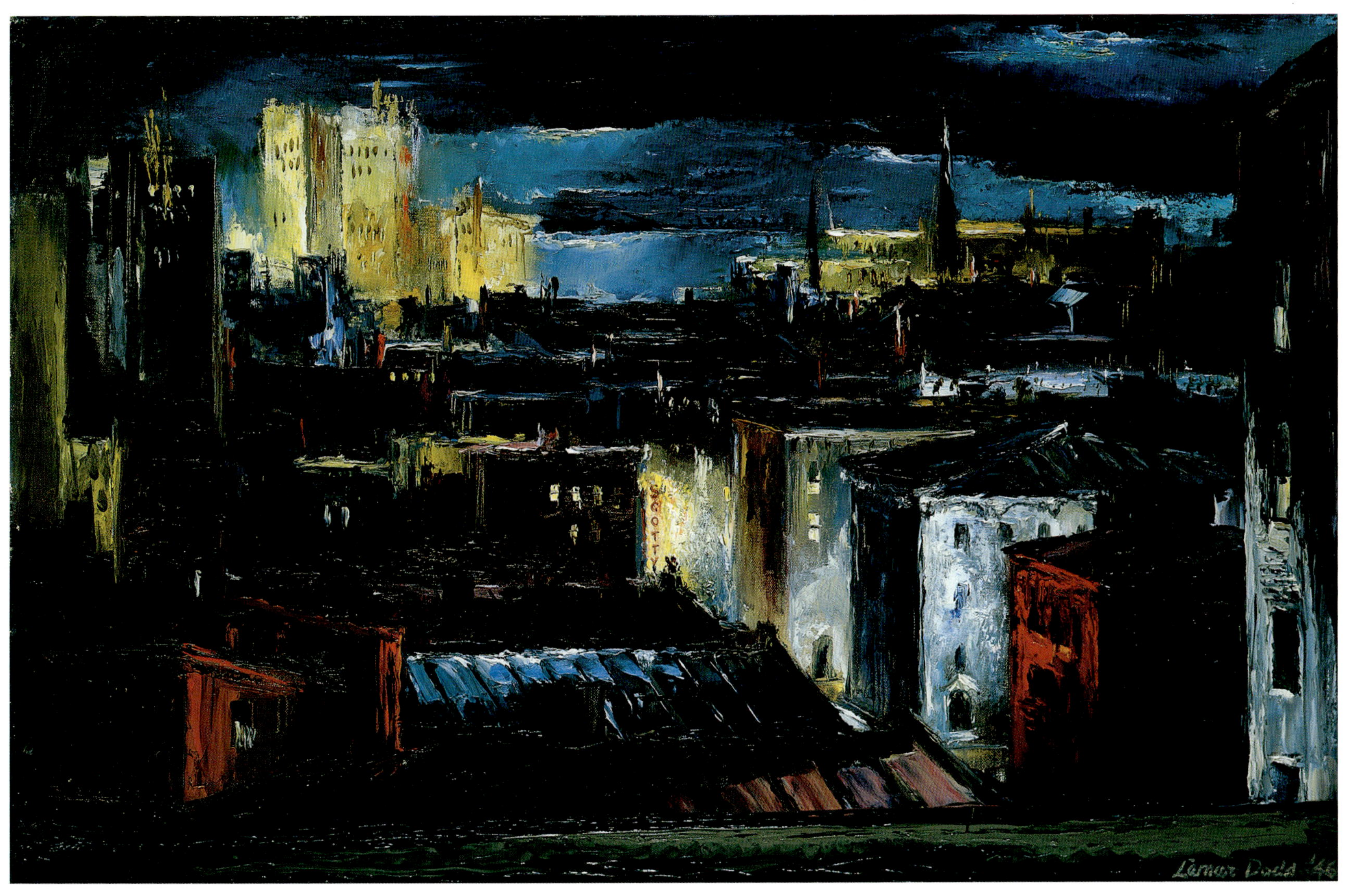

Savannah, 1946
Oil on canvas
20 x 29 ½ in. (51 x 75 cm)
The Montclair Art Museum, Gift of Mrs. Frederick Pleasants

William de Leftwich Dodge

(1867–1935)

William de Leftwich Dodge was one of the most celebrated mural painters of his day. He also produced plein-air landscape paintings, such as *Summer Day under Spanish Moss*, in the then-popular style of the Impressionists. At the turn of the twentieth century, artistic tastes were eclectic. Many artists, including Dodge, were trained in academic techniques, which they used in the execution of mural commissions; but they were also proficient in the more modern styles, such as Impressionism, which appealed to their upper-middle-class patrons.

After living in Bedford, Virginia, Chicago, and Brooklyn as a boy, Dodge accompanied his mother to Europe, where she studied art. Exposed to art at an early age, he became something of a prodigy. He studied at the Ecole des Beaux-Arts from the age of fifteen and gained entrance to the prestigious atelier of Jean Léon Gérôme when he was eighteen. Gérôme taught a highly academic style for the depiction of classical and historical subjects, favored by the French Salon. Dodge's training prepared him well for the painting of American murals in the style of academic classicism.

In 1889 Dodge returned to New York. In 1891, at the age of 25, he received a commission to paint a mural in Richard Morris Hunt's Administration Building at the 1893 World's Columbian Exposition in Chicago. This commission established his reputation as one of the foremost mural painters in America and led to many subsequent commissions, including murals in the Library of Congress and the New York State Capitol building.

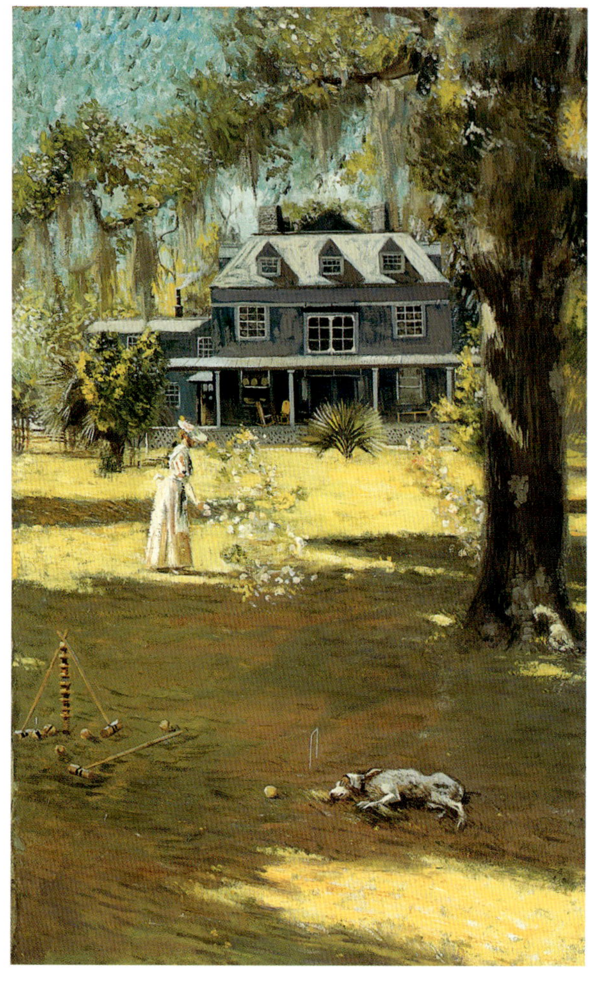

Summer Day under Spanish Moss, c.1915–25
Oil on canvas
40 x 24 in. (102 x 61 cm)
Greenville County Museum of Art,
Museum purchase with funds provided by
Alester G. Furman III, The Pellett Foundation,
and The Museum Association, Inc.

Between 1898 and 1900 Dodge was invited by friends to spend his summers near the home of Claude Monet in Giverny, France, where a number of American Impressionist painters had formed an art colony. Here he began to paint plein-air landscapes, which he would continue to do for the rest of his life. Many of his later subjects were drawn from the gardens at the home and studio he designed for himself at Setauket, Long Island, where he settled in 1906.

Summer Day under Spanish Moss may have been painted on one of the trips Dodge and his wife made to Savannah to visit friends Lilly Livingston and Pierre Lorrillard.[1] The subject of the painting is one of the favorites of the Impressionists: the leisure activities of the upper-middle class, set out-of-doors on a cheerful sunny day. Images such as these may have seemed like antidotes to the anxieties and intrusions of the modern era. The painting exhibits Dodge's grasp of the beaux-arts tradition as well as Impressionism. In particular, his academic training under Gérôme can be seen in the carefully detailed rendering of the house, and his exposure to the style of the French Impressionists is evident in his attention to light effects and use of broken brush strokes in the landscape.

C.L.B.

1. *Memorandum to H.H. DeLorme from Catherine Wade Wahl, Morris Museum of Art*

Walker Evans

(1903–1975)

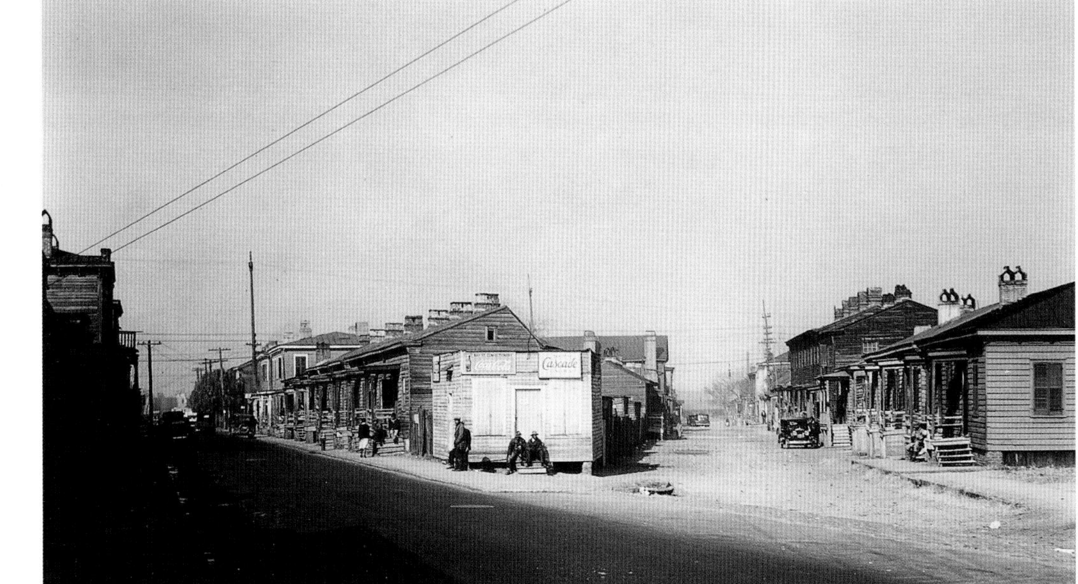

NEGRO QUARTERS, SAVANNAH, n.d.
Silver gelatin photograph
3 ½ x 9 ½ in. (sight)
(9 x 24 cm)
Prints and Photographs Division, Library of Congress

IT IS SAID THAT WALKER EVANS once described his work as "deliberately wrought poetry in the guise of plain, simple fact." Whether this quote is real or apocryphal, it accurately, neatly, and perfectly sums up Evans's philosophy, aesthetic, and working method.

Evans was the founding member and guiding force behind Roy Stryker's team of Farm Security Administration (FSA) photographers, a partner with James Agee in the production of the classic *Let Us Now Praise Famous Men*, a photographer and writer for *Time* and *Fortune* magazines, and a professor of photography at Yale University. His contributions to both documentary and fine art photography are inestimable, and his profound influence continues to resonate today.

While known primarily for his direct, frontal black-and-white images of the Great Depression and rural America, Evans was, in truth, never really a documentary photographer. He was always first and foremost an artist who used the camera to express a personal vision through documentary *style* photographs, a distinction he felt important to make. He consciously and deliberately made photographs of vernacular America in a style that itself seemed artless and vernacular. His seemingly ordinary, anonymous photographs of seemingly ordinary, anonymous people and objects reveal a cool and quiet reverence for everyday life, which to recognize and reveal was his genius and his accomplishment. With his photographs, he singlehandedly created a new American iconography, opening up new subject areas for artistic interpretation, while at the same time strengthening the basic straightforward style adopted by most documentary photographers.

Evans's masterpiece was probably his 1938 Museum of Modern Art exhibition and monograph, *American Photographs*, in which he presented images from all his previous major projects in a brilliant sequence that was a celebration of, and an elegy to, a disappearing America, as well as an indictment of the coming age of mass production and industrialization. The apparent simplicity and directness of the photographs temporarily mask their intellectual and emotional totality. How could these images, a dry and meticulous collection of neutral and anonymous facts, possibly carry such a strong and personal message? This subtle deceptiveness was an important part of Evans's strategy. He wanted the meaning to sneak up on the viewer cumulatively, as though it were the viewer discovering it rather than Evans creating it. This was done as much through the sequencing of the images as through the subject matter of the individual photographs.

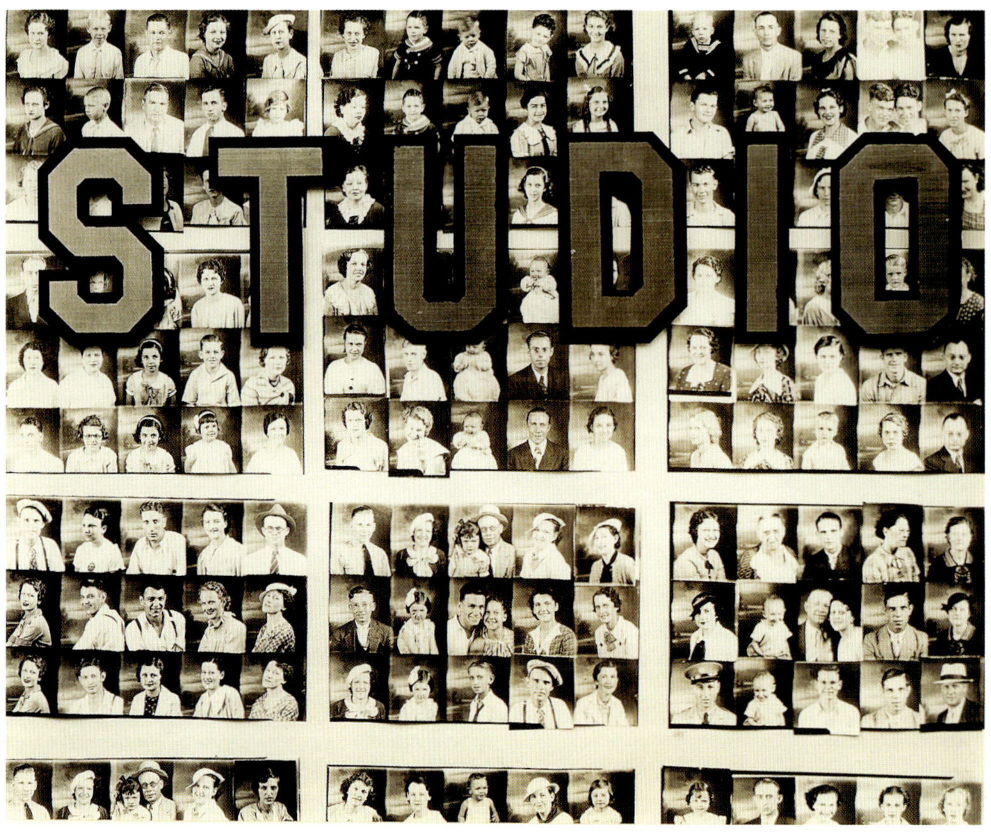

PENNY PICTURE DISPLAY, SAVANNAH, c.1936
Vintage gelatin silver print
7 x 9 in. (18 x 23 cm)
Thomas H. Lee and Ann Tenenbaum Collection

The image entitled *Penny Picture Display, Savannah* is a perfect example. It is the second image in the important opening section of *American Photographs*. The first is of a driver's license photo studio in New York City, which announces the theme of photography itself—not "high art" photography but the most pedestrian and unpretentious kind. *Penny Picture Display* reinforces the idea with a tightly composed display of anonymous portraits—little more than mug shots—with the word "Studio" superimposed over them. Evans is slyly providing the viewer with clues that this is to be a book of photographs *about* photographs and their power to persuade and to bear witness.

Walker Evans's photographs are interesting because they seem so transparent. It is fascinating that a twentieth-century artist, working at the height of modernism, would consciously adopt a personal aesthetic that seemingly denied his presence in the work. Because of his approach, however, Evans's work became a convincing model for factual documentary photography. At the same time it is an eloquent, if understated, personal assessment of the moral condition of the nation at the time. In creating his "deliberately wrought poetry in the guise of plain, simple fact," Evans was following the dictum of Gustave Flaubert, one of his early influences, who said, "An artist must be in his work like God in Creation, invisible and all-powerful; he should be everywhere felt, but nowhere seen."

S.P.M

Daniel Chester French

(1850–1931)

WITH MUCH POMP AND CIRCUMSTANCE, Daniel Chester French's bronze monument to General James Edward Oglethorpe, British soldier and founder of the Colony of Georgia and the city of Savannah, was unveiled and dedicated in Savannah's Chippewa Square on November 23, 1910. The sculptor was in attendance with his collaborator, the architect Henry Bacon, who designed the base for the bronze. Numerous dignitaries, including the governor of Georgia, Joseph M. Brown, who unveiled the monument, also attended. The celebration was marked by three days of activities, including parades, military exercises and exhibitions, a motorcycle race, and a football game.[1]

In 1910 the state of Georgia, the city of Savannah, and several patriotic organizations commissioned French to execute this monument to Oglethorpe. Public monuments such as this dominated sculpture at the turn of the twentieth century as a result of a rise in nationalism after the Civil War and a new interest in the cultivation of art and culture. This period is often referred to as the American Renaissance. The public commemoration of heroes continued through the early years of the twentieth century, culminating in French and Bacon's 1922 Lincoln Memorial in Washington, D.C.

French, who worked in Massachusetts and New York, was undoubtedly America's most famous sculptor at the time of the Oglethorpe monument commission. He first gained attention with his 1875 *Minute Man*, which commemorates the Revolutionary War battle at Concord, Massachusetts. After completing the sculpture, the young artist studied in both Florence and Paris. It was Paris, however, that profoundly influenced French and helped to form his mature style, a combination of American realism and the decorative impulse of the French beaux-arts manner.

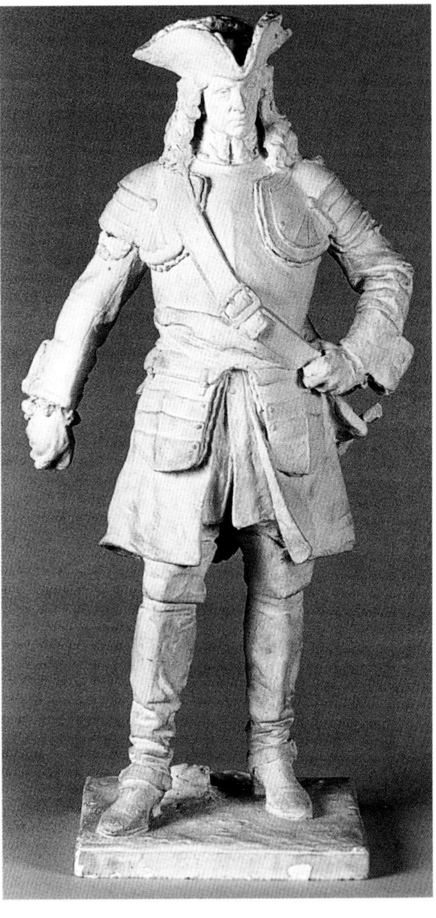

GENERAL JAMES EDWARD OGLETHORPE, 1910
Plaster, 41 x 19 ½ x 12 ½ in.
(104.1 x 50 x 32 cm)
Telfair Museum of Art,
Gift of J. Randolph Anderson, 1926

French's method of producing large-scale bronze sculptures began with a small study or sketch modeled in clay, perhaps ten inches high, in which he worked out the concept and composition. Then he created an approximately three-foot-high clay working model, in which the details of surface, decoration, and composition were resolved; this clay working model was then cast in the more durable medium of plaster. For the full-scale work, French repeated the same process, creating a clay model in which he worked out the final details, cast it in plaster, and then shipped it to a foundry to be cast in bronze.

The Telfair plaster cast represents the interim stage of the process, the working model. This version is still slightly rough—the surfaces are not entirely smooth, and the details are somewhat tentative. Copies can be made from this plaster in any medium. At least one other version exists in plaster, at Chesterwood, French's home and studio in the Berkshires, near Stockbridge, Massachusetts, now preserved as a historic site by the National Trust. The Chesterwood version has been painted to approximate the color of bronze and includes Oglethorpe's sword. Working models such as these provide a glimpse into the creative process of the artist, providing interesting comparisons with successive refinements in the sculptor's conception.

C.L.B.

1. A History of the Erection and Dedication of the Monument to Gen'l James Edward Oglethorpe, Unveiled in Savannah, Ga., November 23, 1910, *Collections of the Georgia Historial Society, v. VII, Part II (Savannah, Ga.: Georgia Historical Society, 1911).*

Reuben Gambrell

(b.1917)

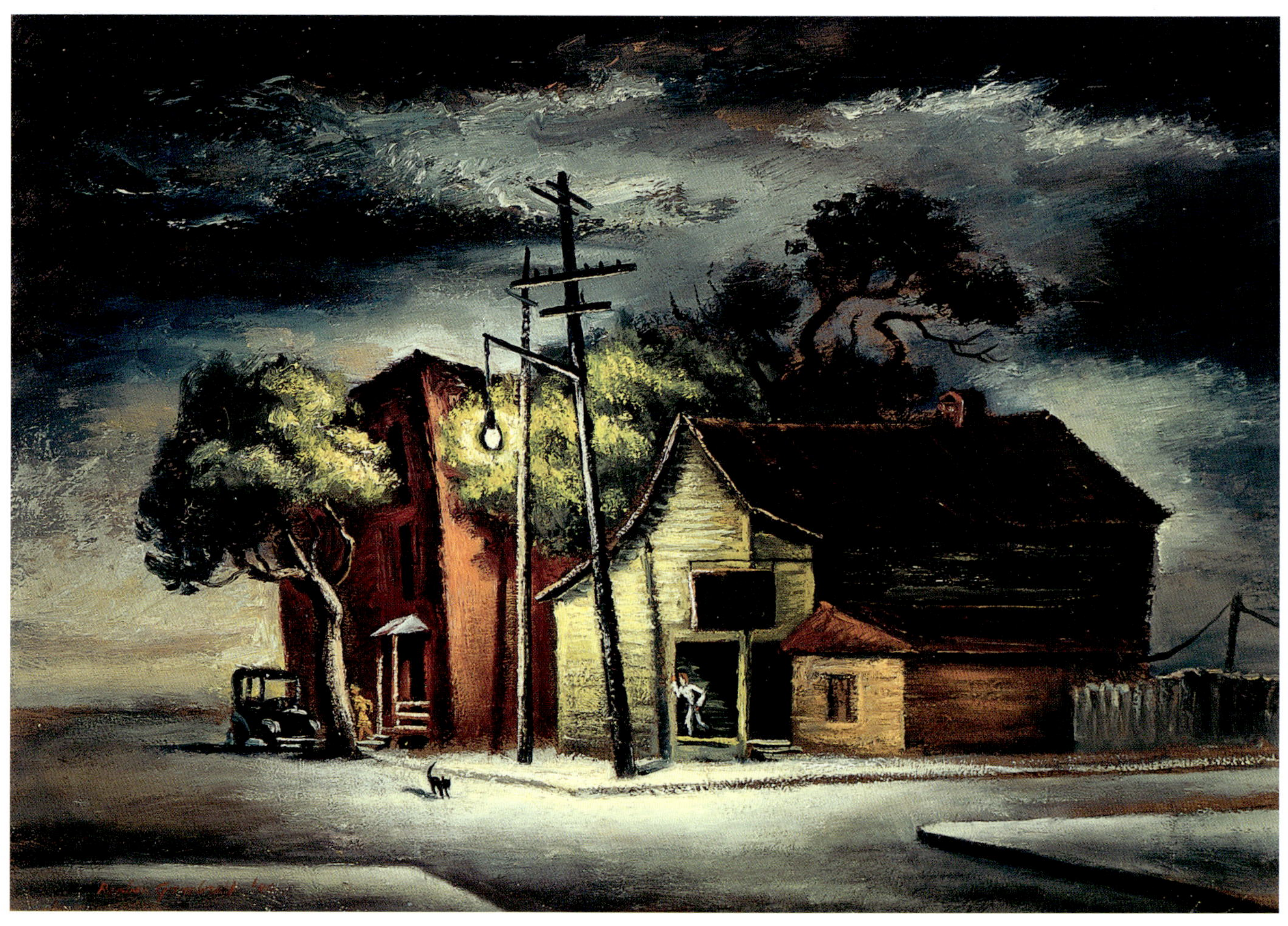

REUBEN GAMBRELL'S VERSATILITY OF STYLE AND SUBJECT marks him as one of the more interesting southern artists of the twentieth century. A student of Lamar Dodd and a follower of modern art movements, Gambrell created works in both an American Scene style as well as a more abstract style. He received a Bachelor of Arts degree from the University of South Carolina and in 1941 was the first person ever to receive a Master of Fine Arts from the University of Georgia. During his studies at the University of Georgia, Lamar Dodd, head of the art department, acted as his sponsor and mentor. Dodd's influence is evident in Gambrell's landscapes. From 1946 to 1947 he taught at the University of Georgia's extension at Hunter

CORNER STORE AT NIGHT, SAVANNAH, 1946
Oil on canvas
20 x 28 in. (51 x 71.1 cm)
Collection of Reuben Gambrell

Army Air Field in Savannah; subsequently he taught at the University of Georgia and at the Telfair Academy.

Gambrell produced several works while teaching at the extension campus, among them the 1946 oil painting *Corner Store at Night, Savannah*. This painting of rural Savannah recalls the blended palette and shadowed style of Lamar Dodd. Gambrell first prepared a wash drawing at the actual location, and after returning to his studio executed the oil. Striving to capture a contemporary American landscape in an honest and simple style, he contrasts the solid forms of the storefronts against a collage of colors in the night sky.

During his sojourn in Savannah, Gambrell worked with Anna Hunter, Frances Anderson, Jane Hopkins, and Ted Waters. Fellow artists Alexander Brook and Gina Knee offered critiques to his classes at the extension campus. A strong supporter of the Savannah Art Association and the Telfair School of Art, Gambrell sees these organizations as the driving force of the Savannah art community.

In the early 1950s Cubism—in particular, the art of Pablo Picasso—influenced Gambrell toward a more abstract style. Picasso's *Girl before Mirror* (Museum of Modern Art, New York) was the inspiration for the artist's *Embrace,*[1] a figural composition of two nudes, a man and a woman, before a mirror. For this work, Gambrell used pencil sketches he had made of models at the American University in Washington and the Telfair School of Art to construct the two characters locked in a passionate embrace. He adapted Picasso's composition as well as his vivid colors. Intense pigments and blended tonalities form a mass of colors that lend power to the work.

Reuben Gambrell presently lives in Columbia, South Carolina.

K.L.H.

1. *Telephone interview with Reuben Gambrell, May 9, 1996.*

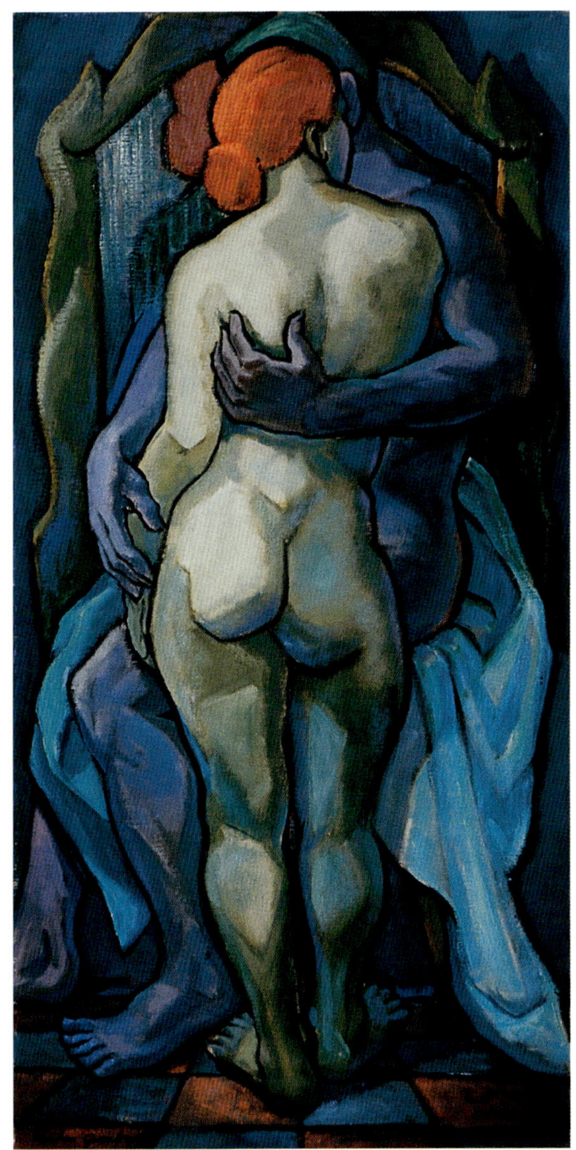

EMBRACE, 1953
Oil on canvas
36 x 18 in. (91.4 x 46 cm)
Collection of Ms. Fran McDonald

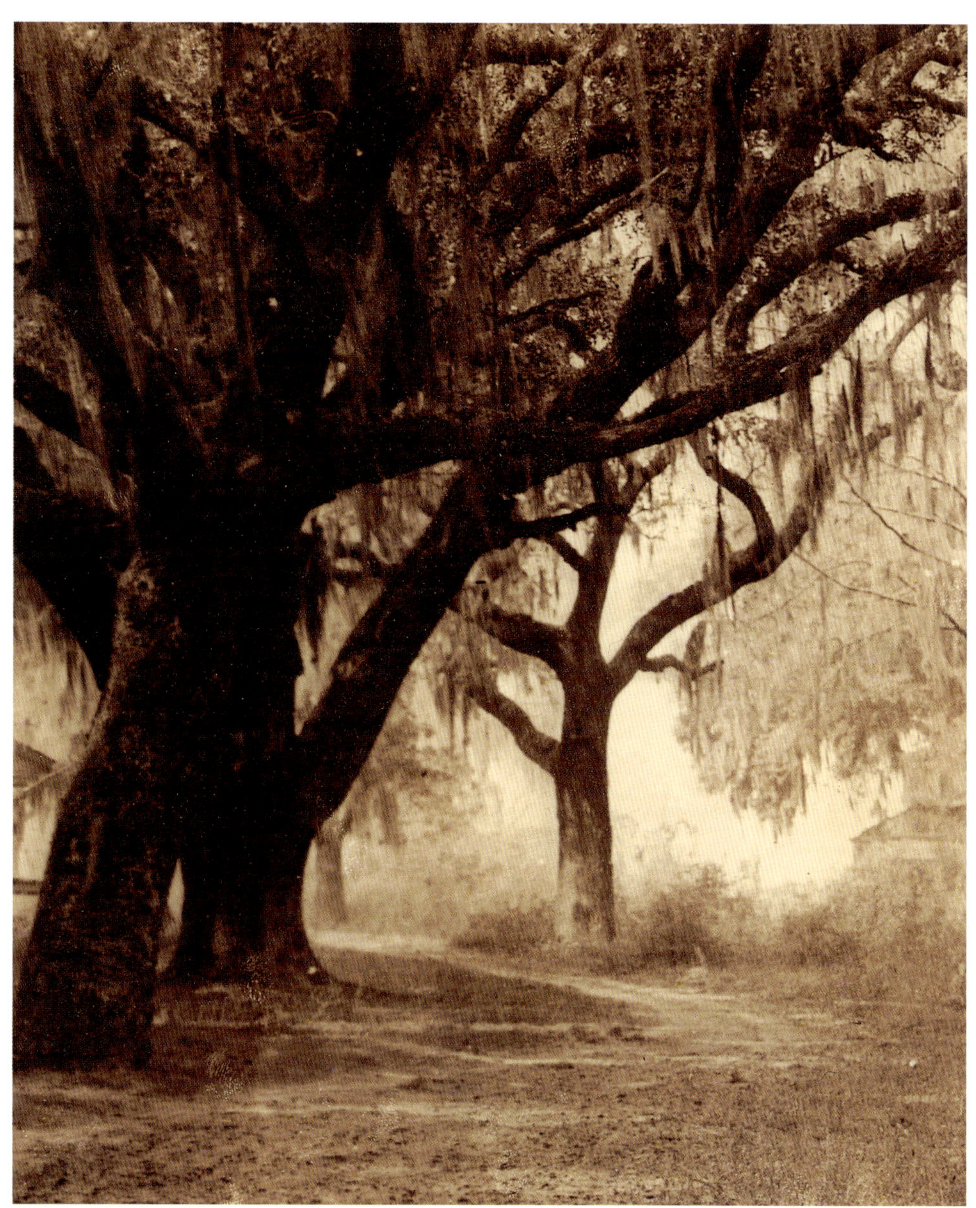

Colerain Plantation, Savannah, GA, 1911
Photograph, silver print
9 ½ x 7 ¾ in. (24.1 x 20 cm)
Collection of Francis D. McNairy

Edgerton Chester Garvin
(1882–1950)

In many of his photographs Edgerton Garvin concentrated on capturing the southern landscape in a poetic and evocative way, much as would an Impressionist painter working in oil. In his logbook he pasted an excerpt from a magazine article that was, perhaps, a reminder or concrete description of his own aesthetic:

> The imagination is more quickly stimulated by a little mystery regarding at least a few elements of the composition than by absolute clarity of delineation, which tells all at a glance and so leaves no food for further thought.[1]

The mystery he sought to convey in his works is immediately perceived in *Colerain Plantation, Savannah, GA*.[2] Here Garvin has captured the almost eerie silence of a deserted estate dominated by ancient oaks draped in Spanish moss. Through use of a soft focus—a technique commonly used by pictorialist photographers in the early years of the century—he has created a work of haunting beauty.

An Ohio native who trained as a civil engineer, Garvin adopted photography as an avocation from 1909 to 1947. He traveled through coastal Georgia and Florida and found many enticing subjects, including the landscapes and cityscapes of Savannah, Augusta, and Brunswick, Georgia, and Fernandina, Florida. He also photographed people and occasions, such as an early car race in Savannah and the flight of a biplane in Augusta. Many of Garvin's images are unabashedly romantic. His photographs have only come to light in the past eighteen years.

P.D.K.

1. *Quoted in Beth Bassett, "Edgerton Chester Garvin: Photographer,"* Brown's Guide to Georgia *(June 1980): 33.*
2. *Garvin spelled the name of the site, "Colrain." It is Colerain, a plantation on the west side of Savannah that has since been razed.*

William O. Golding

(1874–1943)

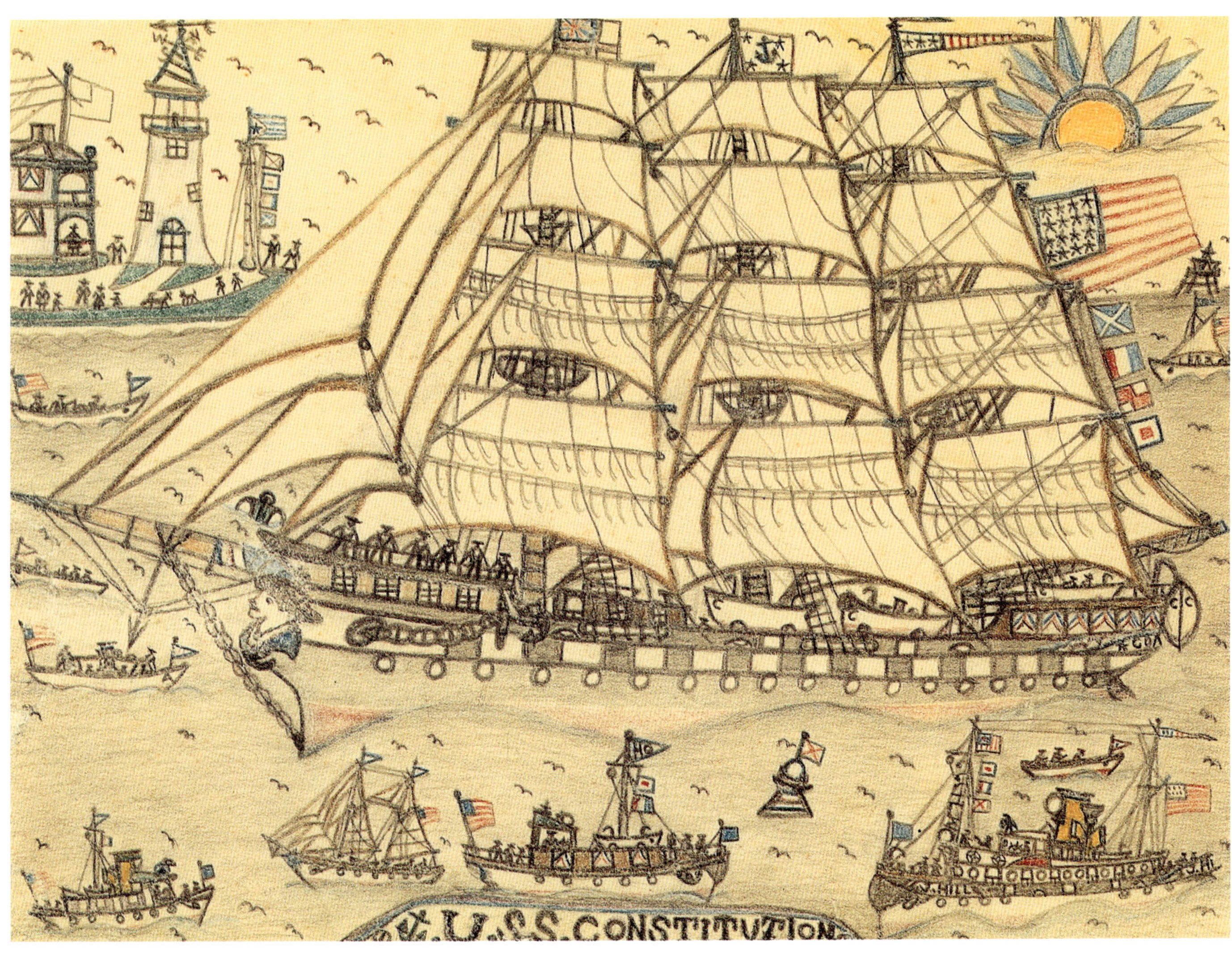

U.S.S. Constitution, 1933
Colored pencil on paper
8 ⅝ x 11 ⅞ in. (22 x 30.2 cm)
Collection of Rita Trotz

William Golding's reputation rests on a group of approximately sixty color drawings made during the years 1932–39, while he was a patient at the Marine Hospital in Savannah. Golding (whose name may have been Golden)[1] was fifty-nine and suffering from bronchitis and other ailments when he was encouraged to draw from memory by the hospital's recreation director, Margaret Stiles, an influential member of the Savannah Art Club. Stiles purchased his works for small sums, and apparently exhibited them.

Golding's work does not seem to draw from the marine painting tradition so much as it reinvents the genre in very personal terms. His images are detailed descriptions of ships he had seen or served on. The featured vessel is often presented disproportionately large compared to other vessels surrounding it. The works are often imaginatively composed to include specific remem-

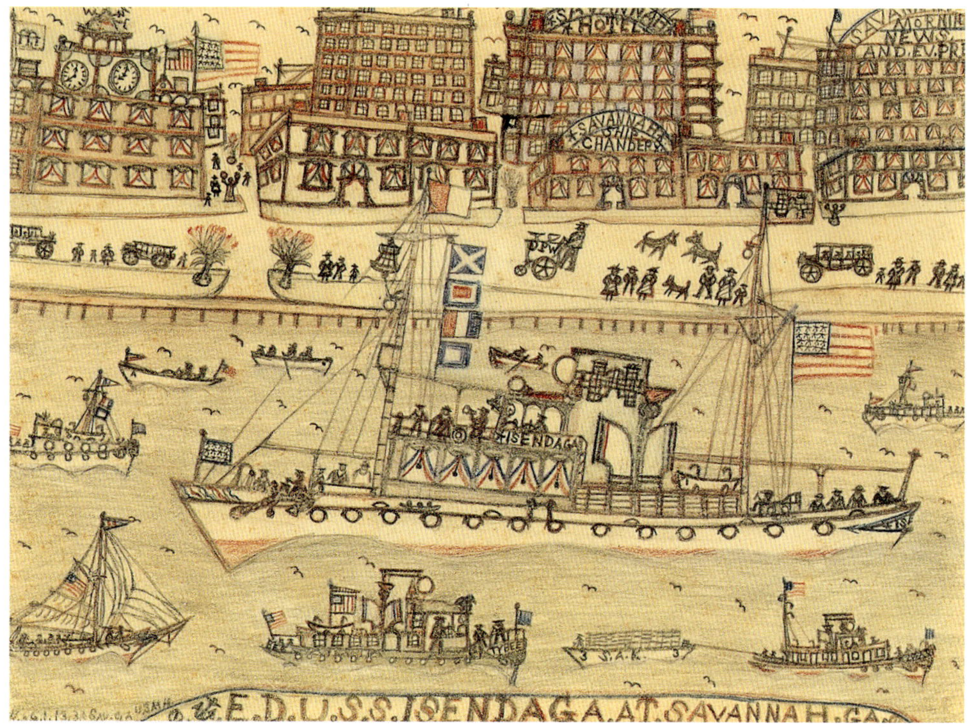

U.S.S. Isendaga, 1934
Colored pencil on paper
8 ¾ x 11 ¾ in. (22.2 x 30 cm)
Collection of Rita Trotz

St. Yacht Rosalie, 1935
Colored pencil on paper
8 ½ x 11 ¾ in. (22 x 30 cm)
Collection of Mr. and Mrs. David E. Miller, Jr.

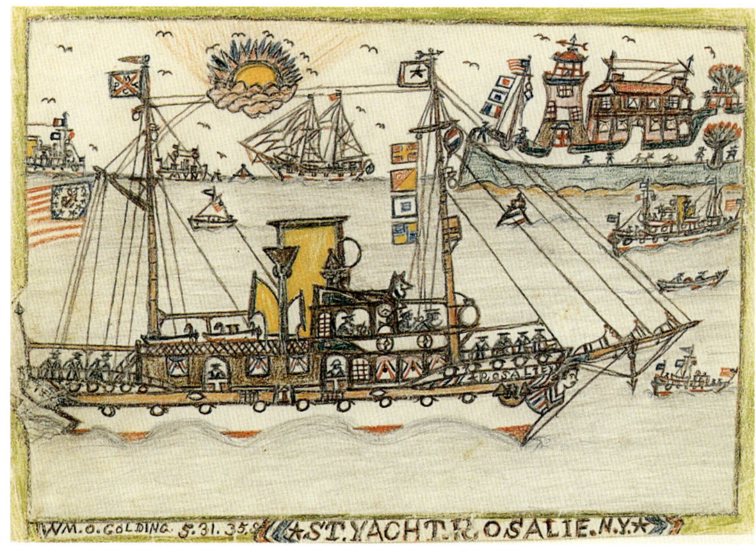

brances: sailing ships chasing whales in the arctic, South Seas ports with erupting volcanoes, and Chinese architecture.

Golding's works chronicle twenty-two years at sea that began with his abduction from the Savannah port in 1882.

> I never saw home again until March 25, 1904. I came home to Savannah and all that time since I left home I have been all over the world. . . . All that time I never accumulated any fortune but hard knocks, hardship and a lot of experience. Was in all kinds of ships, from a whaler to a man-of-war, so I have had my time knocking around the world.[2]

The artist apparently saw all or most of the sights he recorded, an inference we may draw from one of his letters in which he mentioned that he could not draw Bali or Hawaii as he had never seen them. In all likelihood, Golding did see the *U.S.S. Constitution*, which visited Savannah during Georgia's bicentennial celebration in 1933. The *U.S.S. Isendaga*, a coast guard cutter, is shown on the Savannah River, with many of the city's businesses included in the background. In another letter, Golding said that he had drawn two versions of this image because the first one had seemed "a little dark."[3] Golding repeated other images as well, often making changes in composition or color. The extent to which Golding may have been influenced by popular maritime images is unclear, although many of his compositions include drawn frames and name plaques, complete with screws. His last works date from 1939.

H.H.D.

1. *Kai Olsen, "Black Savannah Seamen Captured Ports of Call in Pencil and Crayon,"* Savannah News-Press, *August 24, 1975, p. 1F.*
2. *Anna Wadsworth,* Missing Pieces: Georgia Folk art 1776–1976 *(Atlanta: Georgia Council for the Arts and Humanities, 1976), 47.*
3. *Ibid.*

William Gray

(active early 20th century, Savannah)

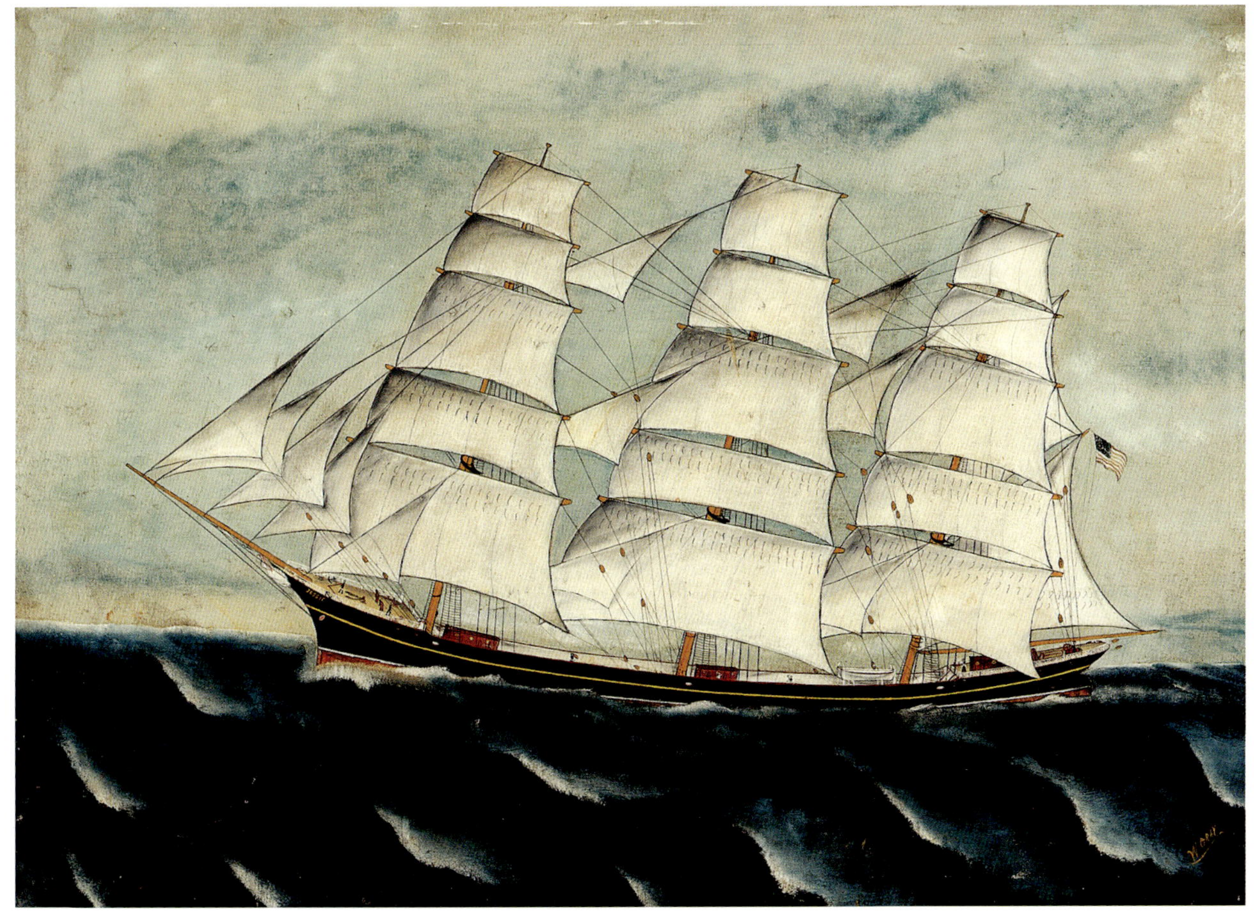

S.S. Jesse, early twentieth century
Oil on canvas
28 ⅜ x 39 in. (72.1 x 99.1 cm)
Collection of H. Paul Blatner

Purchased from the artist's niece in 1979, this painting of the sailing vessel *S.S. Jesse*, fits into the tradition of amateur paintings of marine images taken from popular print sources. Unlike the images of another African American artist who depicted marine subjects in Savannah, William O. Golding, Gray's work does not bear the colorful signs and inventions of memory painting. Nevertheless, in this port city, Gray certainly had the opportunity to view and perhaps serve on such a vessel. The *S.S. Jesse* is depicted at sea, manned by a crew of tiny rudimentary figures. The conventionalized, undulating waves in the foreground create a pleasing pattern, which diverts the viewer's attention from the unevenly painted horizon.

A number of African Americans named William Gray are listed in the Savannah city directories of the early twentieth century. The 1921 directory lists a William Gray employed by the Ocean Steamship Company.

H.H.D.

William Halsey
(b.1915)

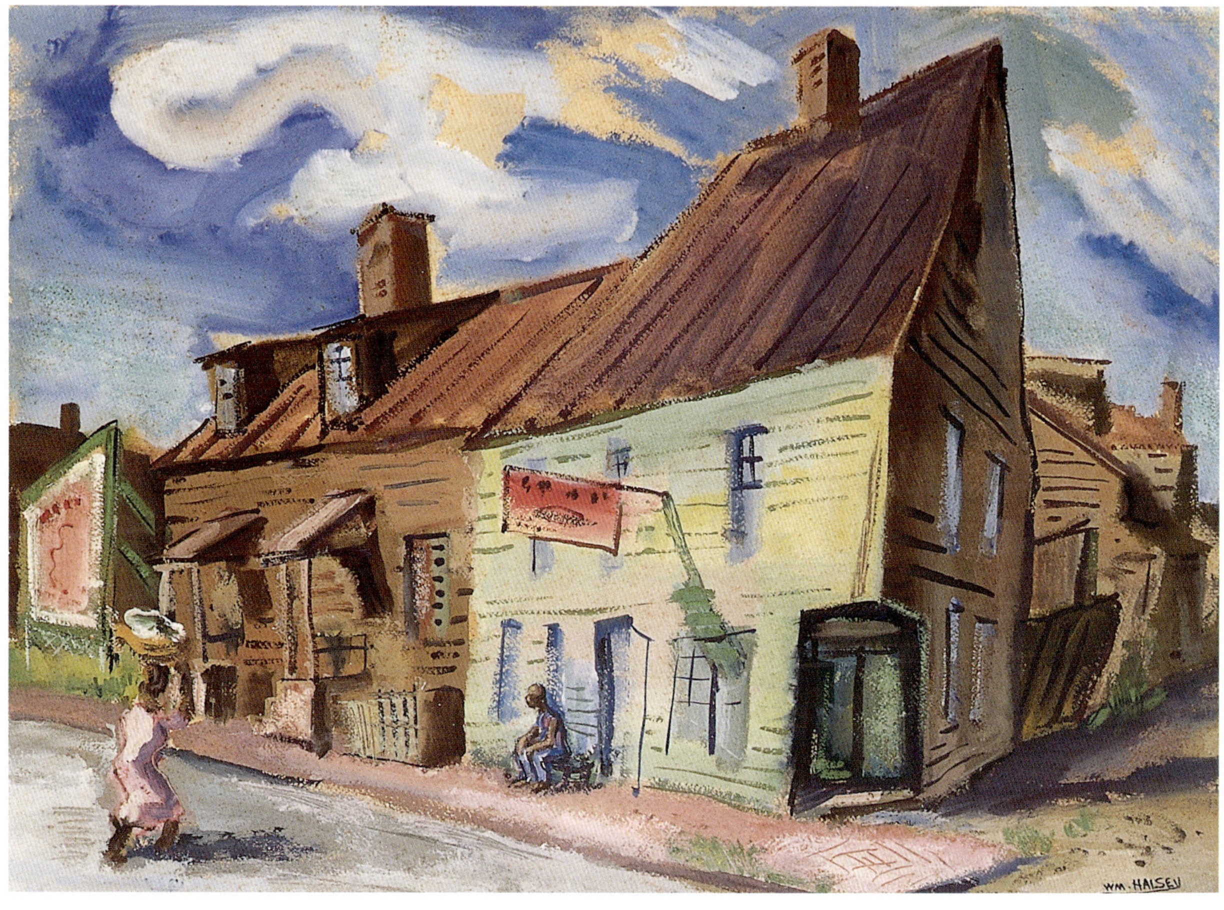

SUMMERTIME SAVANNAH, 1943
Watercolor on Paper
23 x 31 in. (58.4 x 79 cm)
Collection of William Halsey

WILLIAM HALSEY'S ARTISTIC PRODUCTION spans six decades, during which he charted an aesthetic course from abstracted scene painting to highly personal and mythic nonobjective works. Early in his career he was influenced by the venerable Charleston artist Elizabeth O'Neill Verner, a painter and printmaker who specialized in Charleston scenes. Although he adopted to some degree the older scene painter's subject matter, Halsey showed an early affinity for abstraction and individualistic treatment of observed forms. He studied at the University of South Carolina, and at the Boston Museum School, where he was appointed an assistant instructor. In 1939, the last year of his studies in Boston, Halsey married fellow South Carolinian and classmate Corrie McCallum, and received a prestigious fellowship for studies abroad. To avoid the escalating conflict in Europe, the Halseys chose to travel in Mexico—an experience that would have a profound effect on both artists. The couple initially returned to Charleston, and in September 1942 relocated to Savannah, where Halsey held positions simultaneously as director of the art school at the Telfair Academy and art instructor at the Pape School.

Halsey painted a number of works his first year in Savannah and had a one-artist exhibition at the Telfair Academy in 1942. A reviewer for the *Savannah News-Press* noted Halsey's ability to use "every method available from classical influences to modern technique to tell his story, and he has given life to his interpretation without sacrificing technique or boasting of his ability to modernize his subjects."[1] The two works in the current exhibition seem to bear this statement out. *Night Shadows* of 1942, a purchase-prize winner in the 1943 Association of Georgia Artists exhibition at the Telfair, is a somewhat abstracted interpretation of Savannah's oak-lined streets, an amalgam likely painted from memory rather than on site.[2] In contrast, the 1943 watercolor *Summertime Savannah* recalls Halsey's earlier scene paintings and was based on sketches from life. The two-point perspective and exaggerated lean of the foreground building expressively convey the ramshackle nature of the city's decaying neighborhoods, a favorite subject for visiting and local artists.

Halsey's production slowed as war approached. He took a job as timekeeper at the Savannah shipyards in 1943. After the war, the Halseys returned to Charleston, where they were instrumental in developing the art department of the College of Charleston. Halsey's paintings and sculpture evolved toward an expressionist, nonobjective style reflecting the influence of a variety of cultures experienced through his wide travels.

H.H.D.

1. *"Halsey's Paintings Have Versatility,"* Savannah News-Press, *December 1, 1942.*
2. *Telephone interview with the artist, April 1996.*

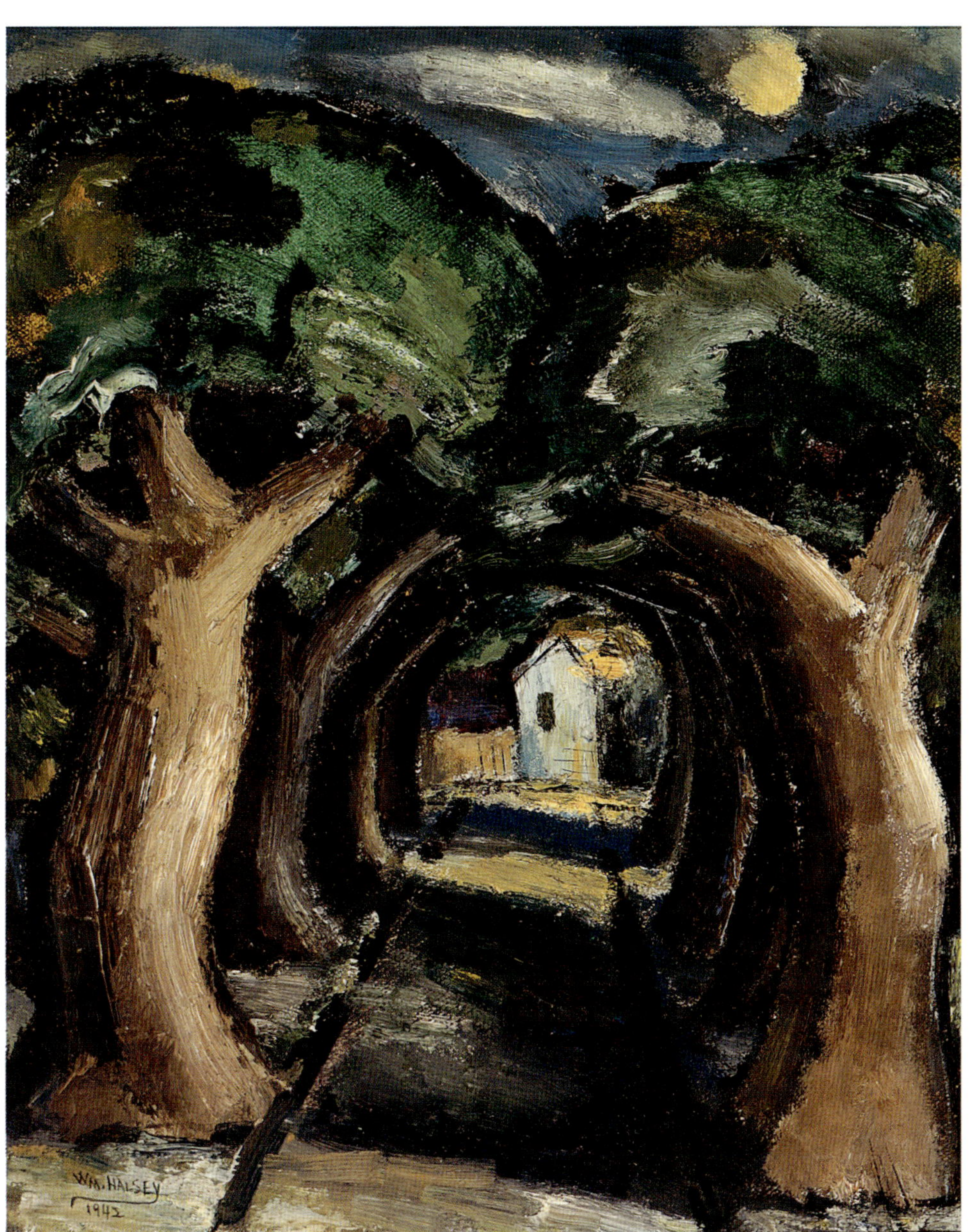

Night Shadows, 1942
Oil on Canvas
20 x 16 in. (51 x 41 cm)
Telfair Museum of Art, Museum Purchase, 1943

Phillip J. Hampton

(b.1922)

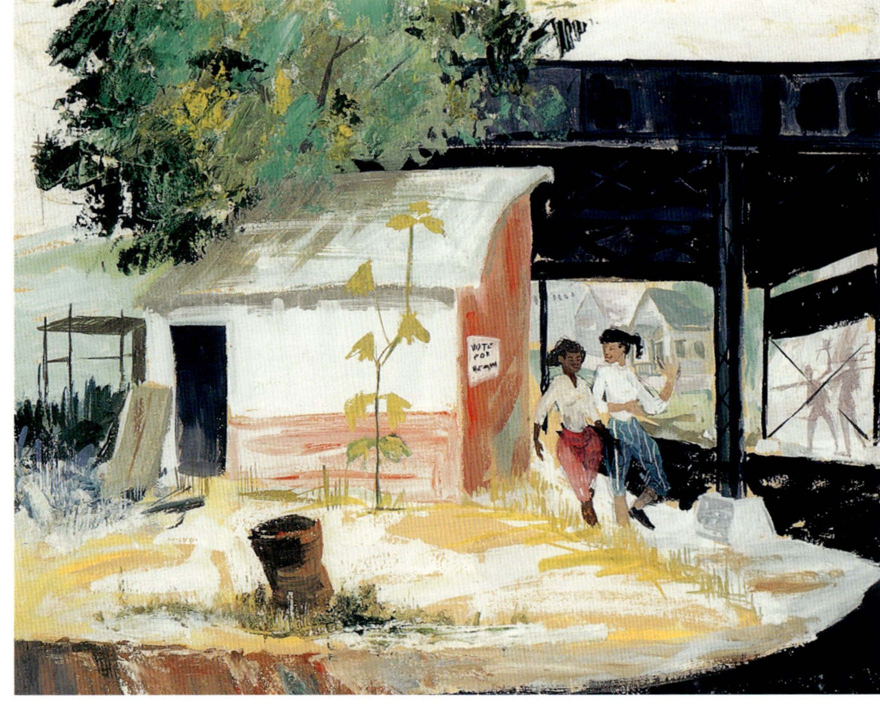

YOUNG GIRLS OF SAVANNAH, 1954
Gouache on paper
13 x 17 in. (sight)
(33 x 43.2 cm)
Collection of Mrs. Louise Lautier Owens

PHILLIP HAMPTON shaped the art department of Savannah State College during his tenure there as professor and director of the department from 1952 to 1969. A well-respected educator and a talented painter and printmaker, he has organized numerous exhibitions of art by African Americans, including one at the Telfair in the 1960s. Hampton's long participation in the struggle for the recognition and exhibition of African American artists' work led to his early and eager participation in the National Conference of Artists, a group founded in Atlanta in 1957 to support African American artists. Hampton has said:

> American Negro artists need the recognition and greater understanding that surveys of their work should bring. It is only through recognition as a group that we will eventually become known as artists who are incidently Negroes.[1]

Born in Kansas City, Missouri, Hampton received his BFA and MFA from Kansas City Art Institute following studies at Citrus Junior College in California, Kansas State College, and Drake University in Iowa. He came to Savannah directly after receiving his graduate degree. He found the city "unusual"; after becoming accustomed to the pace of the people, he began to enjoy the city so much that he remained for seventeen years.[2] In addition to teaching at Savannah State, he offered instruction at the Jewish Educational Alliance and for the Savannah Art Association. He went on to the University of Southern Illinois at Edwardsville, where he is today professor emeritus.

Hampton worked in a variety of media—various types of paint and printmaking processes—but it is his facility in watercolor and gouache that seem to stand out.[3] *Young Girls of Savannah* is a superlative example of the artist's mastery of the medium. A painting of an everyday scene, it shows two young women walking on Gwinnett Street. An elevated railroad crossing fills the upper right of the composition; a small building; complete with a political sign, anchors the image. That nothing is centered indicates Hampton's admiration of Asian art and its characteristic asymmetry.[4]

Hampton has influenced young artists of several generations through his forty-year teaching career. He has steadfastly promoted art to students, visitors to exhibitions he organized, and all who come in contact with him.

P.D.K.

1. *Quoted in Cedric Dover,* American Negro Art *(Greenwich, Conn.: New York Graphic Society, 1960; reprinted, 1972), 51.*
2. *Conversation with the artist, May 22, 1996.*
3. *Conversation with Dr. Floyd Campbell, Howard University Art Department, May 21, 1996.*
4. *Alma S. Thomas, "Philip [sic] Hampton—Painter, Lithographer, Educator,"* Savannah Morning News-Evening Press Magazine, *March 12, 1967.*

Harry Leslie Hoffman

(1871–1964)

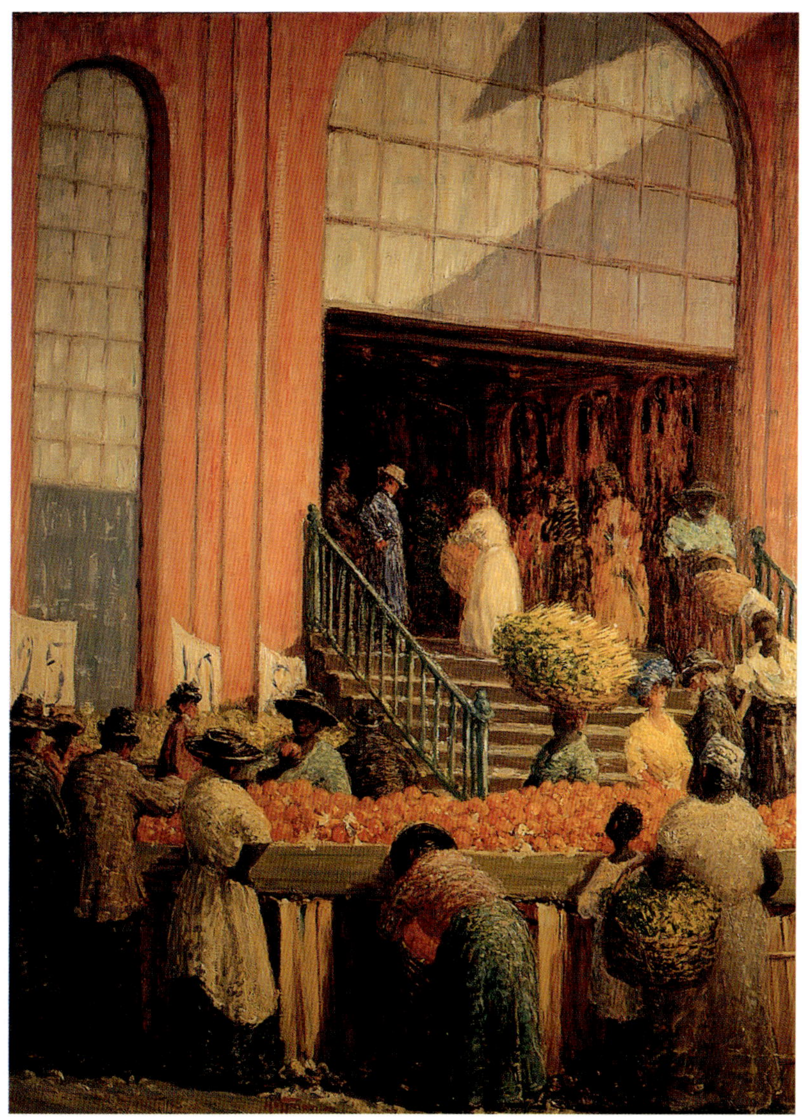

Savannah Market, c.1914–15
Oil on canvas
40 x 30 in. (102 x 76.2 cm)
Collection of Richard and Kay Tarr, Greenwood, South Carolina

Harry Leslie Hoffman, an American Impressionist who worked in Savannah during the winters of 1914 and 1915, trained at Yale with John Ferguson Weir and at the Art Students League with Frank Vincent DuMond. While attending the Académie Julian in Paris, Hoffman had his first solo exhibition at the American Art Association in 1903. One year earlier, he first visited Old Lyme, Connecticut, where he became involved with the town's art colony. He returned to Old Lyme every summer until 1910, when he and his wife settled there and remained until his death fifty-four years later. The predominant style practiced in Old Lyme was Impressionism. The American Impressionist Childe Hassam, a member of the colony, greatly influenced Hoffman, as did other Old Lyme artists, including Wilson Henry Irvine, William Chadwick, and Alphonse Jorgons.

Hoffman's Savannah paintings are loosely painted and brightly colored. *Savannah Market* shows shoppers at the Old City Market, which was erected in the mid-1800s and demolished in 1954. Evident here is Hoffman's preferred technique of applying color in layers of short dashes and his interest in light effects. Some of the same types of figures that appear in the market scene are shown in Hoffman's *Savannah Street Scene*. The house is a typical example of a downtown Savannah home from the 1850s. Although the colors are lighter here, the thick, broken application of paint is the same as in *Savannah Market*.

By the 1920s, Hoffman had become interested in painting underwater scenes. He made watercolor studies for his oil paintings by floating a glass-bottom bucket in the water and drawing what he observed.[1] He traveled to the Galapagos Islands, British Guiana, Bermuda, and Nassau in search of a variety of underwater subjects.

Hoffman was a member of many different artist groups, including Allied Artists of America, New York Water Color Club, and the American Water Color Society. His awards include a gold medal at the Panama-Pacific Exhibition in San Francisco in 1915, and the Lyme Art Association's Eaton Purchase Prize in 1924. In 1930 Hoffman became an Associate of the National Academy of Design. Late in his career, he helped to establish a museum of the work of Old Lyme artists in the Griswold House, a boarding house in the colony where many of the artists, including Hoffman, had lived and worked.

J.A.

1. Connecticut and American Impressionsim (*Storrs, Conn.: The William Benton Museum of Art, 1980*), 163.

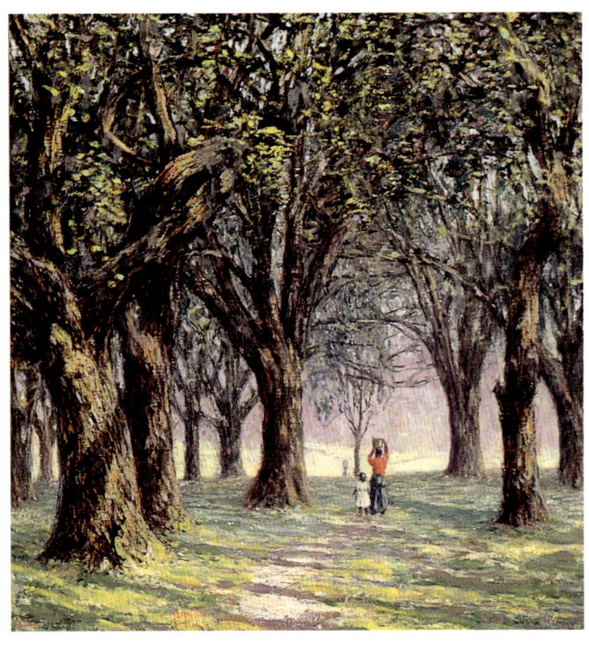

The Hermitage, c.1914–15
Oil on canvas
26 x 24 in. (66 x 61 cm)
Collection of Mr. and Mrs. Robert S. Jepson, Jr.

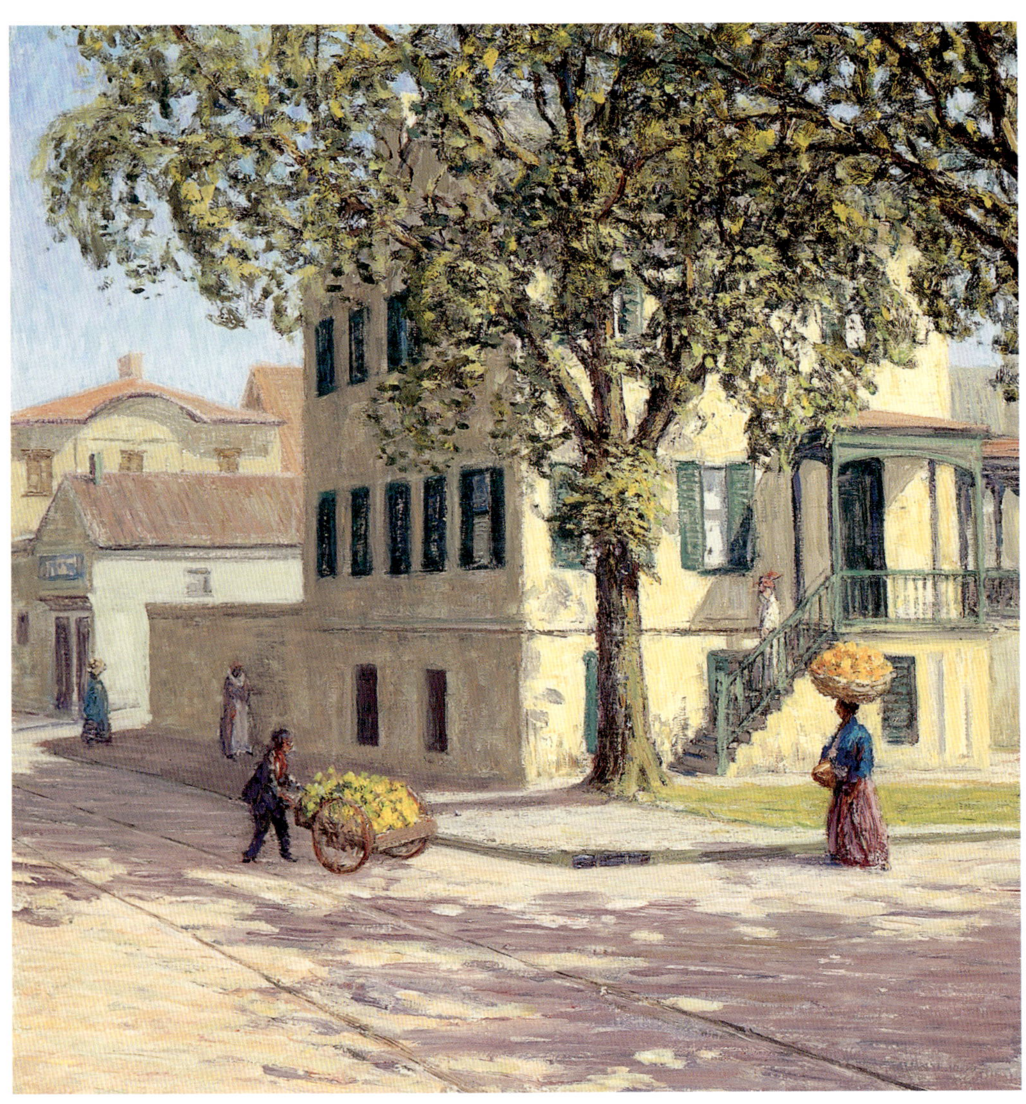

Savannah Street Scene, c.1914
Oil on canvas
26 x 24 in. (66 x 61 cm)
Collection of Mr. and Mrs. Robert S. Jepson, Jr.

Emil Holzhauer

(1887–1986)

EMIL HOLZHAUER WAS A PAINTER of the American Scene known for his rural and urban images of the post-Depression era. Born in Germany in 1887, Holzhauer worked as a jewelry apprentice before moving to New York in 1906 to pursue a painting career. In 1909 he joined Robert Henri's school of art, where he studied with Henri and students such as Edward Hopper, George Bellows, and Rockwell Kent. Holzhauer participated in the Armory Show of 1913 and had a one-artist show in New York in 1915. During the 1920s he traveled throughout Europe, where he was exposed to the styles of Van Gogh, Cézanne, and other Post-Impressionists. Holzhauer returned to the United States in the 1940s and moved to North Carolina to teach at the Asheville School for Boys. He exhibited extensively; major venues include the Whitney Museum of American Art, the Art Institute of Chicago, the Corcoran Gallery of Art, and the High Museum of Art. He received Carnegie Foundation Grants in 1947 and 1949, which allowed him to continue to travel and to paint.

After moving to Macon, Georgia, in 1942, Holzhauer became a professor of art at Wesleyan College. He "found the light in the South intriguing . . . such color . . . so much space . . . so much to paint."[1] During his travels in Georgia he created *Church Spires*, an urban scene combining treetops, rooftops, and soaring spires. As a follower of Robert Henri, Holzhauer learned to record a scene with honesty and realism while showing its beauty. This tight composition includes signs of industrial devel-

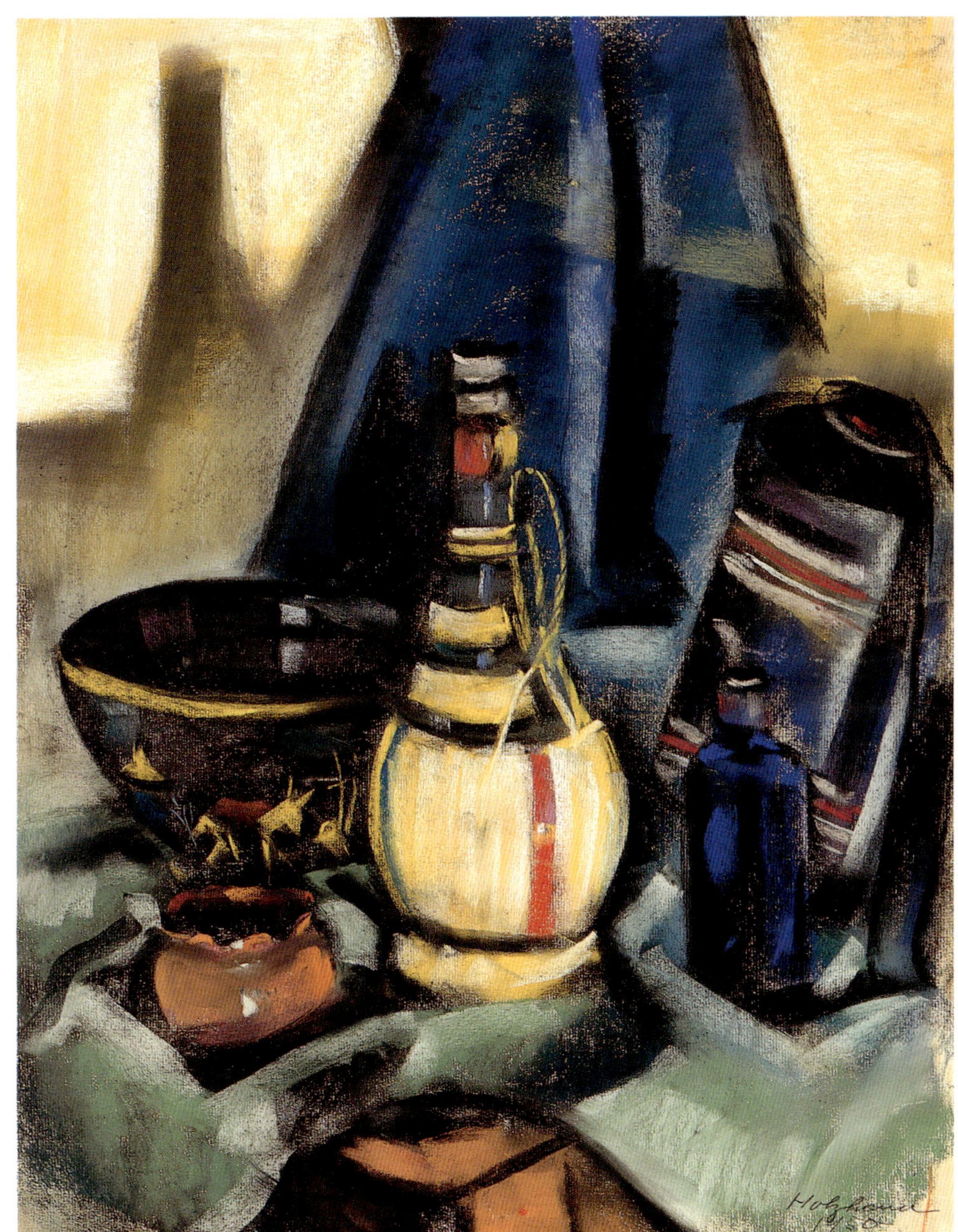

STILL LIFE, 1950
Pastel on paper
24 1/16 x 18 1/4 in. (61.1 x 46.4 cm)
Telfair Museum of Art,
Gift of the Savannah Art Association, 1951

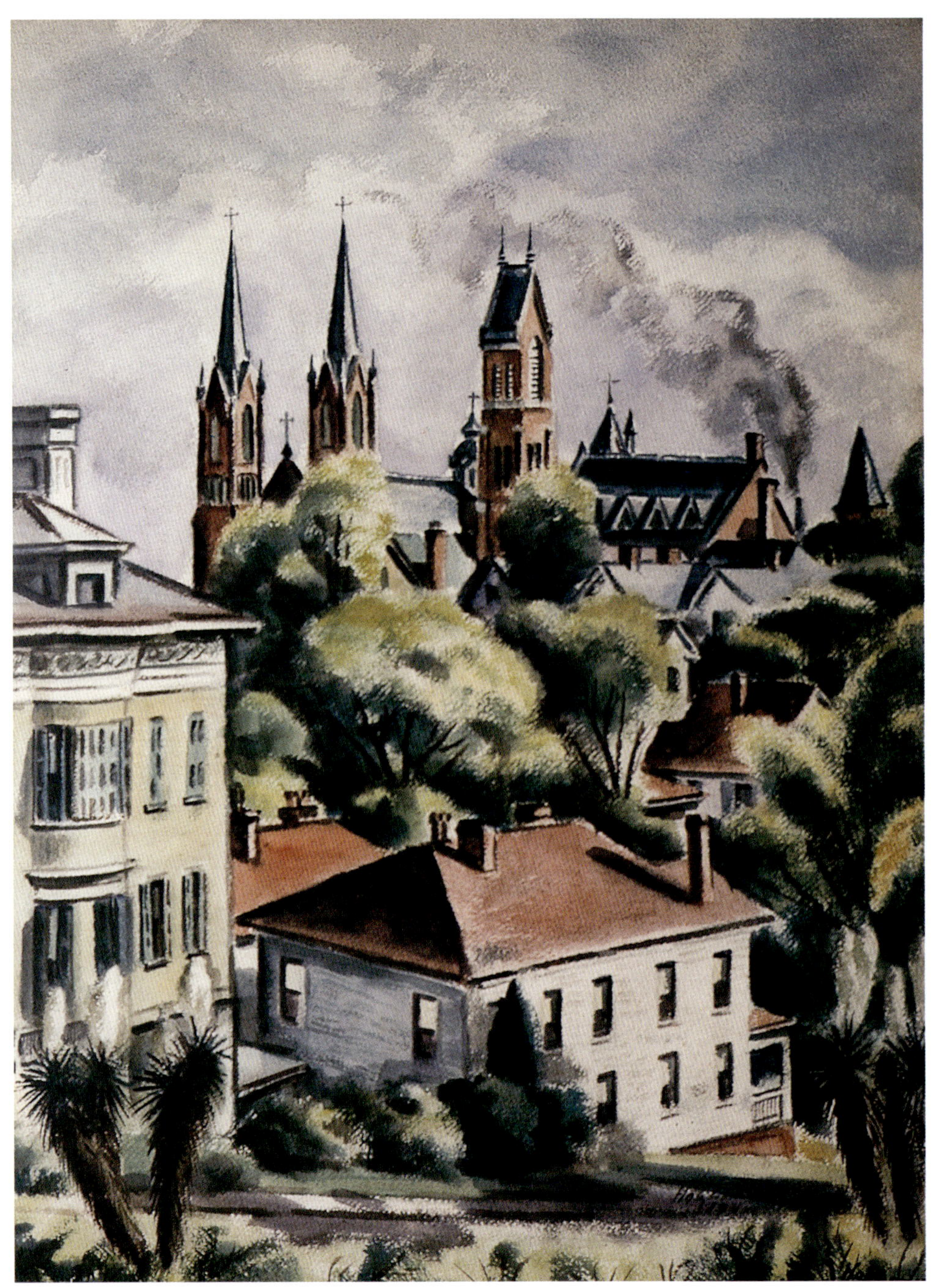

opment. Translucent colors applied with minimal brush strokes bathe this serene southern cityscape, a subject that fascinated Holzhauer throughout his career.

In 1950 he accepted a summer teaching position at the Telfair school. During his tenure, he painted *Still Life*, a pastel composition of bottles, bowls, and drapery, in which solid forms are contrasted with gently folded fabric and great attention is given to texture and surface.

Still Life and *Church Spires* show the breadth of Holzhauer's style and his command of his chosen media. Toward the end of his career, Holzhauer settled in Niceville, Florida, and continued to paint and exhibit until failing eyesight forced him to retire in 1968.

K.L.H.

1. *Mary Takach,* Emil Holzhauer, A Retrospective *(Pensacola: Pensacola Museum of Art, 1982), n.p.*

CHURCH SPIRES, 1944
Watercolor on paper
29 ⅜ x 21 ⅜ in. (sight) (75 x 54.3 cm)
Collection of the Museum of Arts and Sciences, Macon, Georgia, Gift of Dr. Roy T. Ward

Anna Hunter

(1892–1985)

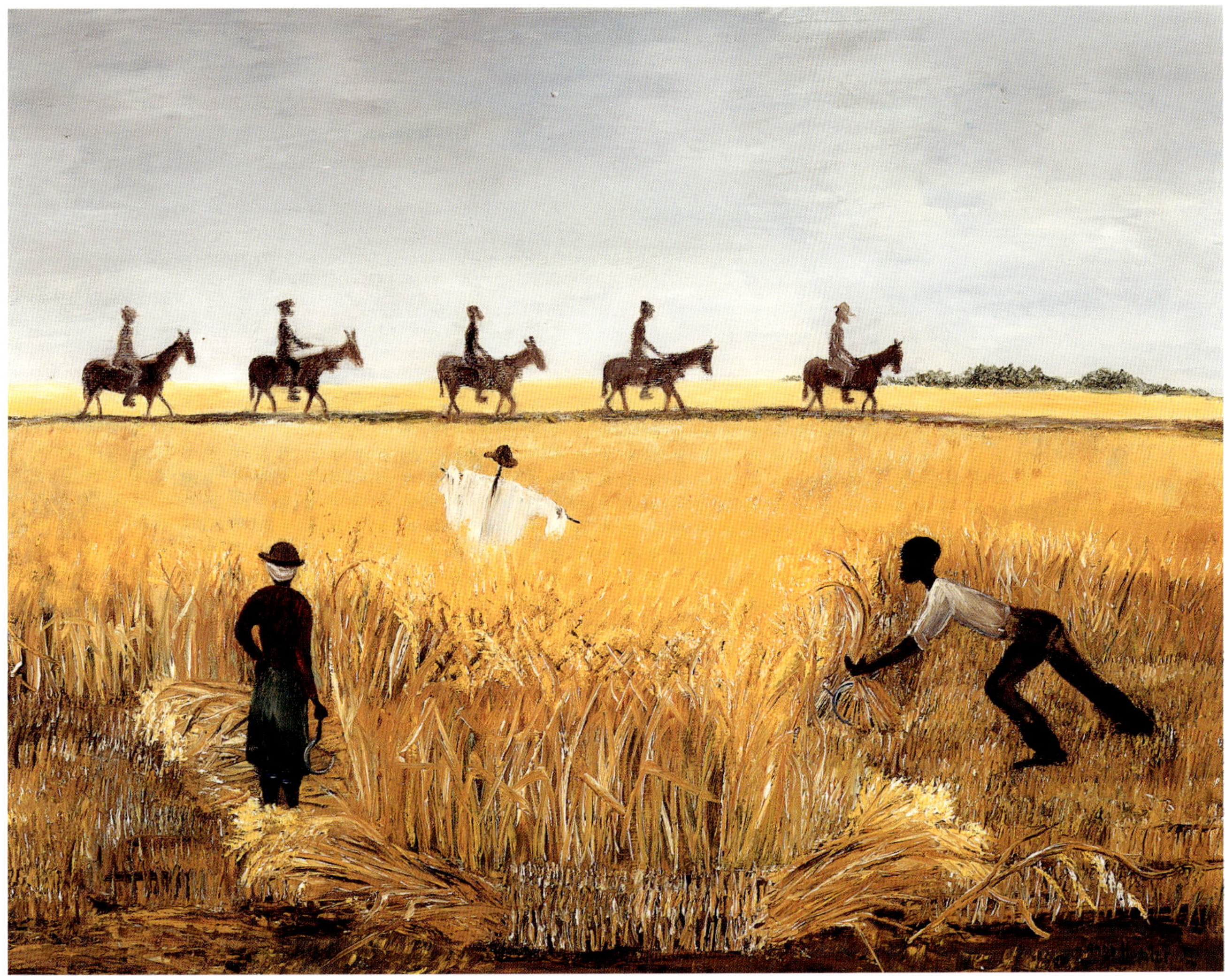

Recessional, c.1948–50
Oil on canvas
22 x 28 in. (56 x 71.1 cm)
Telfair Museum of Art, Museum Purchase, 1952

Anna Hunter came to painting later in life. She had already made a career as a newspaper writer, married and had children and grandchildren, and served in Europe in the Red Cross during World War II before she took up a brush in 1946. Her favorite subjects were the people and scenes of coastal Georgia and South Carolina. Hunter wanted to record what she deemed a vanishing, simple way of life, especially the rice culture.

Primarily a self-taught artist, Hunter had written art reviews for the *Savannah News-Press* and decided that it was necessary to better understand her subject by physically experiencing the application of paint to canvas. She enrolled in a children's class at the Telfair

Academy under the direction of Augusta Oelschig. She related that she "became fascinated by the whole idea, and . . . decided to keep it up."[1] She kept it up the rest of her life, exhibiting with the Savannah Art Association and the Association of Georgia Artists. She showed her work in New York at an interior design studio and in several venues throughout the Southeast, including, in later years, the Telfair Academy.

Beyond that early introduction to painting with Oelschig, Hunter received guidance from Reuben Gambrell during his tenure at the University of Georgia, Savannah extension campus, and at the Telfair. (Gambrell remembers her as a "vital" woman.) She also studied pastel briefly with Emil Holzhauer at the museum. Hunter nevertheless retained a "primitive" style of picture making, that earned her the name "Grandma Moses of the South," a title she apparently did not relish.

Hunter's works struck a chord for visitors to her studio and exhibitions—for her popularity has not waned in five decades. Over this time, technical deficiencies have been overlooked because of the charm and genuine feeling that she communicated in her paintings. One reviewer wrote that "the artist's evident facility of creating a mood . . . cannot fail to affect even the most casual spectator. . . . The immediate fresh appeal, the intimate fresh quality of her paintings are . . . particularly important factors of her well-deserved success."[2]

In many of her paintings, Anna Hunter endeavored to preserve a "simple" way of life in a simple, yet somehow sophisticated style—what Harry DeLorme in this catalogue characterizes as arguably "faux-naive." Her involvement in the Historic Savannah Foundation in the mid-1950s (she was a founding member) paralleled her need to preserve a passing way of life, an element of history.

Through her articles for the local newspaper and her paintings, Anna Hunter recorded and cherished the cultural legacy of the Savannah she helped to create.

P.D.K.

1. *Mardelle Musk, "Newspaperwoman Turns Artist,"* Charleston Evening Post, *October 13, 1950.*
2. *Kyra Kuhar, "Paintings by Savannah Artist Are Shown at Gibbes Gallery,"* Charleston Courier, *October 16, 1950.*

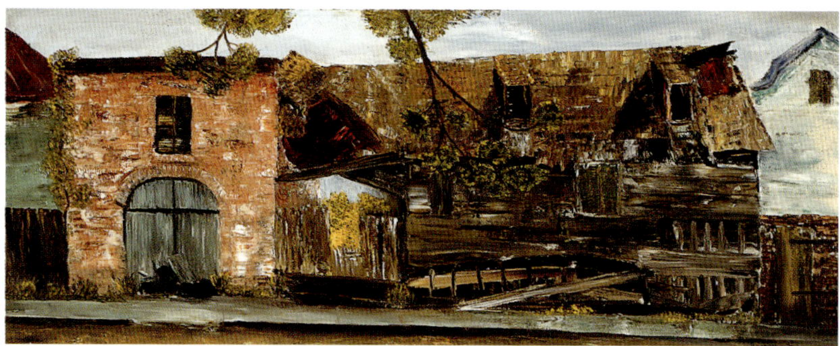

Warehouses, c.1959
Oil on canvas
13 ⅞ x 34 ¼ in. (35.2 x 87 cm)
Collection of Virginia and John Duncan

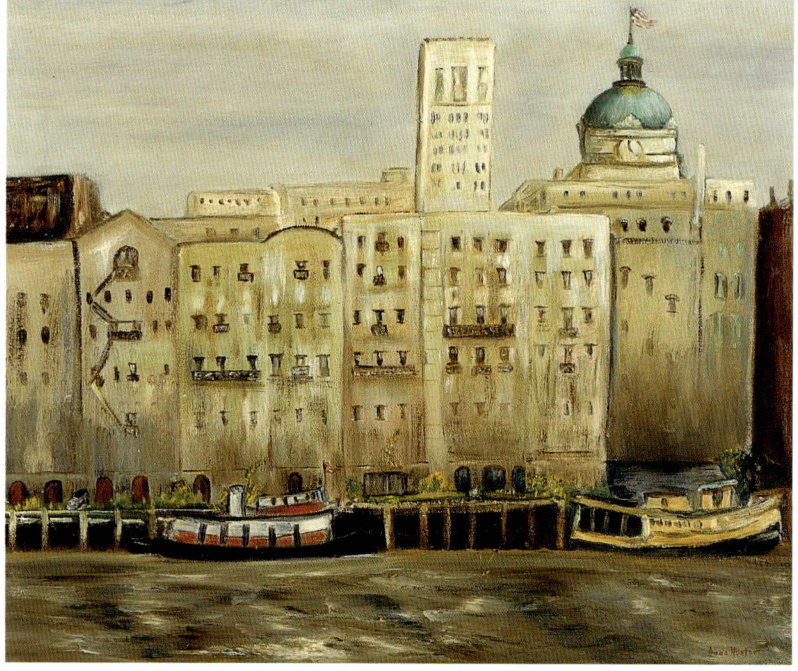

From Seaboard Docks, c.1953
Oil on canvas
20 x 24 in. (51 x 61 cm)
Telfair Museum of Art, Gift of Dr. and Mrs. Lawrence Lee, Dr. and Mrs. Peter Scardino, Mr. and Mrs. Malcolm Bell, Jr., Mr. J. Daniel Zarem, and Mrs. Harriet Huston, 1981

Myrtle Jones

(b.1913)

BORN IN WINDER, GEORGIA, northeast of Atlanta, Myrtle Jones did not receive any formal training in art until after she arrived in Savannah and studied with Emil Holzhauer at the Telfair Academy in 1950. She continues to paint today. Her love for her subject—whether a place or a person—shines forth from the canvas or paper.

A few years after moving to Savannah in 1943, Jones joined the Savannah Art Club. Her first indoctrination in the visual arts in Savannah was her acquaintance with the local painters Leonora Quarterman and Rebekah Saunders. She also met Hattie Saussy, a fellow artist who provided artistic guidance and became a lifelong friend and a painting companion on excursions in and around Savannah.

After studying with Holzhauer, Jones took classes at the Telfair with Reuben Gambrell (a professor from the University of Georgia), Ferdinand Warren (from Agnes Scott College), Bill Hendrix (of St. Simon's Island), and Leonard Delonga (also of the University of Georgia). However, Jones considers herself to be "mainly self-taught" because "the courses were short."[1] By 1959, she had painting students of her own.

Myrtle Jones plunged herself head first into the local art scene. She showed with the Savannah Art Club beginning in 1950 and continuing into the 1990s; she also participated in regional exhibitions, including those of the Association of Georgia Artists, among others. A very early work, *Rooftops*, painted under Holzhauer at the Telfair in 1951, won first prize in an exhibition at the High Museum of Art in Atlanta. The painting exhibits the artist's exploration of modernist concerns with line and block forms while not relinquishing the representational aspects of an urban view of Savannah. Thus the artist creates a dialogue between two and three dimensions in the painting.

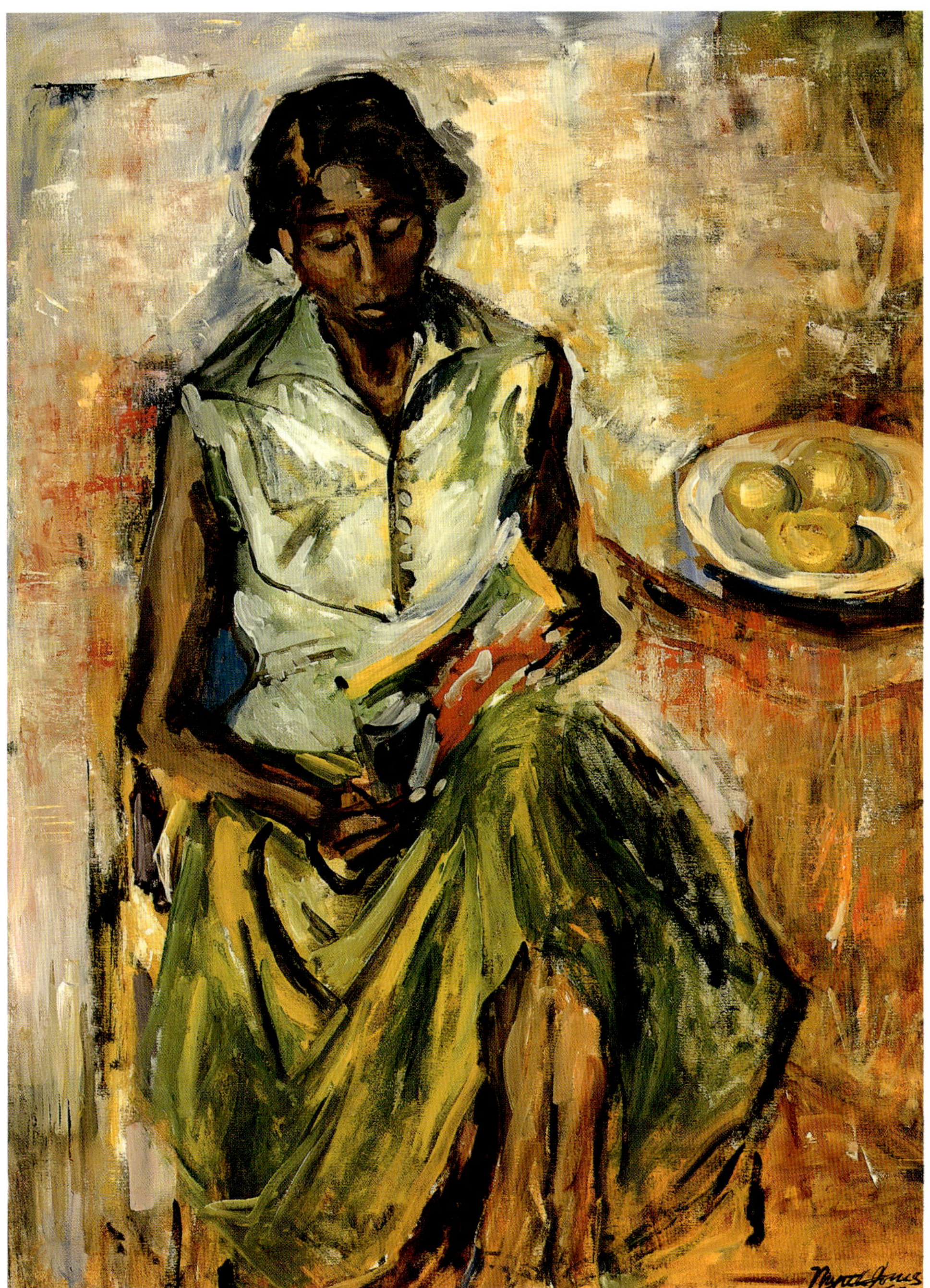

ESSIE READING, c.1959
Oil on canvas
36 x 26 in. (91.4 x 66 cm)
Collection of Virginia and John Duncan

ROOFTOPS, c.1951
Oil on canvas
16 x 20 in. (41 x 51 cm)
Collection of H. Paul Blatner

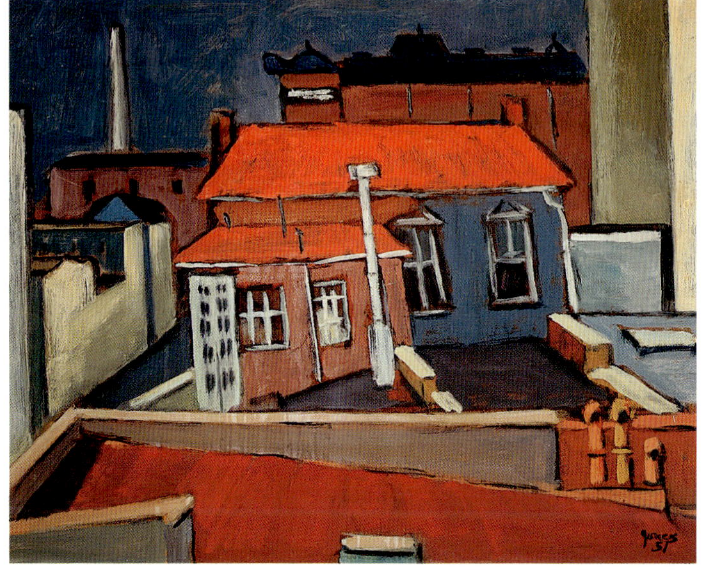

A similar conversation takes place in a painting entitled *Essie Reading*. Here Jones depicts her housekeeper in a quiet moment, seated, with her eyes cast downward. The upper portion of her body is convincingly rendered as three-dimensional, yet her legs seem to melt into the pattern of brush strokes at the bottom of the canvas. Likewise, the solidity of the fruit still life at the center right stands in contrast to the flat layers of color in the background just above. A very colorful painting, *Essie Reading* retains the dark outlining of the figures seen in *Card Players*. Jones calls this effect part of her "dark and bold period."[2] Essie's contemplative mood can also be seen in other portraits from that time, including *Portrait of Joan*.

Although Myrtle Jones's love of art began at an early age, it was not until she moved to Savannah that she could pursue her dream of becoming a painter. A difficult childhood and adult tribulations did not deter her. She has become a beloved Savannah institution.

P.D.K.

1. *Myrtle Jones,* A Savannah Experience: An Artistic Expression of My Life in Savannah *(Savannah, Ga.: M.J. King, 1995), 13.*
2. *Ibid., 39.*

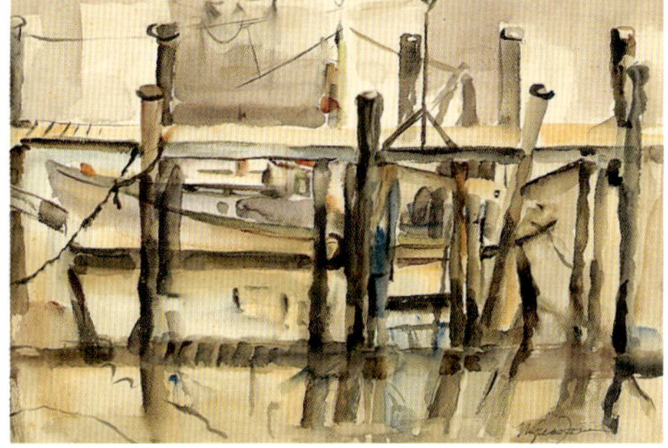

SHRIMP BOATS, c.1951–52
Watercolor on paper
13 ½ x 19 ¼ in. (sight)
(34.3 x 49 cm)
Collection of Myrtle Jones

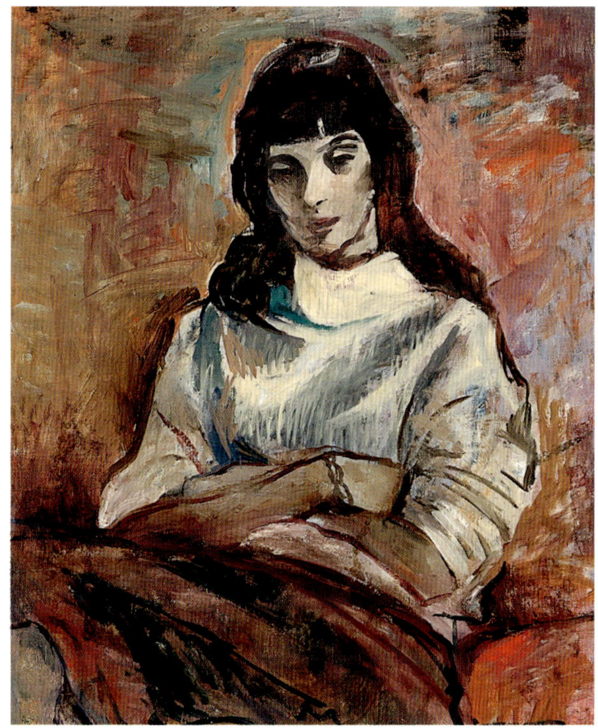

PORTRAIT OF JOAN, 1950s
Oil on masonite
30 x 24 in. (76.2 x 61 cm)
Collection of Myrtle Jones

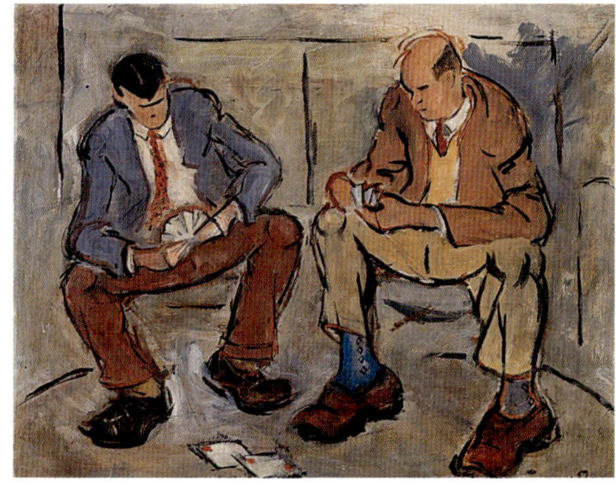

CARD PLAYERS, c.1954
Casein on canvas
18 x 22 in. (46 x 56 cm)
Collection of Ms. Martha McNeil

Mary Comer Lane
(1881–1966)

In *The Fountain*, Mary Comer Lane describes the scene that is the focal point of Savannah's Forsyth Park, a refuge of peace and serenity. Here people are seen enjoying the park, some preferring the shade and others strolling in the sun. Lane's park is infused with sunlight that catches blooming azaleas, trees, and a mother and her children. The artist's spontaneous strokes of color are reminiscent of Auguste Renoir's Impressionist style.

Lane's interest in drawing and painting began in early childhood when she received her first lessons from local artist Emma Wilkins. As she grew up she attended boarding school in Massachusetts and later enrolled at Smith College, neither of which offered art instruction. After her marriage to Mills B. Lane in 1906 she was deeply immersed in family and children, although she did find time to study art in summer classes at Gloucester, Massachusetts, with Henry Bayley Snell.

In 1920 she was instrumental in the founding of the Savannah Art Club, which brought in visiting painters to teach. Among these were Eliot Clark, William Chadwick, and Hilda Belcher. Lane exhibited her work with the Savannah Art Club and also with the Association of Georgia Artists.

After her husband's death in 1945, Lane traveled and painted extensively. Works executed during a trip to the Rocky Mountains led to a one-artist show at the Telfair in 1948. Lane actively participated in the arts of Savannah until her death in 1966.

D.B.

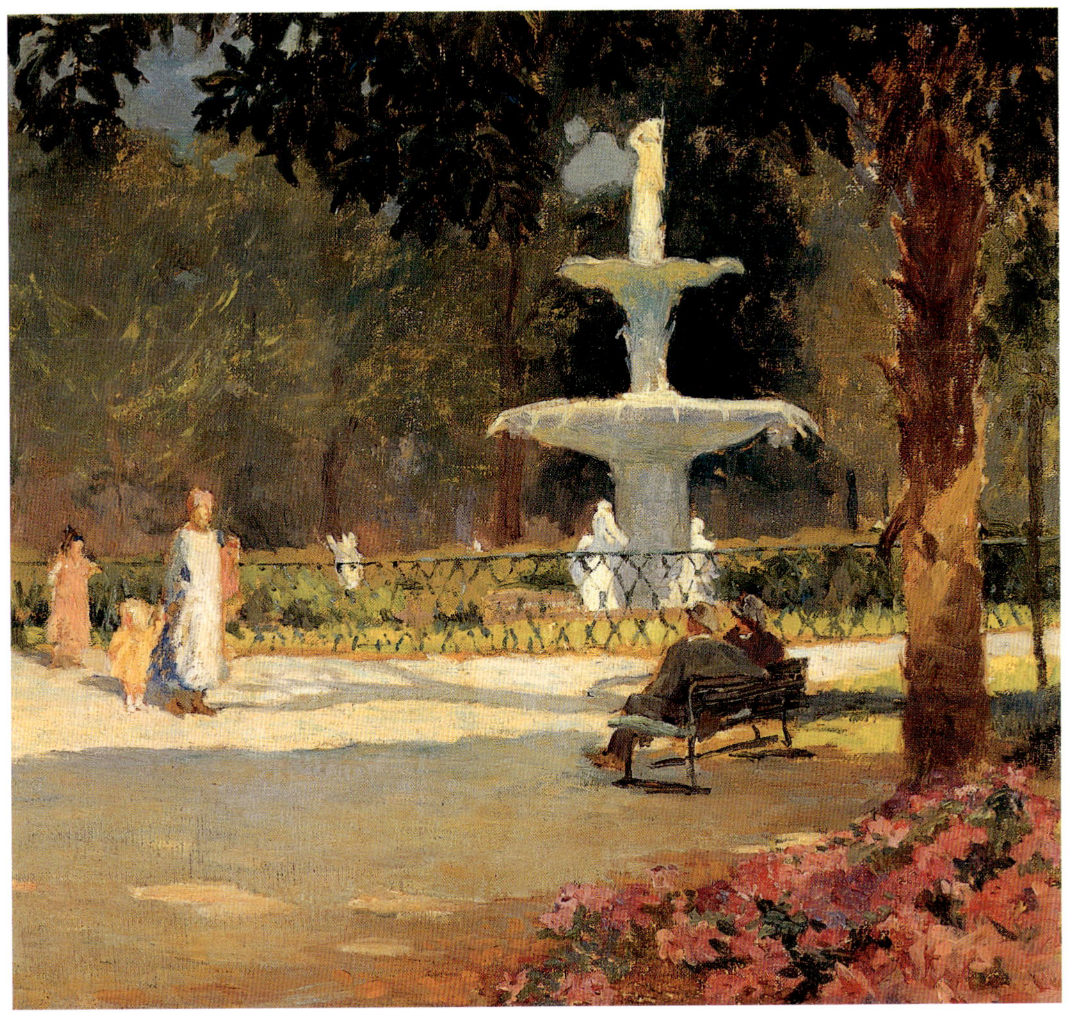

The Fountain, n.d.
Oil on canvas
26 ½ x 28 ¼ in. (67.3 x 72 cm)
The Family of Mary Lane Morrison

Walter Ronald Locke

(1883–?)

ETCHER AND PAINTER WALTER RONALD LOCKE, a Winchester, Massachusetts, native, made his home in Tarpon Springs, Florida. His early training was under the tutelage of Alfred Hutty, an etcher who had studios in Charleston, South Carolina, and Woodstock, New York; and Louis Kronberg, a painter from New York.

Locke's print, *In Savannah, GA*, shows the persistence of the etching style of James Abbott McNeill Whistler into the twentieth century. Whistler's influence on both American and European printmaking after the turn of the century was pervasive. Locke's teacher, Hutty, studied at the Art Students League in New York under William Merritt Chase, who had been profoundly influenced by Whistler in his early development as an artist. The delicately etched tonal ranges in the work of Locke evince the continuing inspiration of the Whistlerian style. Locke, however, diverged somewhat from Whistler's pure aestheticism by his choice of urban scenes in Depression-era America.

Urban subjects became increasingly popular in American art after 1900. Historically, this trend coincided with a mass migration of the population to America's urban centers. In the 1920s all aspects of the American scene became popular themes for artists, and in the 1930s many turned to the depiction of the plight of the poor. In the etching *In Savannah, GA*, Locke depicts a run-down house in Savannah owned by a woman who made her living during the Depression by selling sweets and other goods from a shop on the ground floor of her home. Sanders Confection Shop, operated by Ada Butler Sanders, at 245 Price Street,[1] bears a sign that is clearly legible in the print. Other signs nearby indicate the sale of wood, coal, and ice cream.

Like Whistler, who favored views of peasants and the back alleys of Venice over the more typical tourist scenes, Locke chose to depict daily life in Savannah rather than the more often depicted grand historical architecture of the city. Clearly he was very much a part of the tendency in American art of the 1930s to illustrate the conditions of living in America during the Great Depression.

C.L.B.

IN SAVANNAH, GA, 1934
Etching on paper
9 ¼ x 6 ⅞ in. (plate) (24 x 18 cm)
Telfair Museum of Art

1. Information supplied by Dr. John Duncan, Savannah, Ga., from the 1930 Savannah directory.

Juliette Gordon Low

(1860–1927)

A NATIVE OF SAVANNAH, Juliette Gordon Low, the well-known founder of the Girl Scouts of America, was also a talented artist, proficient in many different media. Her artistic skills came naturally; except for a few art classes in various finishing schools she attended, she was virtually self-taught.

Low's abilities are exemplified in the portrait bust of her grandfather, William Washington Gordon, who was mayor of Savannah from 1834 to 1836. Low portrays him in the classical manner, according to the tradition that began with Roman art, wherein life-size portrait busts of Roman leaders convey the dignity and intellect of the sitter. This mode was revived in late-eighteenth- and early-nineteenth-century neoclassicism by artists such as Jean-Antoine Houdon, a French sculptor who came to America in 1785. Houdon is known in this country for his portrait busts of George Washington, Benjamin Franklin, and Thomas Jefferson. This form of representation continued through the nineteenth century and into the twentieth.

Low's bronze portrait portrays Gordon in contemporary nineteenth-century clothing. Her firm modeling of his face reflects strength of character, yet the most striking element of the portrait is the subject's eyes. Here Low captures a sincere sense of kindness and concern. In this way Low's portrait bust differs from many sculptures of government leaders, probably because she is commemorating the sitter not only as a civic leader but also as a loving grandfather.

D.B.

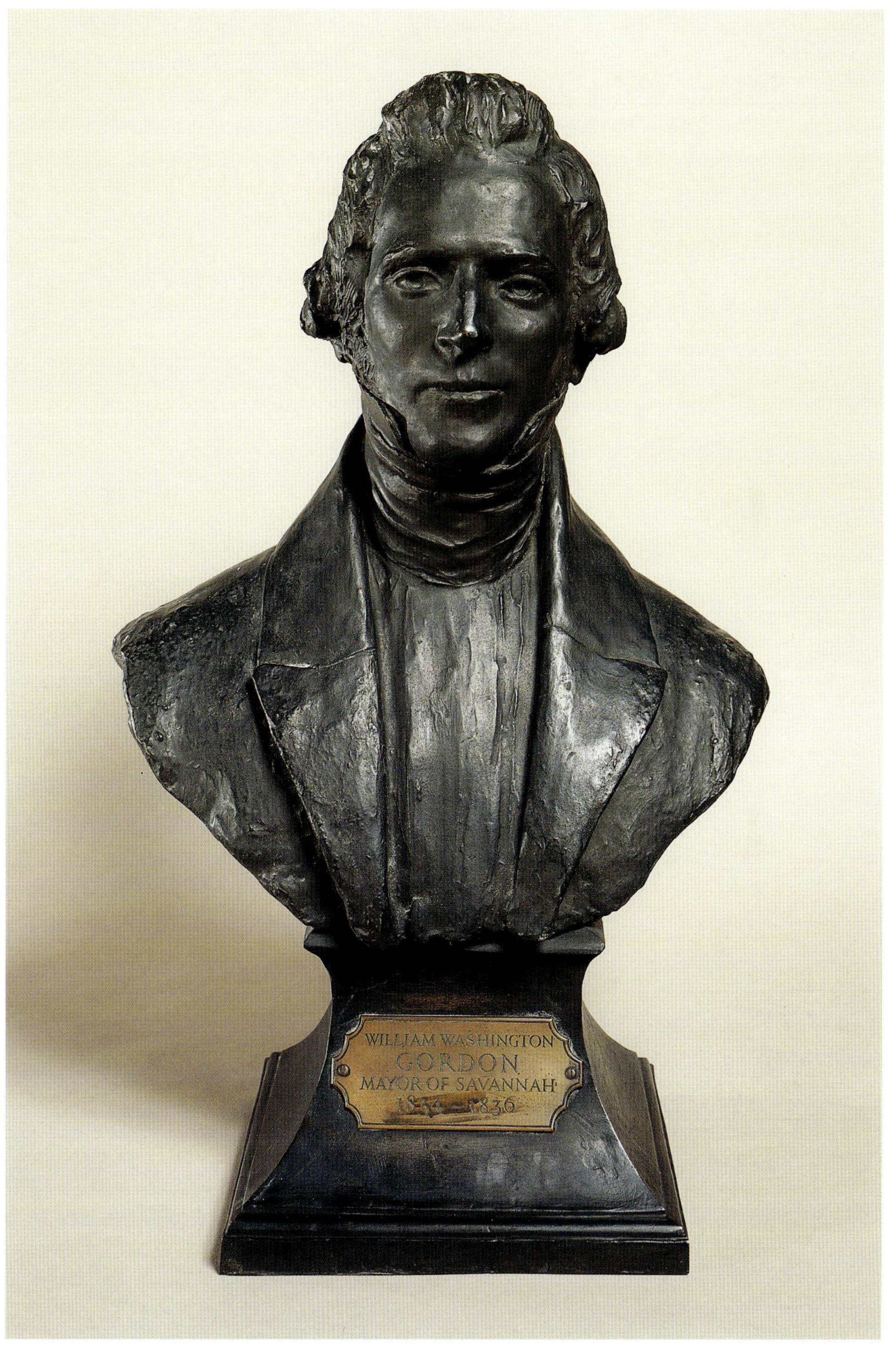

WILLIAM WASHINGTON GORDON, cast in 1926
Bronze
29 x 17 ½ x 11 ¼ in. (74 x 45 x 29 cm)
Collection of the City of Savannah

Bolton McBryde

(b.1910)

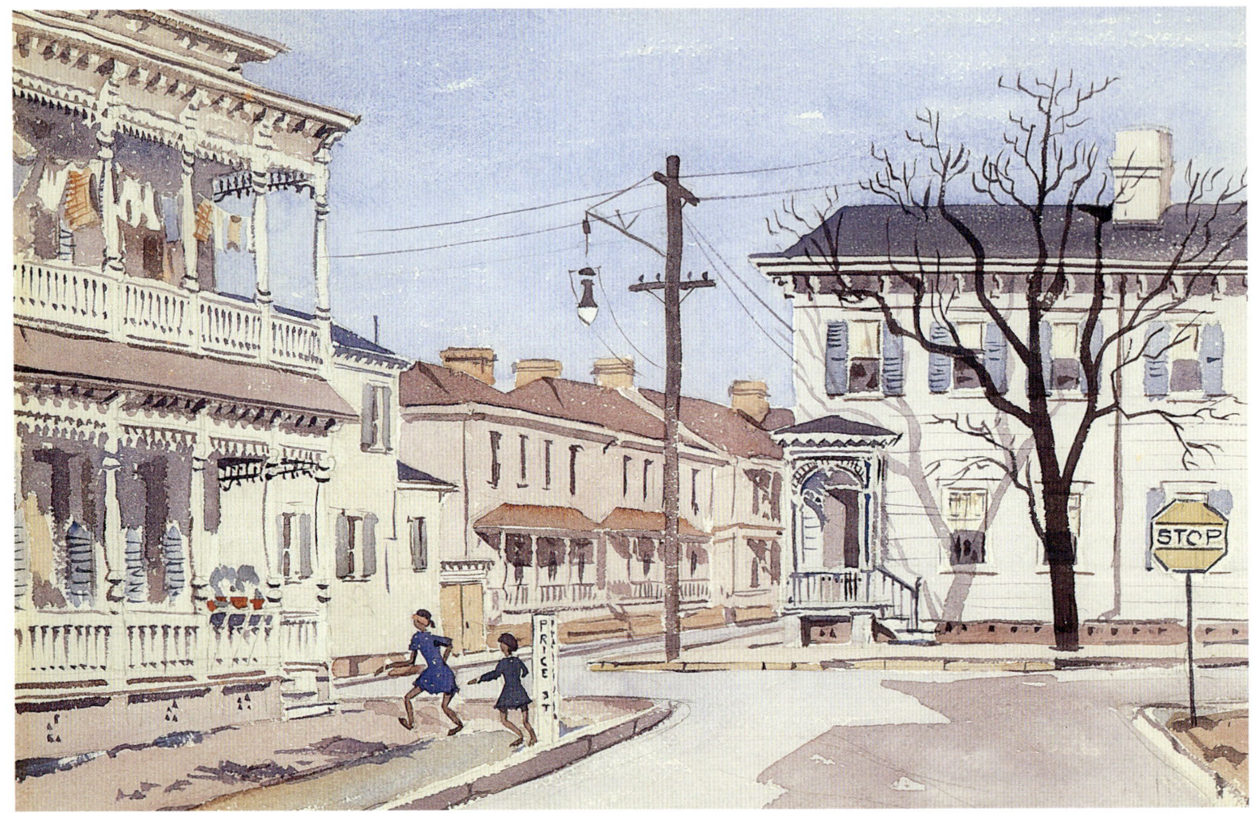

PRICE STREET, 1947
Watercolor on paper
13 ⅛ x 20 ⅝ in. (sight) (33.3 x 52.4 cm)
Collection of Mr. and Mrs. John E. Cay III

IN THE WATERCOLOR *Price Street*, Bolton McBryde of Beaufort, South Carolina, depicts an idyllic scene of a middle-class neighborhood in 1940s Savannah. The house in the right middle ground still stands at the southeast corner of Price and Gaston Streets, as does the building directly across the street to the north, but the elaborate Victorian structure on the left and the houses farther down Gaston Street have been demolished.

The carefully rendered architectural details, which are still extant in the surviving structures, evince McBryde's concern with fidelity to the object. He first made a pencil sketch to establish the composition and delineate the architectural features; then he applied large areas of watercolor using a wash technique and leaving areas of white paper exposed to create highlights. Details were rendered with a dry brush. His limited palette of cool hues creates a sense of serenity and calm. Running children and fluttering laundry animate the otherwise quiescent scene.

The watercolor style and the subjects painted by Bolton McBryde are reminiscent of the work of Edward Hopper, a foremost painter of the American Scene. Hopper too used watercolor to depict the architectural landscape, and often created nostalgic views of Victorian homes. However, while many of Hopper's paintings have a sense of melancholy and isolation, McBryde's works are views of an ideal America. Children playing on a pristine street with freshly painted houses illustrate the prevailing sense of hope for peace and prosperity in post-World War II America.

C.L.B.

Corrie McCallum
(b.1914)

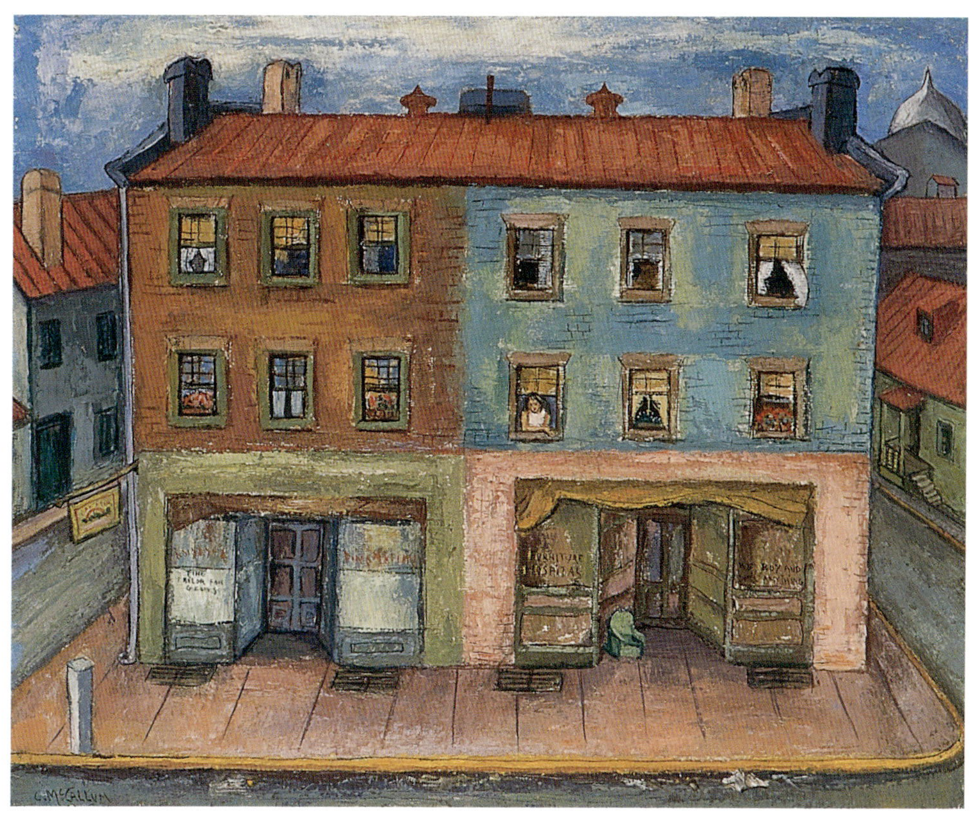

FURNITURE HOSPITAL, 1943
Oil on Panel
20 x 24 in. (51 x 61 cm)
Collection of Corrie McCallum

SOUTH CAROLINA NATIVE Corrie McCallum has been a major figure in art and art education in Charleston, South Carolina, since the 1940s. She began her professional training in art at the University of South Carolina, where she met her future husband, artist William Halsey. After leaving the university to be an administrator for the Works Progress Administration (WPA), she continued her studies at the prestigious Boston Museum School. McCallum and Halsey married in 1939 and embarked on an extended exploration of Mexico, where the couple remained until 1941. In 1942, the Halseys moved to Savannah and both worked initially for the Telfair Academy. McCallum was assistant to the museum's director and taught children's art classes for the museum school.

From the west windows of the museum's third floor studios, McCallum painted *Furniture Hospital*, a work depicting one of Savannah's charmingly disheveled structures. *Furniture Hospital* differs markedly from other paintings of Savannah's urban scene of the period. McCallum's lively pastel colors are more upbeat than the somber grays that create a pervading sense of tragedy in the work of Alexander Brook and other realists working in Savannah. Her approach to painting at this time may have been influenced by her recent Mexican experience. She has said "Mexico introduced me to textures and to weighty things, early things, early colors, early forms that were strong."[1] *Furniture Hospital* is neither overtly abstract nor straightforwardly realistic. Rather it is a "distillation"—to use McCallum's word—of the scene observed.[2]

The artist's intuitive use of color points to her later production in which she paints from an internal, rather than external, reality. McCallum's lyrical sense of color is still evident in her exuberant nonobjective paintings of the 1990s.

H.H.D.

1. *Angela Mack,* Corrie McCallum: A Life in Art *(Charleston, S.C.: Gibbes Museum of Art, 1994), 6.*
2. *Telephone interview with the artist, April 1996.*

Henry Lee McFee

(1886–1953)

HENRY LEE MCFEE was a well-known modernist painter who worked in the Woodstock, New York, art colony for nearly thirty years. Thanks to a trust supplied by his uncle, a wealthy St. Louis industrialist and philanthropist, McFee was able to pursue a career in art free from financial constraints. Little is known about McFee's life until the summer of 1909, when he first traveled to Woodstock to study at the Art Students League summer extension program under Birge Harrison. McFee had hoped that Woodstock would prepare him for further studies in New York City, but he was so taken with the camaraderie he felt among Woodstock artists that he decided to stay.

McFee's earliest paintings followed the dominant trends of American Impressionism and Tonalism. Soon, however, he became more interested in Paul Cézanne's work and began focusing on still-life paintings. McFee's career is typified by his experimentation with many different styles, including Cubism, to which he devoted himself by the early 1920s.

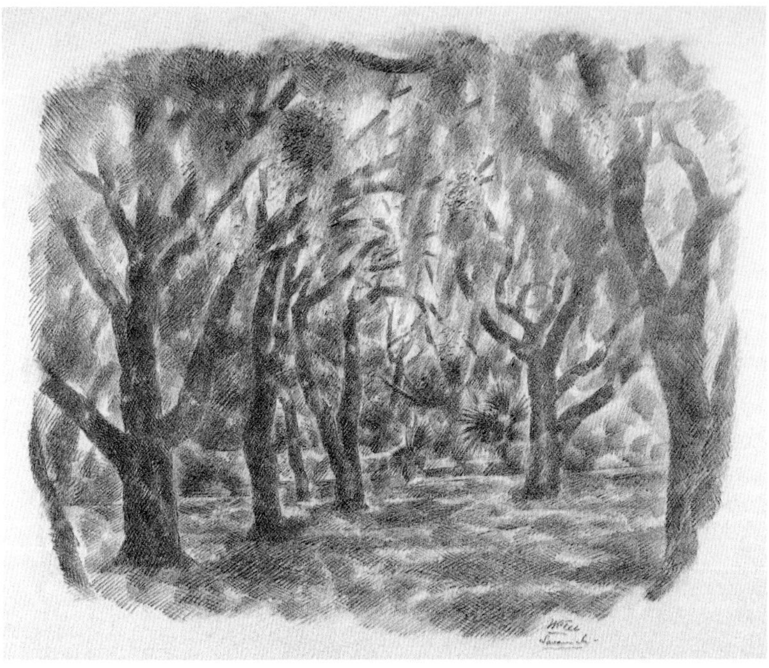

A GROVE, SAVANNAH, late 1930s
Pencil on paper
17 x 19 in. (43.2 x 48.3 cm)
Collection of the Joslyn Art Museum,
Omaha, Nebraska,
Gift of George Barker

McFee came to Savannah in 1936, a turbulent time in his life; he had just divorced his wife and had eloped to Georgia with her niece. This situation apparently caused him some financial difficulties, so McFee turned his attention toward creating an art school in Savannah in 1939. The plan failed, however, due to low enrollment.

Fruit and Leaves and *A Grove, Savannah* are both examples of McFee's late 1930s style. In *Fruit and Leaves*, he uses a simple composition to explore his idea of "object presence," a term he used to describe portraying his subject realistically, with an emphasis on volume and deep color.[1] Both the composition and the use of color reflect the influence of Cézanne's still-life paintings. The work McFee produced during this period has been generally considered less successful than his earlier experiments in Cubism; however, that opinion is changing as his realist paintings are seen to be equally important to modernism.[2]

By 1940 McFee had become frustrated by his lack of motivation to work:

> I have come to the conclusion anyhow that I would like to stop thinking and struggling to make things and sit down somewhere in the sun and do exactly nothing but eat, drink, and be entirely comfortable.[3]

McFee relocated to Los Angeles to accept teaching positions at the graduate school at the Claremont Colleges and the Chouinard Art Institute. In 1941 he was awarded a Guggenheim Fellowship. He remained in California, painting and teaching until his death.

J.A.

1. *John Baker,* Henry Lee McFee and Formalist Realism in American Still Life, 1923–1936 (*Lewisburg, Pa.: Bucknell University Press, 1987*).
2. *Ibid.*
3. *Ibid.*

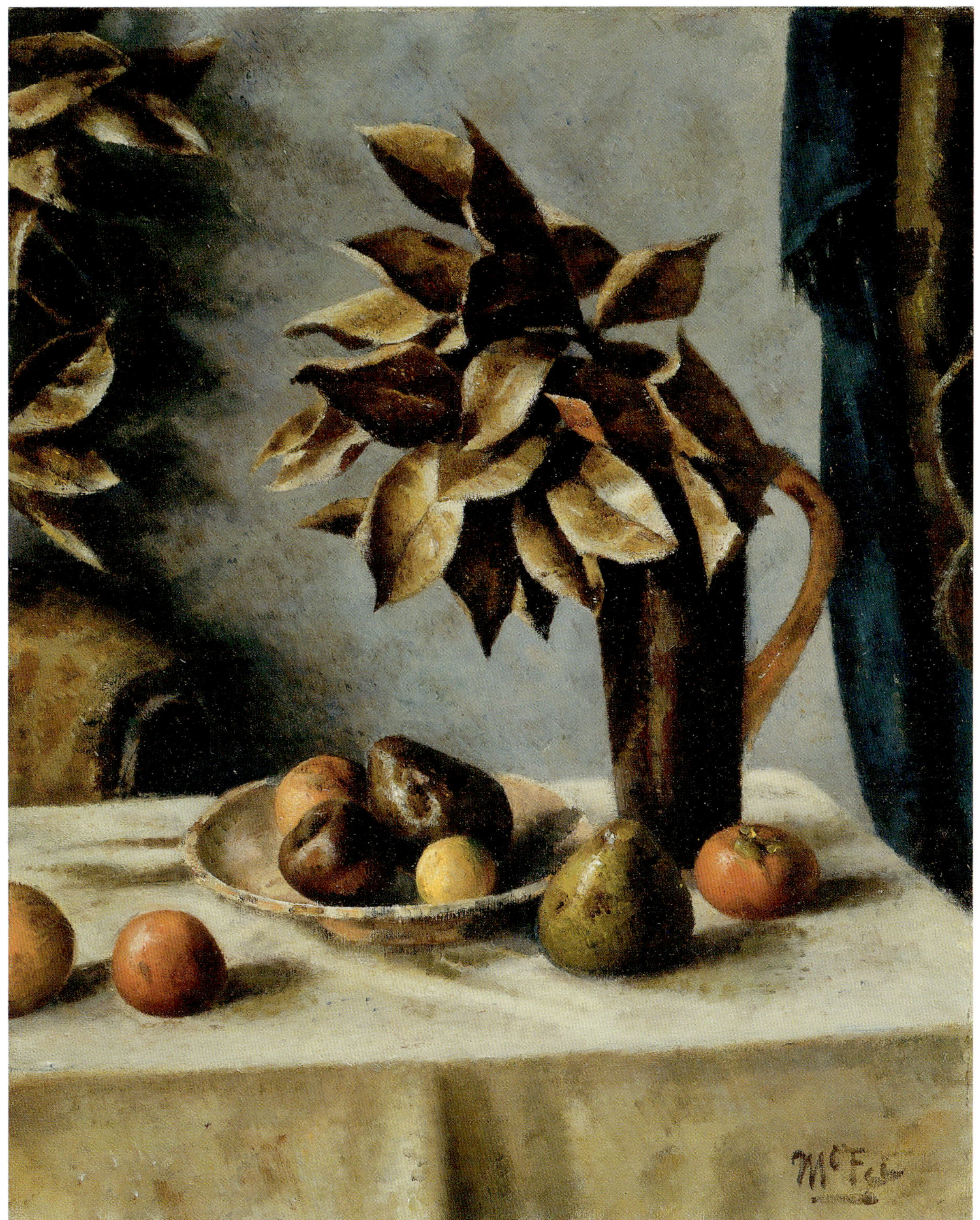

Fruit and Leaves, 1938
Oil on canvas
30 ¼ x 24 ½ in.
(77 x 62.2 cm)
Collection of the Nelson-Atkins
Museum of Art,
Kansas City, Missouri,
Gift of the Friends of Art

Valentino James Molina

(1879–1954)

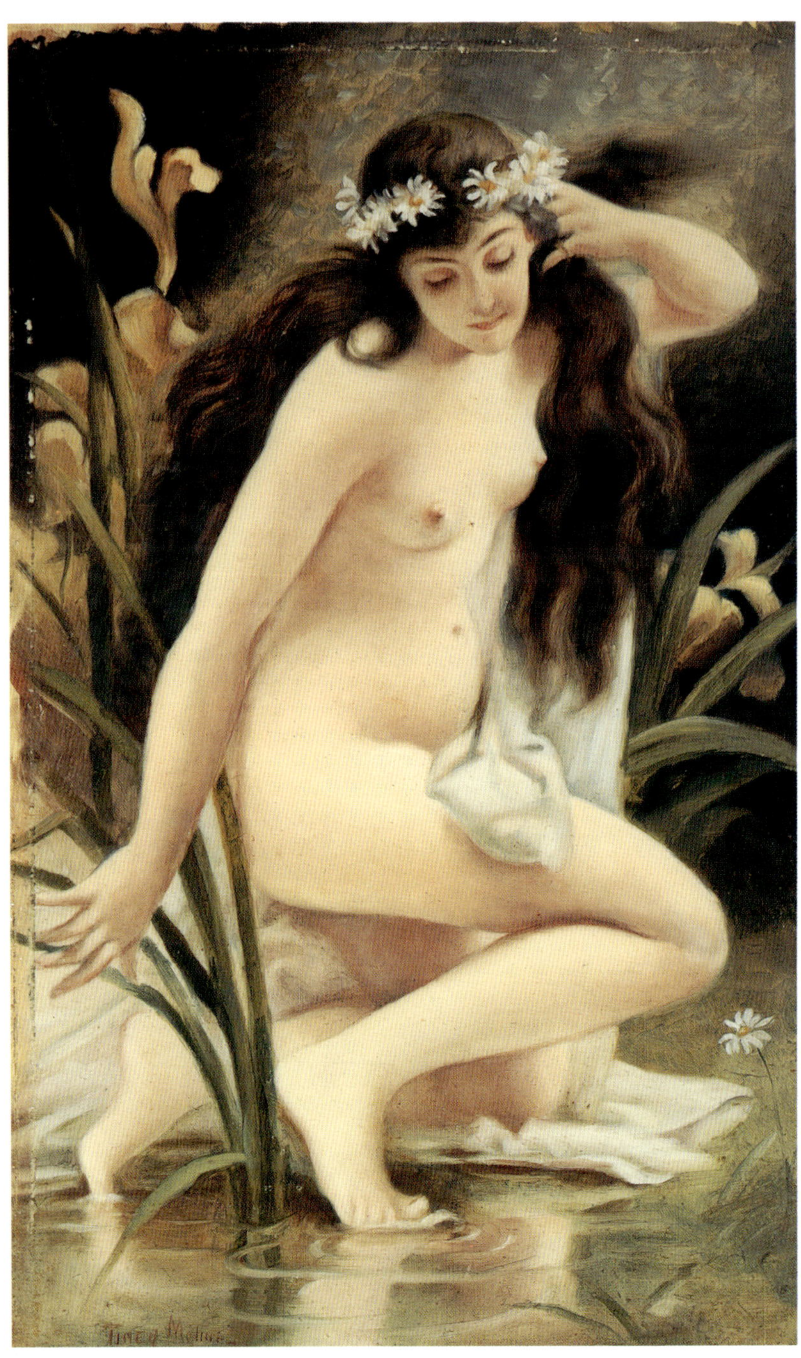

BORN IN POVERTY, Savannah's Valentino James Molina lived a fascinating, cosmopolitan life that included European travel, contacts with the rich and famous, and even scandals. In a Quebec newspaper, Bernard Epps wrote,

> In his villa at Villefranche-sur-Mer on the French Riviera, he was Count Valentino de Molina, wealthy cousin to the King of Spain and a painter of society portraits. In his London studio on Cheyne Walk near that of John Singer Sargent, he was Don Valentino Molina. . . . In Savannah, Georgia, where he was born on September 11, 1879, he was Tiney Molina.[1]

Later, "Tiney" Molina would disavow what had become a hated nickname. That it appears on these two small idyllic nudes, innocently posed in an imaginary landscape setting, helps date the works to those early formative years when the young artist painted *Cupids at Play*, *Andromeda*, and the work that created a Savannah scandal, the monumental six-foot-tall canvas of a nude, titled *Cleopatra*, reportedly painted in the basement of Savannah's Cathedral of St. John the Baptist.

It was the picture of Cleopatra that enabled the talented Molina, whose education consisted of lessons at the Savannah Art Club and copying the Telfair Academy's most noted paintings, to acquire a patron, Mrs. Helen Lucke.[2] Mrs. Lucke, who wintered in Florida and often stopped in Savannah en route, was shown *Cleopatra* by her friend Mrs. Gignilliat, whose son was a supporter of the artist. Upon meeting Molina, Mrs. Lucke was impressed by his manners, charm, and good looks—as well as his talent. Mrs. Lucke introduced him to a new lifestyle. She took the young artist to her home in Lennoxville, Quebec, which she shared with her sister, and he was given a top-floor studio. The sisters also took Molina to London, Spain, France, and Italy. In Paris he studied at the Académie Julian under Jean Paul Laurens and Lucien Simon; he also joined the American Art Association and the Cercle International des Arts.

Fortune continued to smile on Molina. He married a New York debutante, Dorothy Keene Taylor, whose father built them a home

UNTITLED (KNEELING FEMALE NUDE), c.1900–1905
Oil on ivorine
8 ¼ x 5 ¼ in. (21 x 13.3 cm)
Collection of Ben N. Adams

and studio and is said to have helped Molina exhibit at New York's Milch Galleries. Portraits, often of royalty, landscapes, and sunlit nudes were his specialties. A scandalous divorce and life on the Riviera followed, and then another marriage. At the end of 1938, with war imminent, the Molinas settled in Jacksonville, Florida.

In 1947 the couple moved to Savannah and Molina was welcomed back to the Telfair with an exhibition. Paintings in the exhibition—*Capri; Beach in Maine; Spanish Dancer, Madrid; Rock Garden, Brittany;* and *Son of a Sheik, North Africa*—attest to a life of travel.

Sadly, Molina's life ended in poverty. A 1968 talk written by Tom Gignilliat, who was president of the Telfair Board in 1947 and whose mother had known Mrs. Lucke, included the recitation of chapters from the artist's memoirs, based upon his scrapbooks. Gignilliat also related the attempts by Savannahians to help Molina and his wife. Commenting on the dinner that was held for the artist when he moved to Savannah, Gignilliat said:

> Tino was at his best. He regaled us with tales of coronations and royal christenings, contrasting this life with the bitter poverty of his boyhood here in Savannah, and then his voice took on a wicked edge and he said, 'Tonight, Valentino Molina is back in the place of his birth. He is arranging for a show of his paintings—in the Telfair Academy. He is the house guest of a Gignilliat. He is having supper with a Ravenel . . . and with a Colquitt—in the Oglethorpe Club! Valentino Molina has arrived.'[3]

D.L.

1. *Bernard Epps, "Count Valentino de Molina,"* The (Quebec) Township Sun, *March 1986, p. 25.*
2. *A portrait of Mrs. Lucke, by Molina, has remained in the Telfair since its donation by Molina in 1947. The Telfair also owns* By the Mediterranean, *another gift of the artist and his wife (in 1954).*
3. *Tom Gignilliat, "Valentino Molina," text of lecture delivered to the Madeira Club, March 13, 1968, p. 5.*

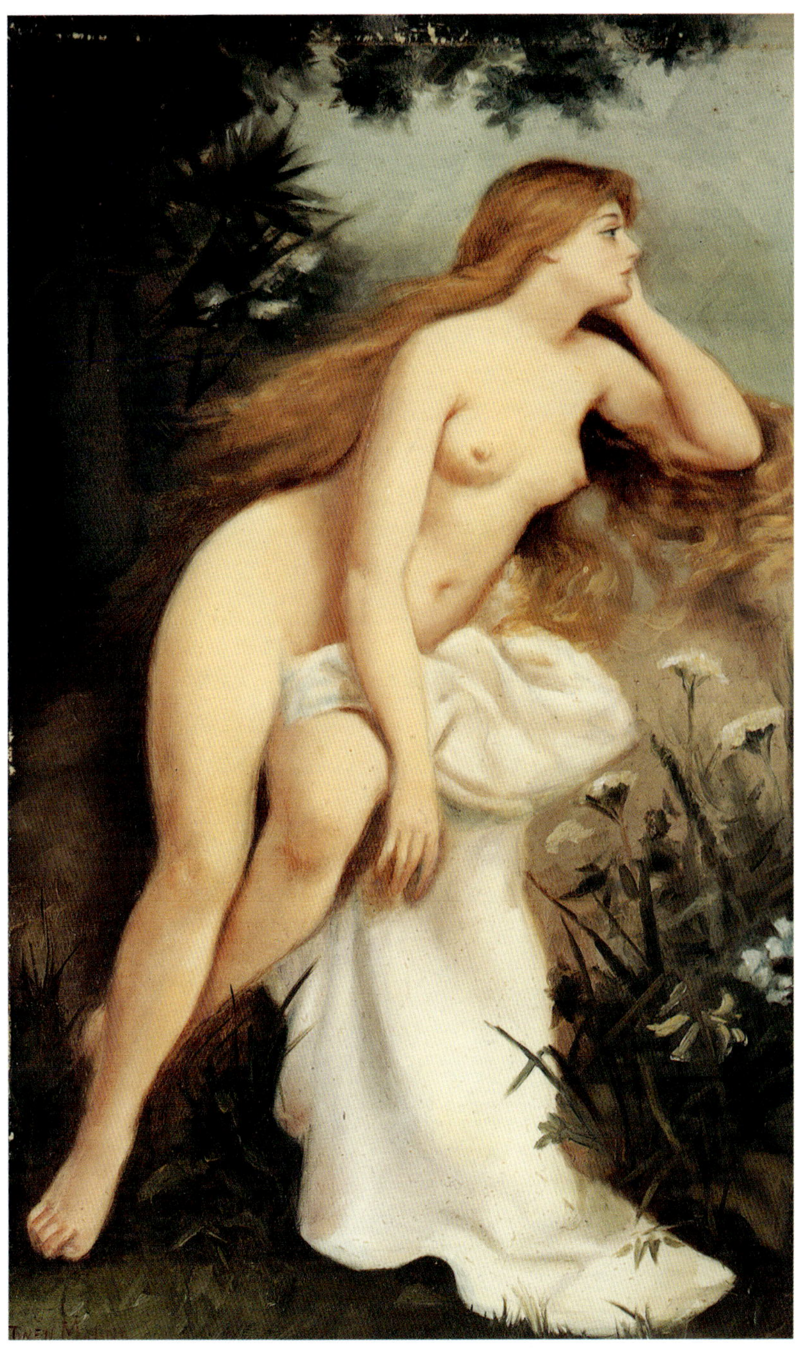

Untitled (Nude Leaning on Rock), c.1900–1905
Oil on ivorine
8 ¼ x 5 ¼ in. (21 x 13.3 cm)
Collection of Ben N. Adams

Christopher P. H. Murphy

(1869–1939)

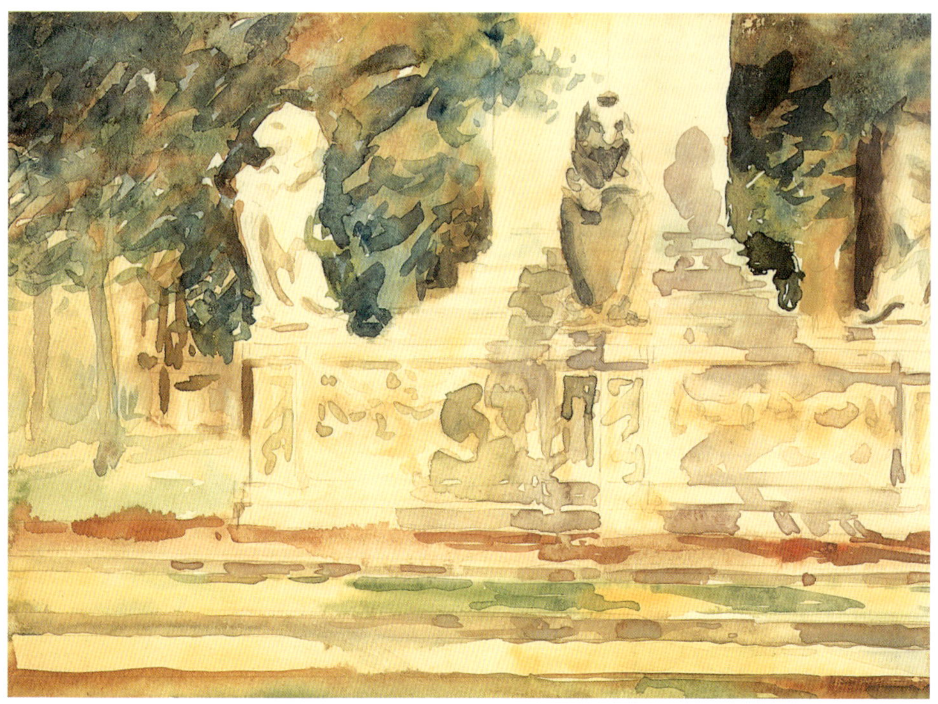

Oglethorpe Monument, Chippewa Square, Savannah, #2, c.1920–30
Watercolor and pencil on illustration board
10 x 12 ½ in. (sight) (25.4 x 32 cm)
Collection of Hunter, Maclean, Exley and Dunn

CHRISTOPHER P. H. MURPHY joined his father's ship chandlery and commercial painting firm in 1888. With each succeeding year he mastered more specialized crafts: sign painting, paper hanging, fresco painting, graining, and decorating. Yet nothing short of the fine arts would satisfy his creative yearning. After his father's death in 1895, Murphy concentrated on learning to make pictures.

By the late nineteenth century, relatively few American artists developed their skills through apprenticeships in crafts. American art students wanted to acquire European-style academic discipline, whether they studied in Europe or America. Because he was tied to the family business, Murphy could not pursue full-time study. He taught himself with books and correspondence courses. He also participated in the Savannah Art Club, gleaning as much expertise as he could from the classes it offered. His outgoing personality made it natural for him to befriend artists who visited Savannah, and he often corresponded with them after they left. When he traveled, Murphy visited museums and exhibitions to study original works by his favorite artists.

Apprehension about being in his mid-forties and older than the other students notwithstanding, Murphy joined a summer class given by Eben Comins at Gloucester in 1915. It was the only uninterrupted instruction he ever received. After the final critique of the course, Murphy wrote to his wife, "There is no doubt that had I gotten a chance, I would be among the best of them [professional artists]."[1] From around 1915 until the early 1930s, Murphy exhibited nationally. The Depression ended his quest for recognition but not his passion for art.

Murphy created all the paintings chosen for this exhibition

near home. Since he painted during moments stolen from a busy professional and family life, his paintings typically reveal intimate insights into nearby surroundings. Murphy's friends, knowing that he reserved the hours after Sunday dinner for still life, brought him bouquets. Depending on what materialized, he painted set pieces of cultivated flowers as in *Still Life (Pink Roses in a Dark Blue Vase)*, or free-style arrangements of southern plants such as hydrangeas, figs, coral vine, honeysuckle, and yellow jasmine.

The ingenious eye of the artist saw a protean world of diversity within a small radius of home. Whether it was a service at Christ Church, a performance by Rosa Ponselle, or roustabouts erecting a big top for a circus in a field near town, events fascinated him. The fire at the DeSoto Hotel occurred just across the alley from his home. At his back door he sketched the incident and later reexplored the subject in oil in the painting titled *Desoto Hotel on Fire*.

Despite his lack of formal training, Murphy realized a sophisticated, beaux-arts style that characterizes *Oglethorpe Monument, Chippewa Square, Savannah, #2*, created literally at his doorstep, and *The Fountain in Forsyth Park, Savannah, #5*, painted within a few blocks of his home. Each painting belongs to a series showing the same subject washed in changing colors and different light. Murphy's ability to use the paper color as positive space, his treatment of the subject by describing a detail rather than the whole, and his ability to exploit the fluid elegance of the watercolor medium owe a great deal to his study of John Singer Sargent. Simultaneously, these techniques evoke a lyrical vision of Savannah that is like no other.

F.S.C.

1. *Christopher P. H. Murphy, letter to Lucile D. Murphy, July 19, 1915, quoted in Feay Shellman,* Christopher P. H. Murphy, 1869–1939: A Retrospective *(Savannah, Ga.: Telfair Academy of Arts and Sciences, 1985), 9.*

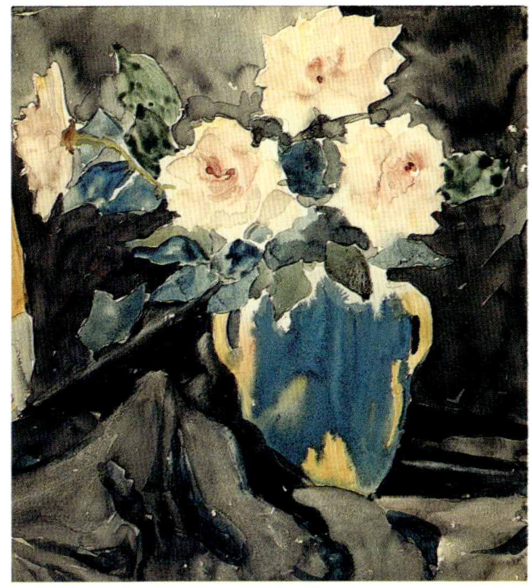

Still Life
(Pink Roses in a Dark Blue Vase), c.1920–30
Watercolor on paper
14 ¾ x 12 ¾ in. (sight)
(38 x 32.4 cm)
Collection of Hunter, Maclean, Exley and Dunn

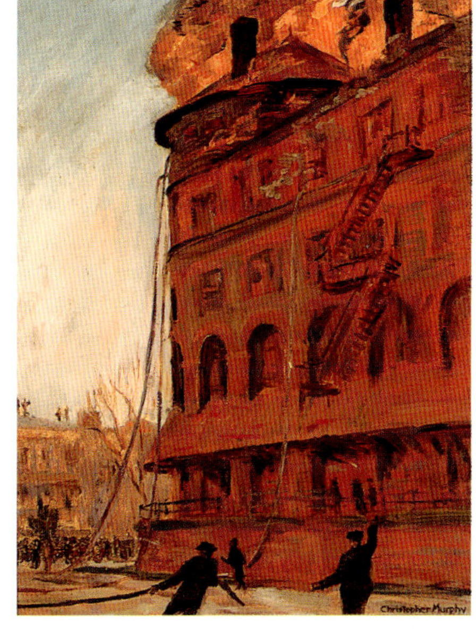

DeSoto Hotel on Fire, c.1926–30
Oil on canvas
19 ½ x 14 ½ in. (sight) (50 x 37 cm)
Collection of
Mr. and Mrs. Leopold Adler II

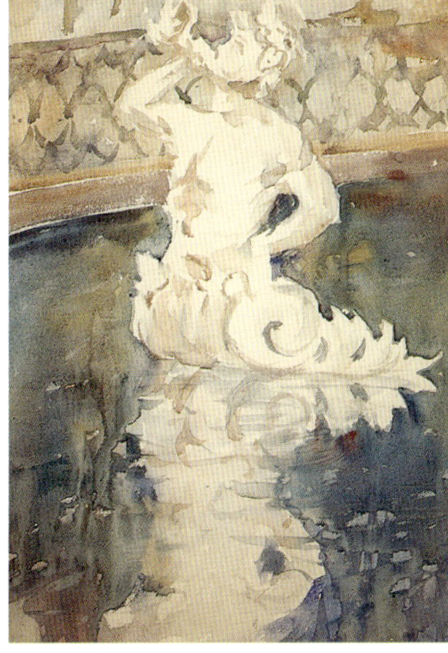

The Fountain in Forsyth Park, Savannah, #5, c.1920–30
Watercolor on paper
16 ½ x 11 ½ in. (sight)
(42 x 29.2 cm)
Collection of Hunter, Maclean, Exley and Dunn

Lucile Desbouillons Murphy

(1873–1956)

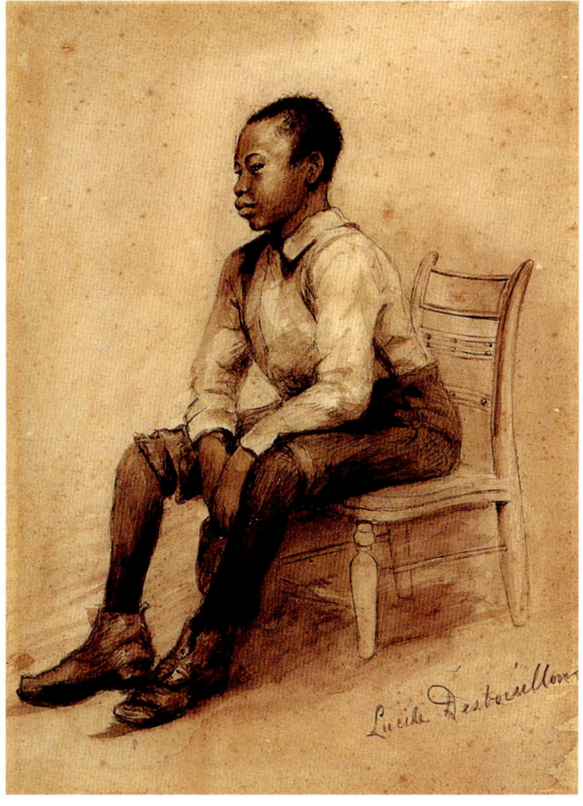

Black Youth Seated on a Chair, c.1900
Sepia wash on paper
12 ⅜ x 9 ¹⁄₁₆ in. (31.4 x 23 cm)
Morris Museum of Art, Augusta, Georgia

Lucile Desbouillons was an adolescent when the serious study of art opened to women in Savannah. Prior to that drawing and watercolor painting had been acceptable accomplishments for young ladies. Yet, as one of four children of bourgeois French immigrants who lived above the family jewelry store, Lucile Desbouillons may have had to forgo the luxury of a drawing master. However, with the 1886 opening of the Telfair Academy of Arts and Sciences, director Carl Brandt initiated classes that offered students like Lucile Desbouillons training modeled on the French academic system. His carefully chosen reproductions of old master paintings and a splendid collection of casts outfitted the Telfair with the best teaching resources in the South.

It was undoubtedly with Brandt's encouragement that Desbouillons and her slightly older confrère, Emma Cheves Wilkins, resolved to spend the summer of 1895 studying art in Paris. As the center of the Western art world, Paris lured many striving artists, and entrepreneurs established countless institutions to satisfy their needs. The two young American women found appropriate housing and company at the American Girls Club and enrolled in a course for foreigners taught by Gustave Courtois. The course incorporated weekly critiques given by Courtois and visiting artists, including Bernard Boutet de Monvel. Probably executed after her return from Paris and before her marriage, *Black Youth Seated on a Chair* showcases Desbouillons's highly finished academic drawing style, which she learned under Brandt and polished in Paris. The unidentified sitter could have been her father's messenger, who was persuaded to sit during a quiet spell; or maybe he was an employee of the Telfair who consented to pose for one of Brandt's classes.

Late in the 1890s, the young sign painter, grainer, decorator, and aspiring artist, Christopher P. H. Murphy, began courting Lucile Desbouillons. After his discharge from military service in the Spanish American War, they married in January 1902. Their first baby was born in December 1902 and six more followed by 1912. That she gave birth to seven surviving children in a decade may explain why there are no other thoroughly worked, academic drawings in her oeuvre.

Although she had little time after her marriage to display her command of academic draftsmanship, Lucile Murphy did not abandon art. A pencil drawing (private collection) by her husband shows the new direction of her work. Murphy sketched her seated in a rocker on the screened porch of the house they rented at Tybee Island during the summer of 1914. With a drawing board on her lap, brush in hand, and a mason jar of water at her side, she sits serenely painting, concentrating intently on her work. She seems unaware that she is being sketched. The after-dinner hours when children napped often allowed just enough time for a quick watercolor before the afternoon breeze blew away the steamy, midday heat and the little ones awakened. Perhaps on this afternoon she was able to complete one of the delicate watercolors of flower subjects that she continued to paint throughout her life.

F.S.C.

Christopher A. D. Murphy

(1902–1973)

ONE SUMMER MORNING IN JUNE 1921, Christopher P. H. Murphy and his first-born child, Christopher A. D. Murphy, departed Savannah for New York. The son would have the prize the father never attained: formal training in art. The elder Murphy looked on proudly as his son enrolled at the Art Students League. During the next ten years, Christopher Murphy alternated between spending extended periods in New York and helping his father with business in Savannah.

Initially his life in New York centered on classes at the Art Students League. Later he won a Tiffany Foundation fellowship. Murphy ultimately landed a job in commercial art. Then came a change. According to his diary entry of Thursday, October 24, 1929, he "got back to Brooklyn . . . [and] saw all the downtown illuminated on account of the great crash on Wall Street."[1] In another diary entry he noted parting from a southbound friend and admitted, "I heartily wished that I were going with him to Savannah."[2] The shrinking economy and homesickness drew Murphy home for good in 1931.

Murphy cultivated an affinity for the graphic arts during his studies at the Art Students League with Joseph Pennell. Perhaps his teacher's massive output of prints portraying cities sparked Murphy's desire to elicit the essence of Savannah in etchings. In 1925, while he was still in New York, Murphy began the ambitious project. Spanning almost fifty years, this oeuvre eventually consisted of innumerable drawings and almost two hundred fifty etchings of different subjects.

All Savannah, rich and poor, emerges in Murphy's urban imagery. Civic monuments and houses grand in scale and style, such as that in *425 Bull Street, Monterey Square*, appear in isolation, without figures. Frequently the picture plane is tilted so the viewer looks up to the subject from a lower vantage point. In contrast, views of poorer sections, as in *Gnarled Oak* (illustrated on half-title page), impart a sense of community. People inhabit these neighborhoods, talking, working, going about the routines of daily life. Yet the anonymity of undifferentiated figures hints at the economic and social fragmentation of the late 1920s and 1930s.

In many images, such as *City Market*, Murphy crafted neutral documents of soon-to-be demolished landmarks. But *In the Name of Progress* (private collection) and other etchings showing half-razed buildings poignantly convey regret and loss. In *Train on Viaduct*, where locomotives and cars join in a face-off against a single horse, the artist pointedly laments the quickening pace of life and changing times.

Ships and the tidal rhythms of the waterways coursed through Murphy's being as naturally as the blood in his veins. Many of his most nostalgic works show life on the river where batteaus and sailing ships are giving way to the pounding engines and steam whistles of freighters. As youths, Murphy and three friends equipped a batteau with a mast and sail. Later they obtained a boat with a cabin for overnight expeditions to places like the ruined forts Jackson and

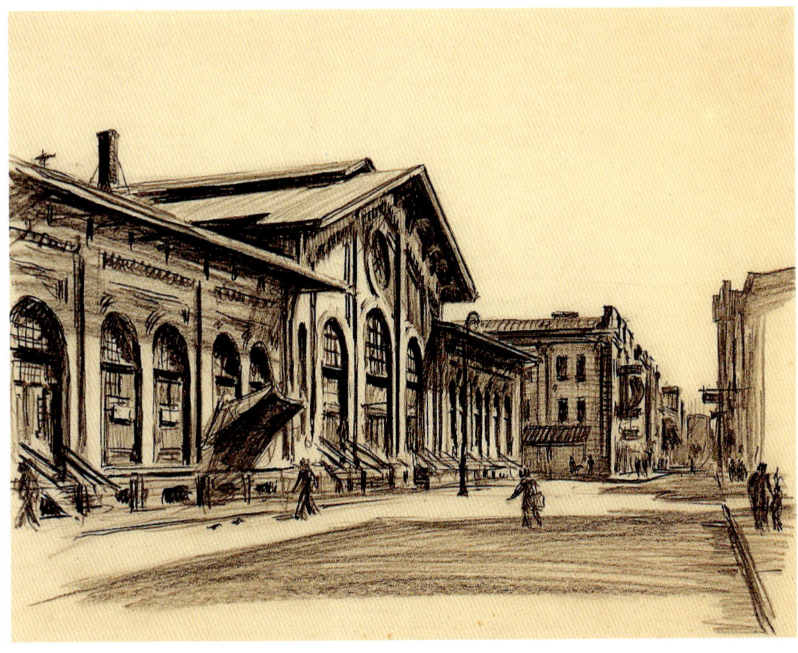

CITY MARKET, n.d.
Charcoal and crayon on paper
11 ½ x 14 in. (sight) (29.2 x 36 cm)
Collection of Mr. and Mrs. Leopold Adler II

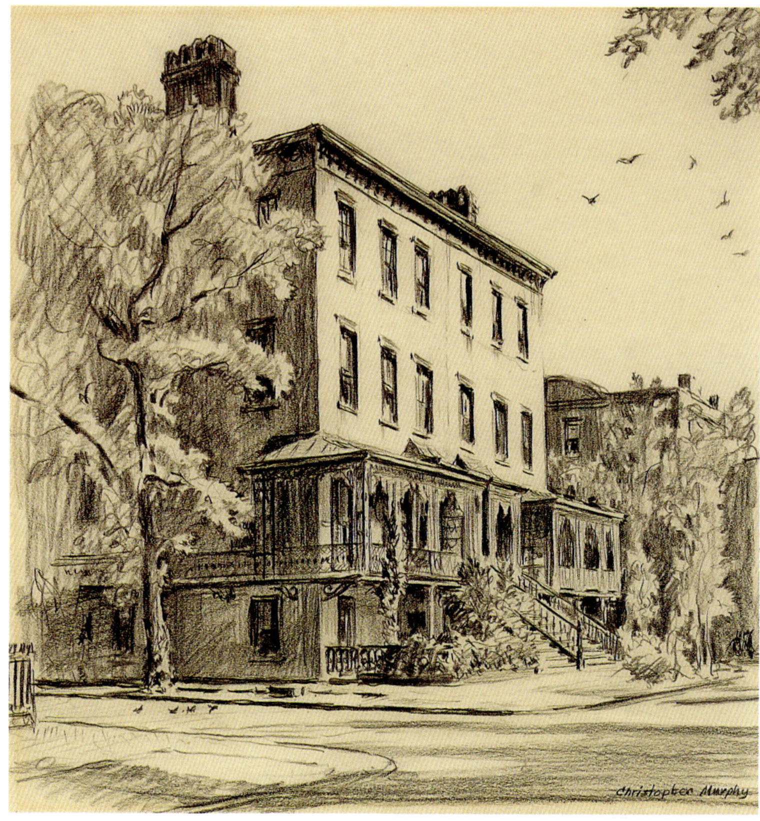

425 Bull Street, Monterey Square, n.d.
Charcoal on paper
10 ⅝ x 10 in. (sight) (27 x 25.4 cm)
Collection of Mr. and Mrs. Leopold Adler II

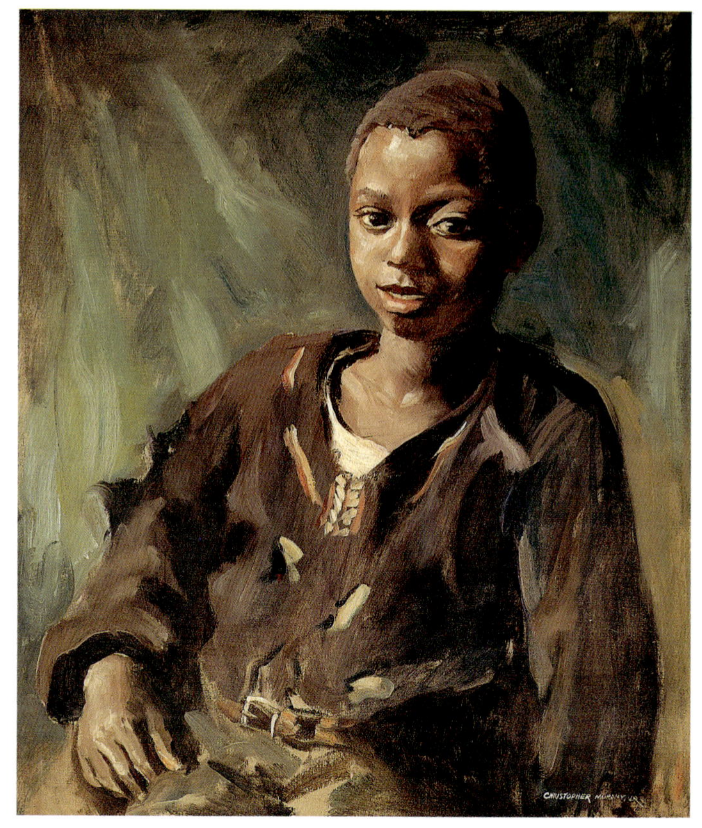

Portrait of a Boy, c.1920–30
Oil on canvas
24 ⅛ x 20 in. (61.3 x 51 cm)
Collection of the Unitarian Universalist Church, Savannah

Pulaski. Murphy made many renderings of these and other sites along the Savannah River, including the Hermitage plantation. After spending so much of his youth on the water, it is not surprising that later in life Murphy perfectly captures pink and yellow late afternoon light washing over the clouds, marshes, and palmetto hammocks in *Landscape*.

The facelessness of humanity in Murphy's prints contrasts with the searching character studies found in his portraits.[3] *Portrait of a Boy* belongs to a group of uncommissioned paintings of black men and boys. The model's bright face and the loose treatment of clothing epitomize the restless, wiggly nature of a boy impatient to explore the whole world that stretches before him.[4] Portrayals of men are less sanguine. In the portrait of Geddes Cooper (private collection), Murphy implies the smoldering anger of African American manhood with the sitter's downturned mouth and slightly drooping eyelids that reflect this subtle undercurrent on the handsome face.

F.S.C.

1. *Christopher A. D. Murphy, Diary, September-November 1929, Murphy family papers, private collection.*
2. *Christopher A. D. Murphy, Diary, November 1929-May 1930.*
3. *Murphy's portrait of his sister is discussed in the entry about Margaret A. Murphy, p.81 of this publication.*
4. *The artist's records identify the sitter as "Little Caesar," Murphy family papers, private collection.*

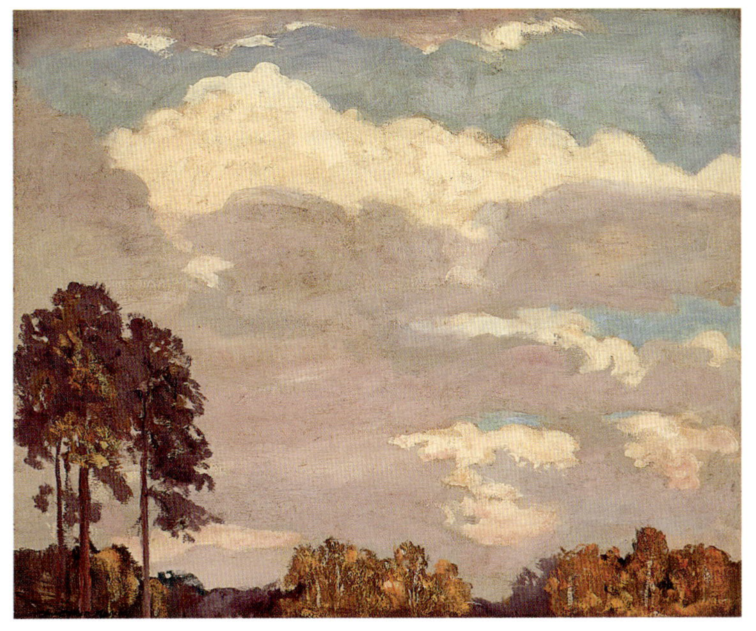

Landscape, n.d.
Oil on canvas
20 ½ x 24 ¼ in. (52.1 x 62 cm)
Collection of Mr. and Mrs. Leopold Adler II

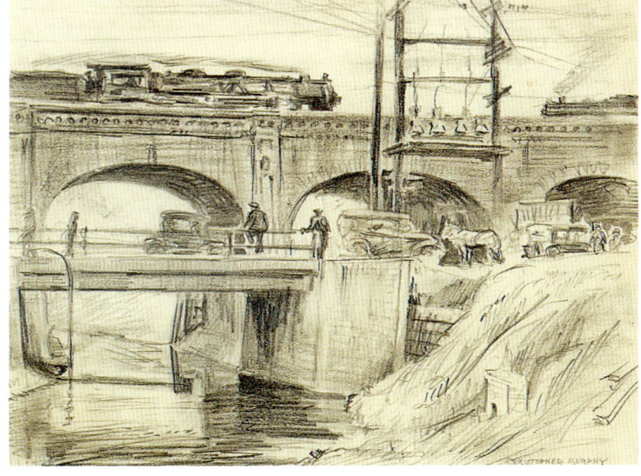

Train on Viaduct, n.d.
Charcoal on paper
8 ⅜ x 11 in. (21.3 x 28 cm)
Collection of Mr. and Mrs. Leopold Adler II

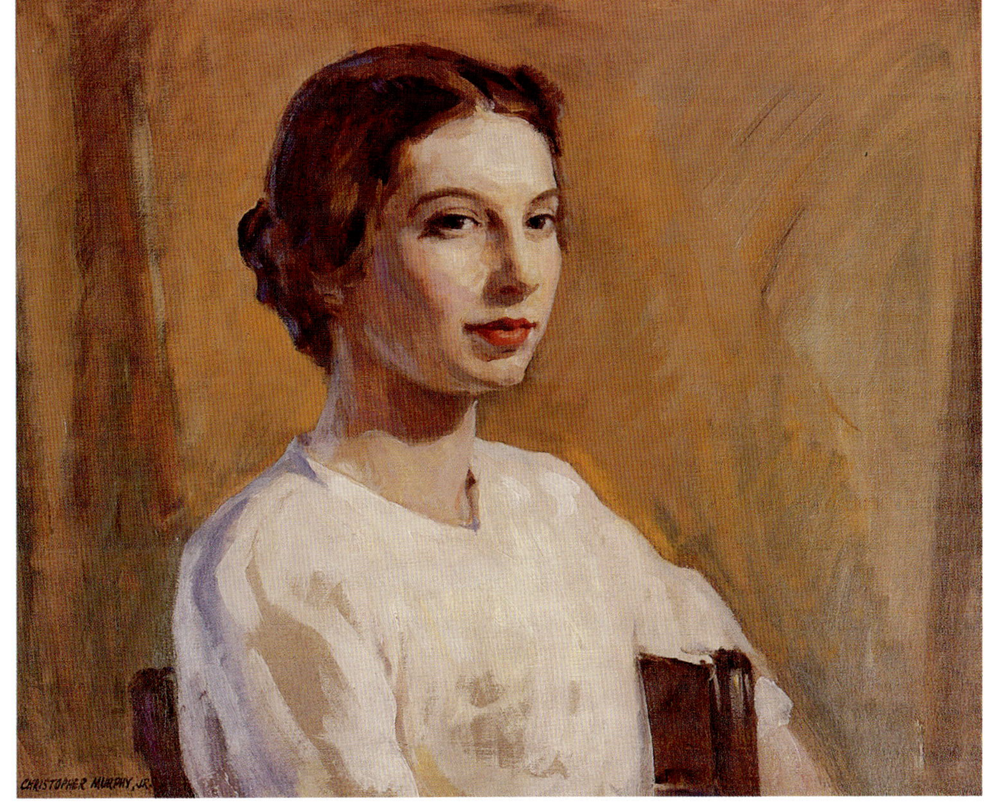

Portrait of the Artist's Sister, Margaret, c.1930–40
Oil on canvas
20 ⅛ x 24 ⅛ in. (51.1 x 61.3 cm)
Telfair Museum of Art,
Gift of Arthur B. Kouwenhoven, 1986

Margaret Augusta Murphy

(1908–1991)

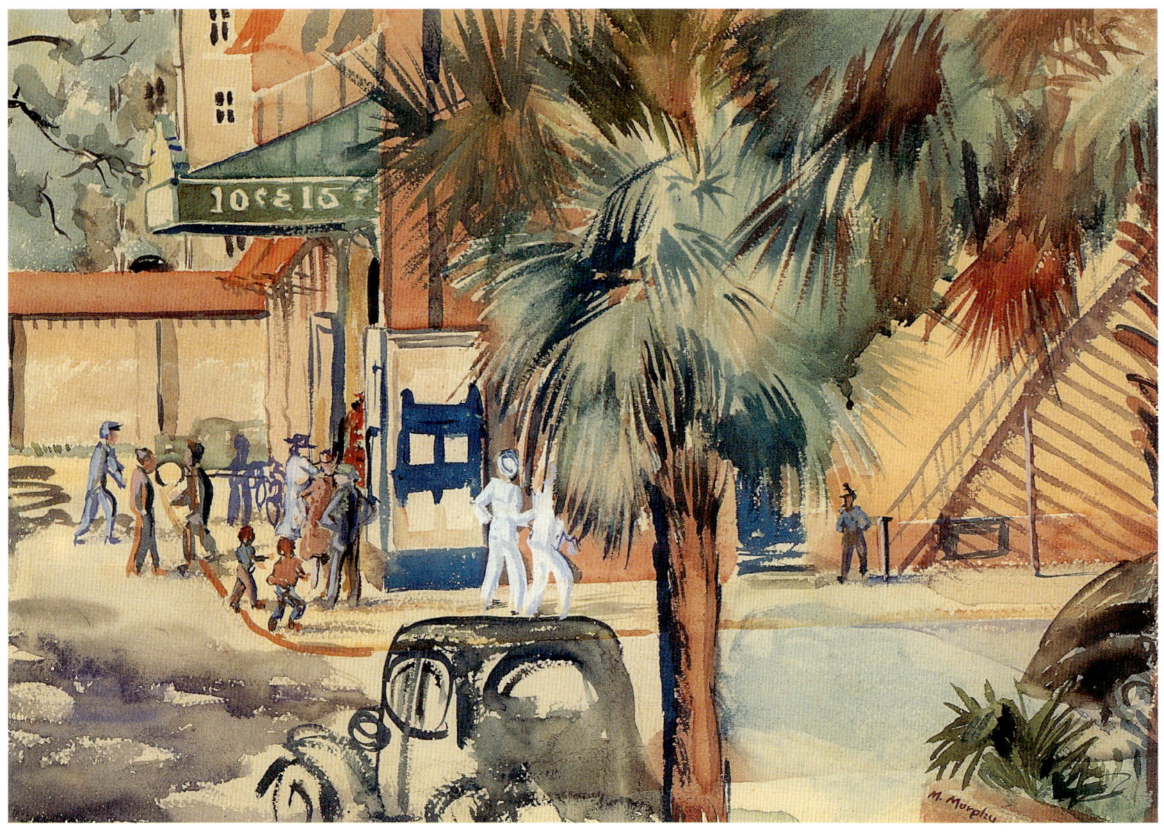

STREET SCENE, SAVANNAH, c.1930–40
Watercolor on paper
14 ½ x 20 ½ in. (37 x 52.1 cm)
Morris Museum of Art, Augusta, Georgia

THE FOURTH OF SEVEN CHILDREN born to Christopher and Lucile Murphy, Margaret Murphy lived in an art-centered world from the time of her earliest memories. Art, artists, art books, and art talk filled the Murphy household. In the fall of 1929 the two most talented of the Murphy children embarked for New York: Margaret studied at the Pratt Institute in Brooklyn; Chris struggled to find patronage for his printmaking and work as a commercial artist as the Depression worsened.

Murphy studied for two years at Pratt before returning to Savannah. In the fall of 1931 she began a career in art education that would span forty years. Although leaving Pratt had been a harsh disappointment for her, the arid economy of the thirties may have wilted, but did not wither, her dreams. In 1942 she graduated from the University of Georgia. Later she completed master's degrees at Columbia University (1955) and the University of Georgia (1971).

During the 1930s, classes and exhibitions at the Telfair were the focus of her life in art. Murphy cultivated her creativity with instruction from visiting painters like Eliot O'Hara. *Street Scene, Savannah* shows the watercolor technique she practiced with O'Hara. Her subject is the view looking north toward the Savannah theater from an upstairs room of the family home her parents purchased in the year of her birth. The Murphys translated the familiar environs of 11 East Perry Street into endlessly ingenious compositions. Her father painted a similar view in the watercolor *The Theater from My Place* (private collection).

> Earning my way has had to dominate so much of my life (as for so many others) that I have had to curb, or forego, a great many things I would have liked to have, or to do. I think this sort of thing affects one's personality very much. On the other hand I put a lot of faith in ideas such as the one expressed in these lines from E. St. V. Millay:
>
> "Think not, nor for a moment let your mind,
> Wearied with thinking, dwell upon the thought,
> That beauty, since 'tis paid for, can be bought."
>
> . . . I believe that statement is true for a great many things. Education for instance.[1]

In his portrait of Murphy (page 79),[2] brother Chris gives a perceptive depiction of the woman who wrote these words. A decorous presence that contradicts the informality of her arm slung over the chair back, the stately carriage of her neck and head, and the subdued colors convey her thoughtful, dignified, serene temperament. She engages the eyes of the viewer, but the gaze is sidelong. Similarly, Murphy's painting *Tybee Beach* reads like an autobiographical statement. From the peripheral region of the sand dunes, the artist's viewpoint, Murphy reveals herself as one who observes life's main events from a distance, away from the center of action. Children's laughter, the sound of the waves, and the smell of salt air come to her indirectly. Unobtrusively making her way through life, Margaret Murphy always put others first.

F.S.C.

1. Margaret A. Murphy. "Autobiographical Sketch," August 7, 1952 (Murphy family papers, private collection).

2. The identity of the sitter in this painting was unknown to the donor who purchased the work directly from Margaret Murphy, the trustee of her brother's estate. When perusing the Christopher Murphy records after Margaret Murphy's death, the author found a photograph of the painting documenting her as the sitter. It is ironic, but entirely consistent with her personality, that Margaret Murphy's presence in the Telfair collection has been until now as an unidentified sitter rather than as an artist.

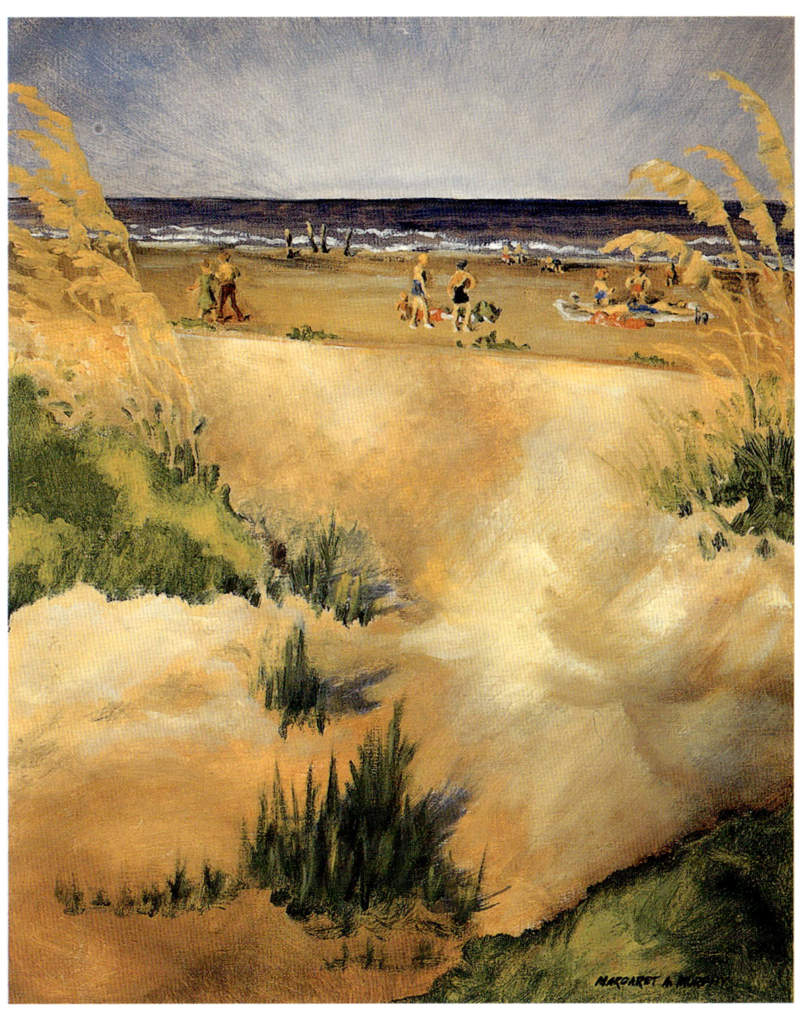

TYBEE BEACH, c.1950–60
Oil on canvas-textured paper
20 x 15 7/8 in. (51 x 40.3 cm)
Morris Museum of Art, Augusta, Georgia

Augusta Oelschig

(b. 1918)

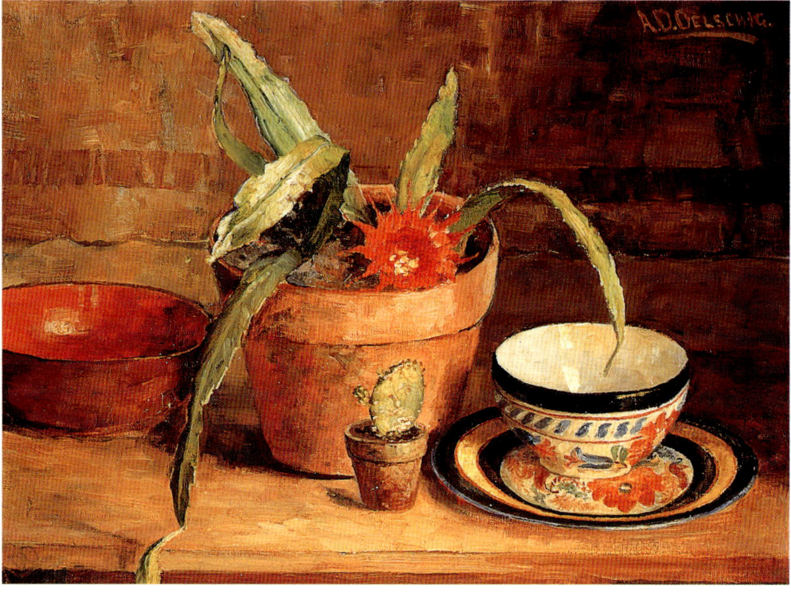

THE CACTUS, 1935
Oil on canvas
17 ½ x 23 ¼ in. (45 x 59.1 cm)
Collection of Milton Mazo, M.D.

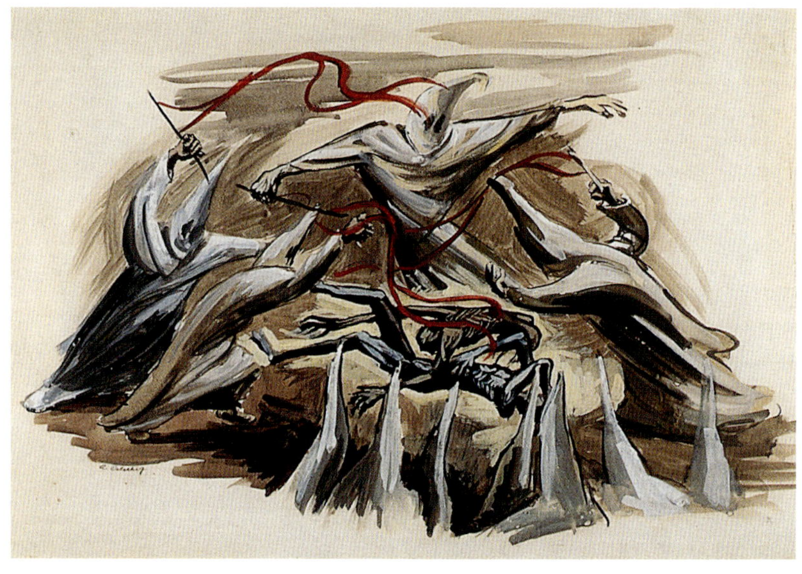

TRAINED LARGELY IN SAVANNAH and Athens, Georgia, Augusta Oelschig produced numerous outstanding works in a variety of modes during the course of her forty-year career as a painter. Although her production as a whole is astonishingly varied and strong, Oelschig alone among the many artists who recorded the American scene in Savannah successfully ventured into the realm of social commentary.

The Cactus, the first work of her college years, was painted during private classes with Emma Cheves Wilkins. After studying with noted painter Lamar Dodd at the University of Georgia from 1937 to 1939, Oelschig returned to Savannah and enrolled in private classes with visiting artist Henry Lee McFee.

McFee's influence is observable in several excellent still-life and figure subjects by Oelschig, including *Gullah Goddess*, which was painted in McFee's class as one of a series depicting the same model in various states of undress. According to Oelschig, McFee's recommended approach was to unify the painting by the mixing of black with each color.[1] The African American subject, and Oelschig's title for this painting have additional significance in the light of her larger body of work, which included numerous representations of African American folklife, such as *Rhythm Diggers*. The largest in a series of paintings and drawings inspired by her observation of the African American religious tradition of "shouting," *Rhythm Diggers* is a scene from a New Year's Eve celebration at Pin Point, south of Savannah.[2] Although Oelschig seems to have interpreted the dance shown here as secular rather than sacred, the unique body movements, the trancelike expressions, and the artist's expressionistic approach suggest something of the impact the experience had on Oelschig.

An extended visit to Mexico with her husband in 1947 and first-hand contact with Mexican muralists, particularly José Clemente Orozco, gave Oelschig the impetus to comment, through her work, on the injustices she observed in the mid-twentieth-century South. *Love Thy Neighbor* of 1948 is one of a series of preparatory works that Oelschig produced for a proposed mural project on the "recent history of Georgia" at Savannah High School. Administrators were shocked by Oelschig's savage images of racial violence, depicting Klansmen whipping contorted black bodies with red suspenders—a

LOVE THY NEIGHBOR, 1948
Gouache on paper
12 ¾ x 18 in. (32.4 x 46 cm)
Collection of Milton Mazo, M.D.

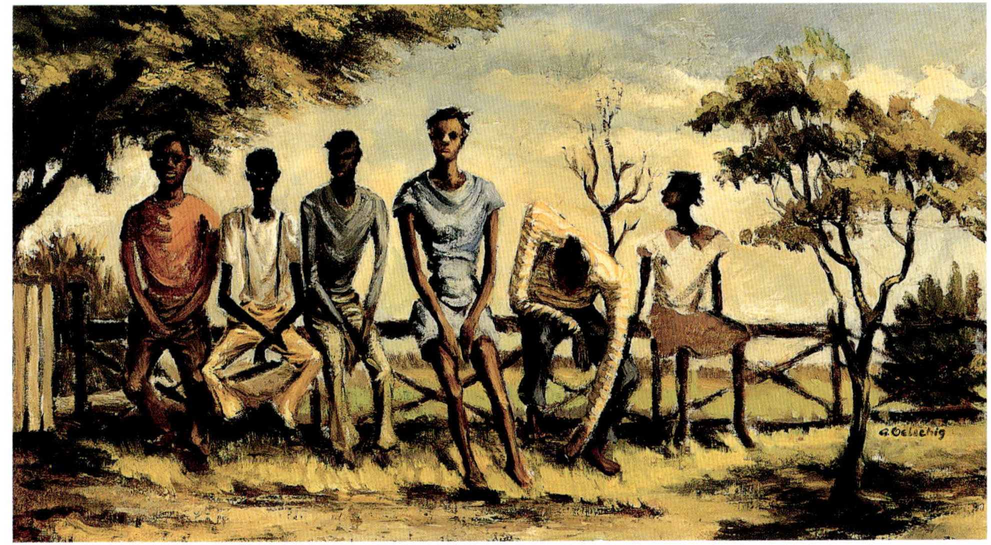

Sparrows, 1953
Oil on canvas
16 x 29 in. (41 x 74 cm)
Collection of the artist, promised gift to the Telfair Museum of Art

very obvious reference to the trademark attire of flamboyant Georgia governors Eugene and Herman Talmadge. The latter was openly endorsed by the Ku Klux Klan in the 1948 gubernatorial election.[3] Other images by the artist entitled *Pietà* show the Christ figure as a lynched black male. Not surprisingly, Oelschig's mural plans were rejected. She left Savannah the same year for New York City, where she spent the next eleven years.

Sparrows, which she began during a return visit to Savannah, continues in the vein of Oelschig's earlier African American genre images; the painting was exhibited in New York to favorable reviews. Even though she was present in New York during the heyday of Abstract Expressionism, Oelschig continued to paint the American scene, and occasionally created powerfully original works of a more personal nature. She returned to Savannah again in 1961 and remained active until health problems prompted her retirement from painting around 1976.

H.H.D.

1. *This and other information in this entry is gleaned from interviews with the artist conducted between June and October 1995.*
2. *Actually a form of sacred dance, "shouting" incorporates specific body movements and call-and-response singing, accompanied by the rhythmic thumping of a broomstick on a wooden floor.*
3. *Donald J. Grant,* The Way It Was in the South: The Black Experience in Georgia *(New York: A Birch Lane Press Book, Carol Publishing Group, 1993), 368.*

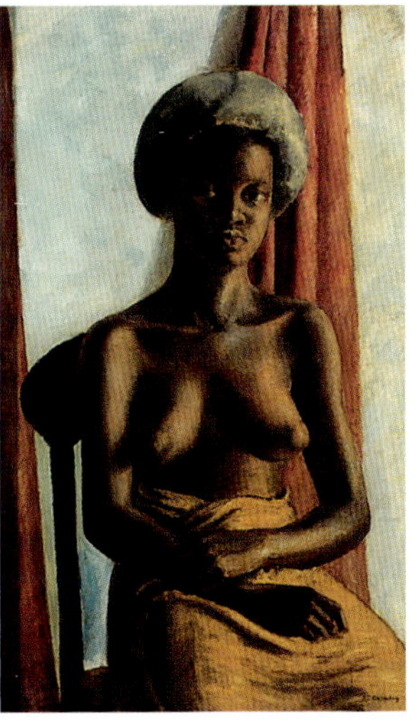

Gullah Goddess, 1939
Oil on canvas
39 ½ x 25 in.
(100.3 x 64 cm)
Collection of the Morris Museum of Art, Augusta, Georgia

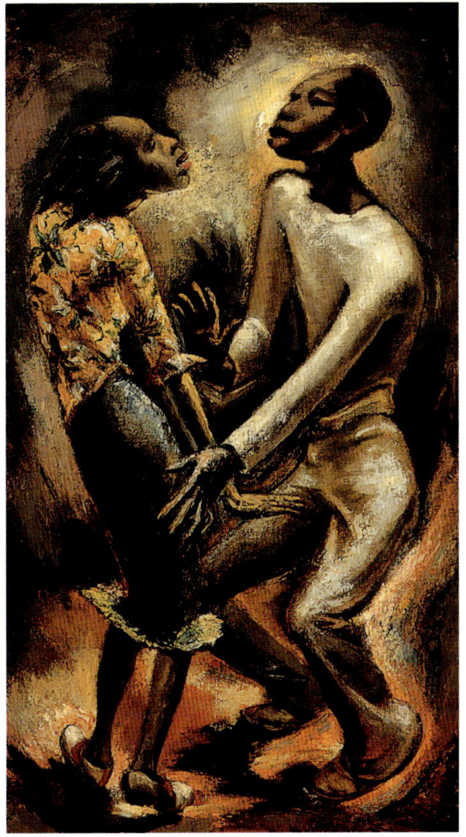

Rhythm Diggers, 1947
Oil on panel
40 x 22 in. (102 x 56 cm)
Collection of the Morris Museum of Art, Augusta, Georgia

Eliot O'Hara

(1890–1969)

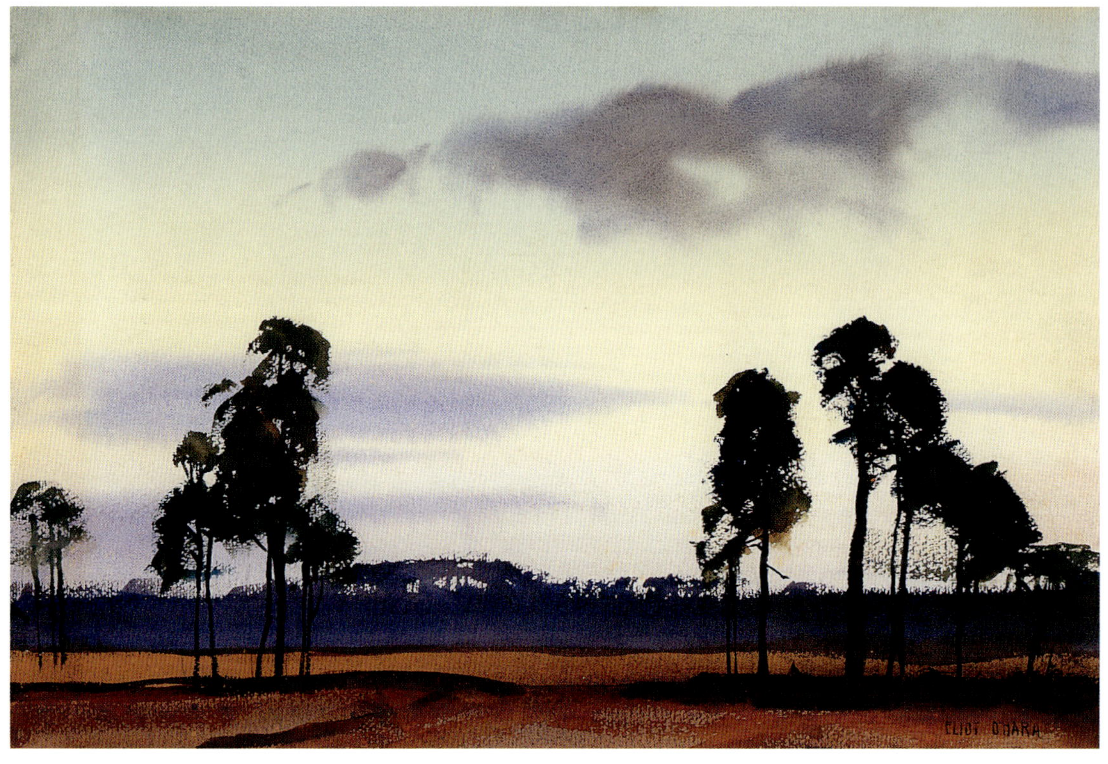

GEORGIA SUNSET
Watercolor on paper
15 x 22 in. (sight) (38.1 x 56 cm)
Telfair Museum of Art, Museum Purchase, 1934

ELIOT O'HARA WAS A TEACHER, A WRITER, AND A PAINTER who worked exclusively in watercolor. A native of Maine, he attended Norwich University before going abroad to study art in Europe. In addition to contributing to *American Artist* magazine, O'Hara wrote several books on watercolor technique and history, including *Making Watercolor Behave* (1932), *Making the Brush Behave* (1935), *Watercolor Fares Forth* (1938), *Art Teacher's Primer* (1939), and *Watercolor at Large* (1946); he also appeared in a series of instructional films. O'Hara taught at the Telfair Academy and at the Art Students League in New York, where Hattie Saussy was among his students. A member of the American Water Color Society, he owned and operated the Watercolor Gallery in Maine from 1932 to 1946 and held exhibitions of both modern and traditional watercolor paintings.

O'Hara's paintings reflect a close observation of nature. He taught his students to take photographs and make color studies outdoors, but to paint indoors for greater control. He also instructed them not to work for more than one hour on a painting or they would risk loss of spontaneity. *Georgia Sunset* is a horizontal composition, a format the artist deemed most appropriate for landscape paintings. His dictums to his students are realized in this work. With washes of translucent color, O'Hara evokes the colors of the setting sun and the dark silhouettes of pine trees.

J.A.

William Rogers
(1865–1952)

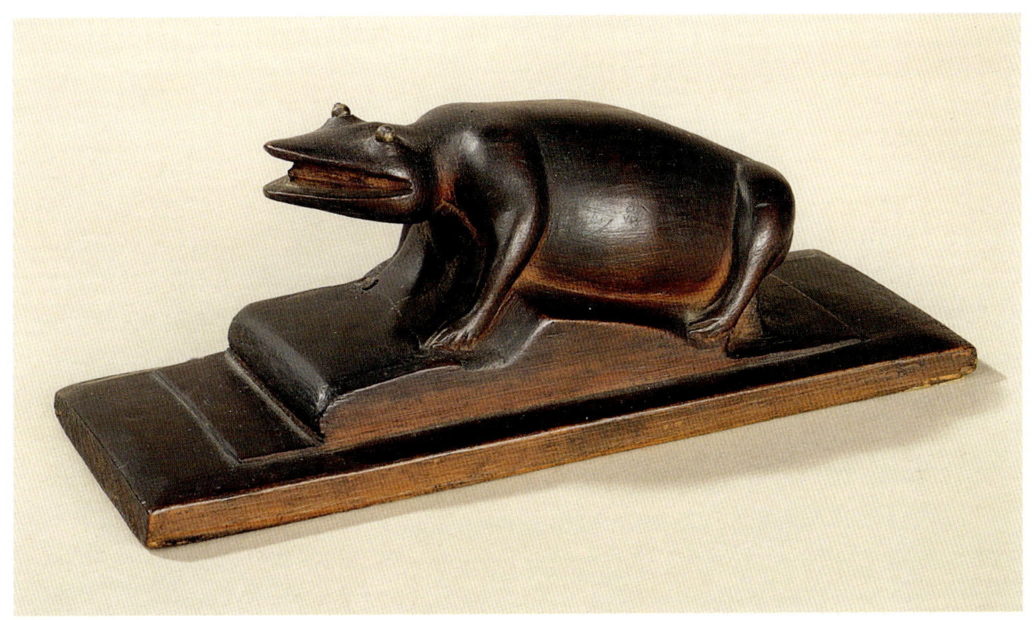

Carved Frog, before 1938
Wood, brass nail heads
L. 8 ½ in. (21 cm)
Collection of Mary Barron Saunders, Joanna, South Carolina

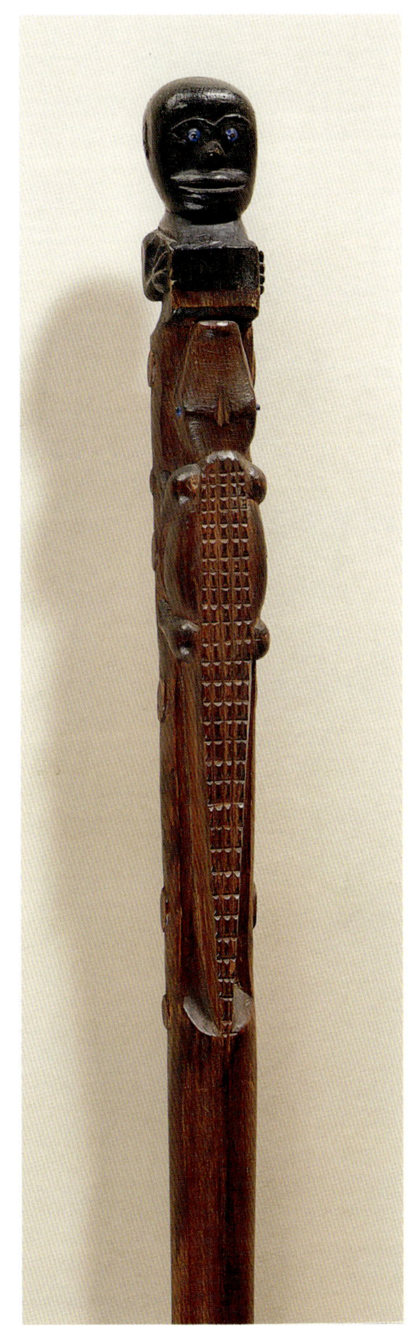

Walking Stick, 1938
Cedar, black paint, stain, blue beads
L. 34 ½ in. (88 cm)
Collection of Mr. and Mrs. Harvey Granger, Jr.

William Rogers has been called the "master carver" of coastal Georgia by numerous contemporary scholars of African American vernacular art. Clearly, Rogers was a man of great significance within his community, where he was known for much more than his carvings. An Atlanta University graduate, he was a carpenter, farmer, state legislator, and later in life, a preacher. It is said that Rogers also worked in Savannah's shipyards. He was the last black representative in the Georgia State legislature before the disenfranchisement of blacks in 1907.[1]

Although Rogers lived in Darien, Georgia, about sixty miles down the coast from Savannah, his work provides an important link with the now-lost works (known only in photographs) of early twentieth-century Savannah carvers. Like the Savannah examples, Rogers's extant carvings may provide some of the strongest physical evidence for the survival of African-influenced carving traditions in the post-Emancipation South. A carpenter by trade, Rogers carved wooden walking sticks, staffs, eating utensils, and small, nonfunctional sculptures in his spare time and after his retirement. When he was interviewed in 1939 by Mary Granger for the Georgia Writers' Project,

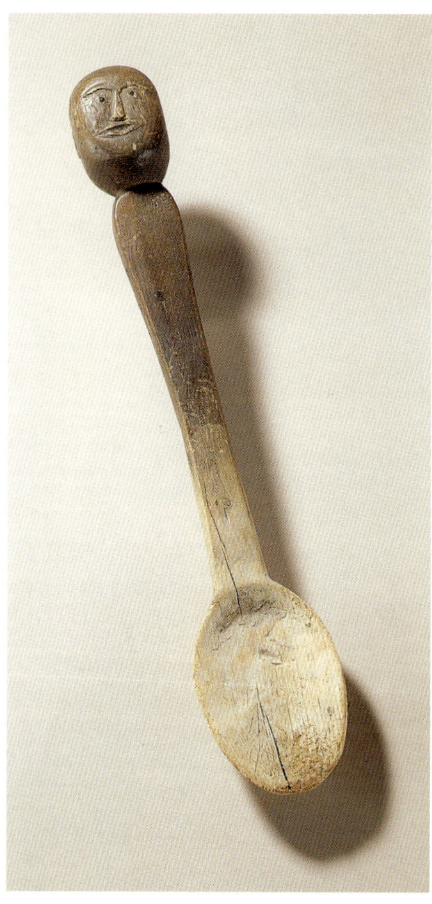

Carved Wooden Spoon,
before 1938
Cedar, nail heads
L. 13 ½ in. (34.3 cm)
Collection of
Mr. and Mrs. Harvey Granger, Jr.

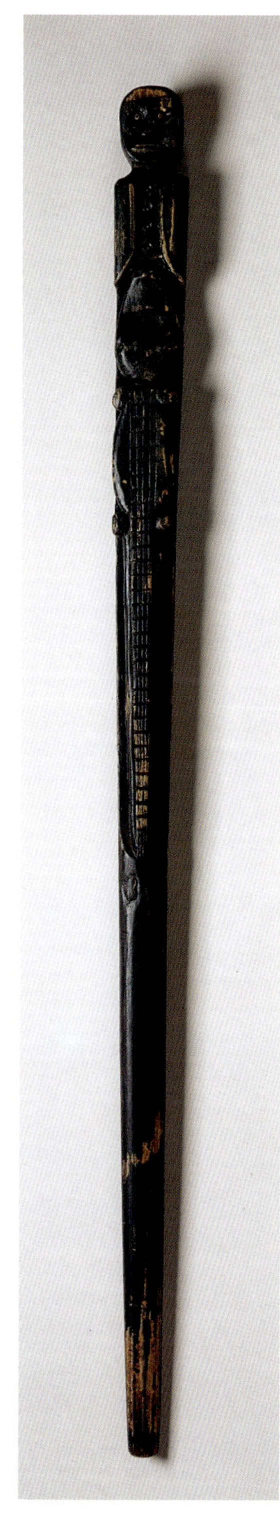

Staff,
c.1935
Wood, black paint, beads
49 x 2 ½ x 2 in.
(125 x 6.4 x 5.1 cm)
Collection of the Columbus Museum,
Columbus, Georgia

Rogers, then seventy-two, was still active. His production had been slowed somewhat by a stroke, but he promised Mary Granger "When I get my hands back into use, I hope to carve a cane, with a 'gator on it like the ones I made long ago."[2] Rogers's comments indicate a history of producing such objects, though it is unknown exactly how he acquired his facility or iconography.

Two existing walking sticks and a staff by Rogers are composed almost identically: each consists of a stout stick with a single alligator carved along its length, terminating in a human torso and head. Each cane also features a series of low-relief lozenges along each side. The *Walking Stick* Rogers carved for Mary Granger is perhaps the strongest because of the greater attention given to the carving of the human figure, which is painted black to contrast with the stained red cedar. A longer *Staff* is the largest of the known pieces, and stylistically relates to the simplified human form on a cane now in the University of California Museum at Berkeley, and to the human head carved on a wooden spoon, also by Rogers.

Another major work, a carving of a frog, has been discussed frequently. Robert Farris Thompson, the eminent art historian of Africa and the African Americas, has compared the frog to a possible African antecedent in the work of Dahomean artists.[3] Thompson, John Michael Vlach, and others are quick to note Rogers's signature use of beads, driven in with small nails, to represent eyes on the frog as well as the cane figures. Again, this feature seems to have African counterparts. The challenge remains for scholars to definitively trace the ancestry of Rogers and his work, if possible, to specific African cultures.

H.H.D.

1. *Donald J. Grant,* The Way It Was in the South: The Black Experience in Georgia *(New York: A Birch Lane Press Book, Carol Publishing Group, 1993), 209–10. Rogers represented MacIntosh County from 1902 to 1907. He valiantly attempted to ward off the Hardwick amendment, which disenfranchised blacks. There would be no other black legislators in Georgia's government until 1962.*
2. *Georgia Writers' Project,* Drums and Shadows: Survival Studies Among Georgia Coastal Negroes *(Athens, Ga.: The University of Georgia Press, 1940; reprinted, Brown Thrasher Books, The University of Georgia Press, 1986), 152. Translated from phonetically spelled dialect in the original text.*
3. *Robert Farris Thompson, "African Influence on the Art of the United States," reprinted in* Afro-American Folk Arts and Crafts *(Jackson, Miss.: University Press of Mississippi, 1983), 45.*

Andrée Ruellan

(b.1905)

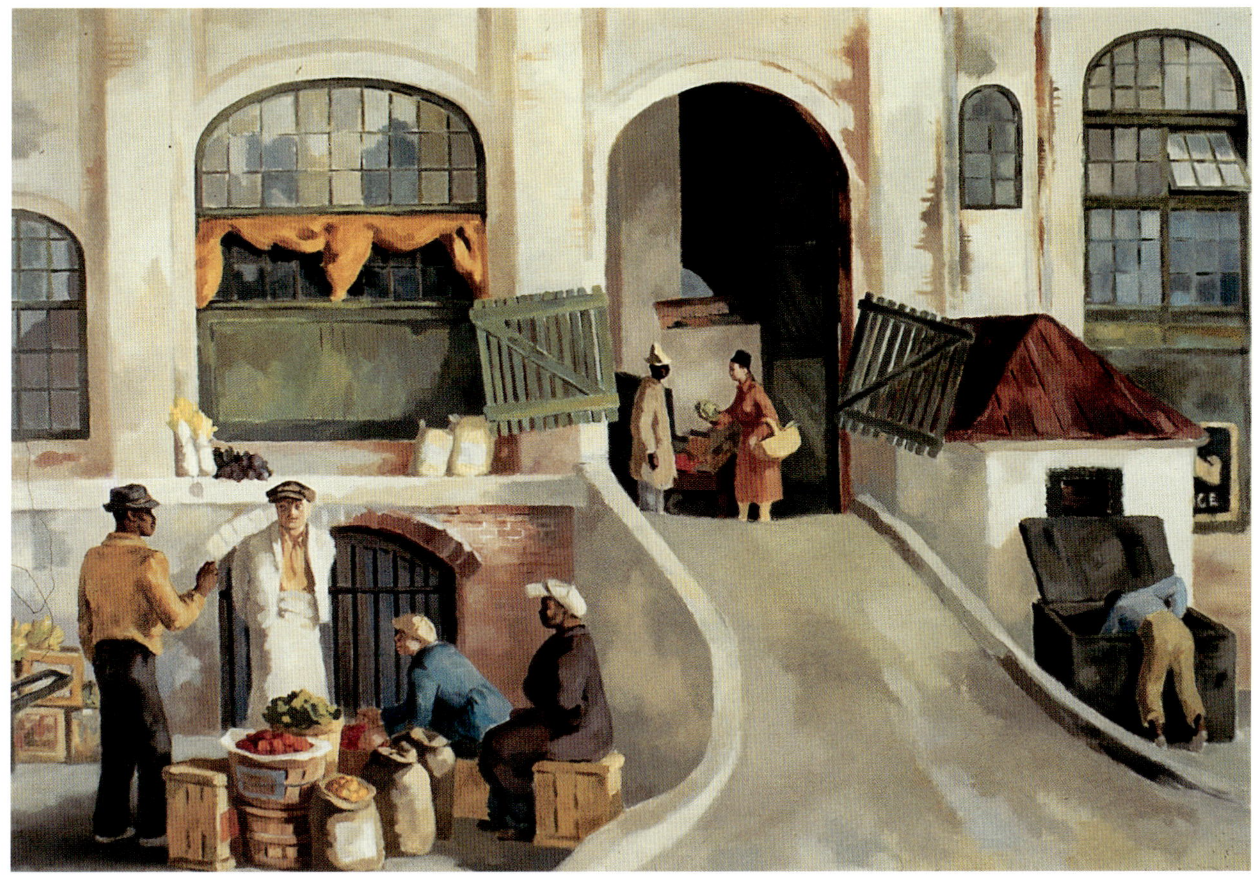

City Market, Savannah, 1942
Oil on canvas
32 x 44 in. (81.3 x 112 cm)
The Schoen Collection, New Orleans, Louisiana

Savannah was not Andrée Ruellan's first introduction to the South. Beginning in the late 1930s, she and her husband and fellow painter, John ("Jack") Taylor, discovered the charms of Charleston, South Carolina. It was in 1941 that Ruellan, Taylor, and Lucette, Andrée's mother, first journeyed farther south to Savannah. Although they stayed only briefly on that first trip, their intense work drawing the local scene provided a wealth of material for many outstanding paintings.[1]

Andrée Ruellan was a true child prodigy. She was studying art by the age of eight and was taken to the Armory Show in New York by her teacher and family friend, Ben Liber. In 1914, she exhibited some drawings (drawing was her first medium of choice) with two of America's leading painters, Robert Henri and George Bellows. Henri invited the young girl to join the exhibition after seeing her work. At age fifteen, Ruellan accepted a scholarship to the Art Students League, choosing concentrated art lessons over high school studies. Two years later, she studied in Rome with Maurice Sterne, a professor at the Art Students League.

Ruellan lived primarily in France from 1923 to 1928. In certain respects, her stay there was a coming home for Ruellan and a foretaste of her future. She was born in New York City to French parents, and in France she would meet her future husband and other artists of the Woodstock Art Association and colony. The couple married in 1929 and moved to the house that Taylor had purchased earlier in Shady, New York, just outside Woodstock.

Many artists who worked at Woodstock and studied in Paris had connections with Savannah, as well as with Ruellan and Taylor. Among these, Jules Pascin, a French American artist, visited Woodstock, and in 1927 lived in the house next to Taylor in Brooklyn. He also visited Savannah. A mutual friend of these three artists who also had connections with Woodstock and the Art Students League was Alexander Brook. It was he who recommended that Ruellan and Taylor visit Savannah. Brook lived and worked there and loved the city, and when Ruellan and Taylor did come to Savannah, they worked with Brook in his studio overlooking the Savannah River.

As with many other artists of the era, Brook, Taylor, and Ruellan were primarily concerned with recording contemporary life in a straightforward manner. American Scene painting, as such painting is now known, dominated art of the 1930s—in Savannah, Woodstock, and throughout the country. Its "honesty, vitality and freshness, not academic finish or modernist liberties, were the virtues artists sought and critics praised."[2] When Ruellan came to the South, she was eager to expand her iconography beyond that of Paris streets and New York City scenes, and embrace a new world. She has remarked that she had seen the south of France and wanted to experience the American South; "in Savannah . . . she found locales with spirit of place, distinguished architecture and a black culture that provided inspiration for a number of her best-known paintings."[3] While in Savannah, she sketched the beautiful fountain of Forsyth Park but was more intrigued by earthier subjects—vendors at the City Market, a pick-up baseball game near the now-destroyed gas tank, or workmen taking a break along the Savannah River. In comparison to Charleston, she found Savannah "rugged,"[4] a word that implies, not so much a lack of refinement but an honest way of living.

To capture the life of downtown streets, Ruellan employed a trick she had learned from Pascin, who advised her to place drawing paper inside a newspaper so that her subjects would be unaware they were being observed. This undercover sketching backfired once for Ruellan in Savannah. On one outing, she and Taylor remained in their car to draw. It was just before the United States entered World War II, and tensions in the city were palpable. The two were reported to the police as possible spies and were arrested. Alexander Brook went down to the station and convinced the constabulary that they were merely artists.

Ruellan found simplicity and honesty not in grand houses but in everyday lives—especially in the African American community, which to her was the most alive. Her sensitivity to that community is recorded in her paintings. She is a reporter who combined an objective eye with an outstanding talent to compose and record. Although she later turned toward a more abstract style related to Yasuo Kuniyoshi, the work inspired by Savannah is a realist's approach to a sometimes charming, sometimes gritty, subject.

P.D.K

The Wind-Up, 1941
Oil on canvas
20 ⅛ x 30 in. (51.1 x 76.2 cm)
The Phillips Collection, Washington, D.C.

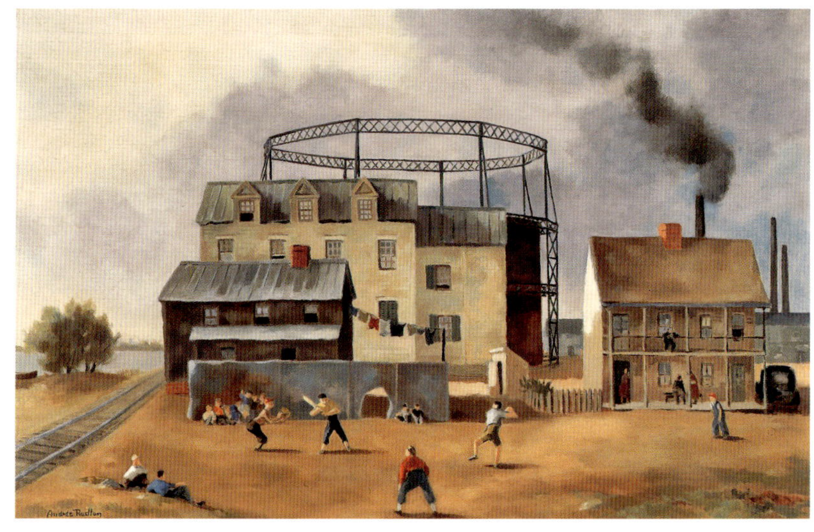

1. Ruellan's practice was to to draw and sketch on site and produce the paintings back in the studio in Shady, N.Y.; she did not paint outdoors. Conversation with the artist, May 7, 1996.

2. Marlene Park, "Andrée Ruellan: Her Life in Art," in Donald Keyes and Marlene Park, Andrée Ruellan *(Athens: Georgia Museum of Art, 1993), 54.*

3. Janis Conner, Andrée Ruellan: Sixty Years of Drawing *(New York: Kraushaar Galleries, 1990), n.p.*

4. Conversation with the artist.

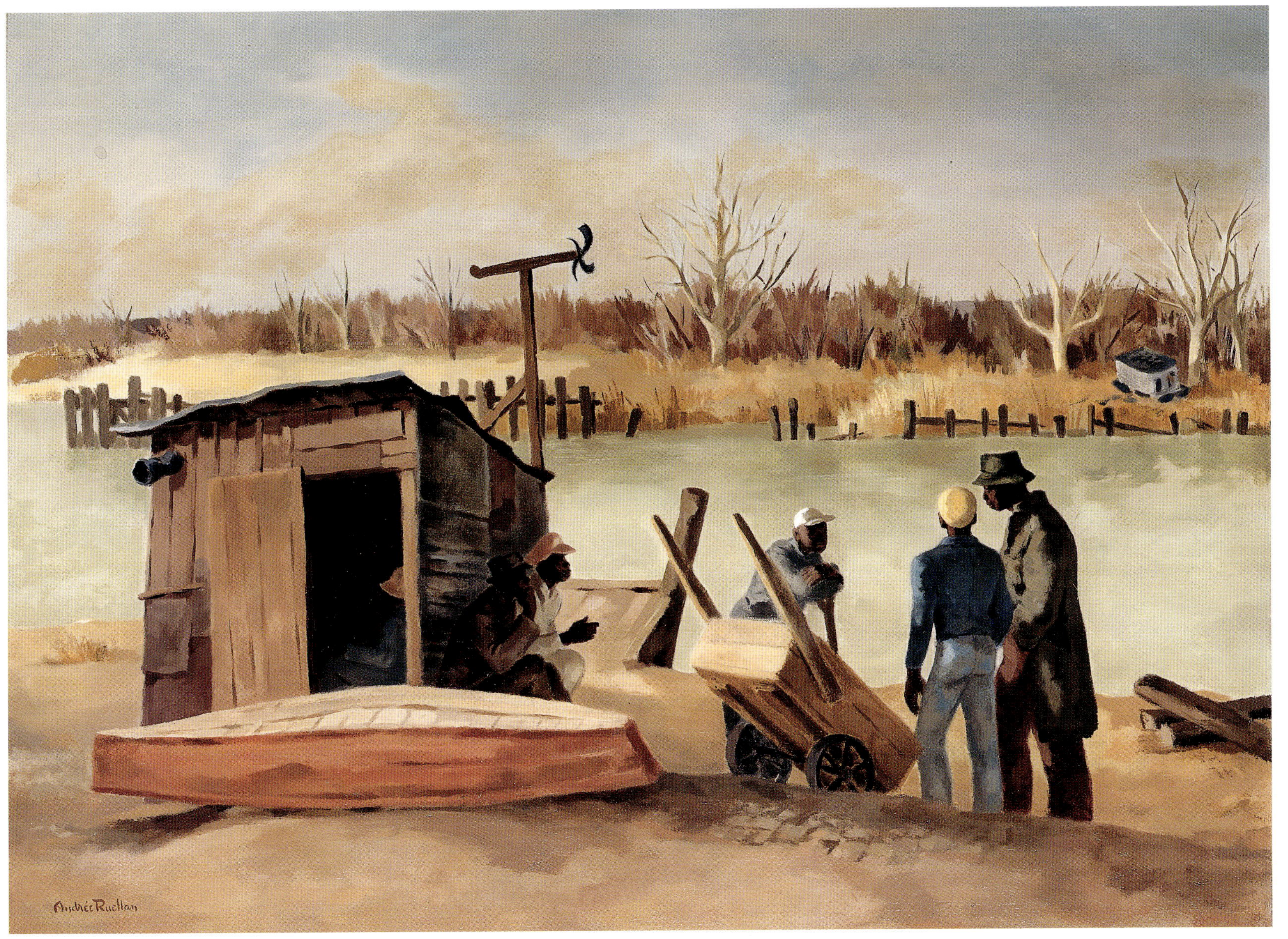

River Men (On the Savannah), 1942
Oil on canvas
18 x 24 in. (46 x 61 cm)
Wichita Art Museum: Purchased with funds donated by the Volunteers of the Gift Shop, Friends of the Wichita Art Museum, Inc.

Hattie Saussy

(1890–1978)

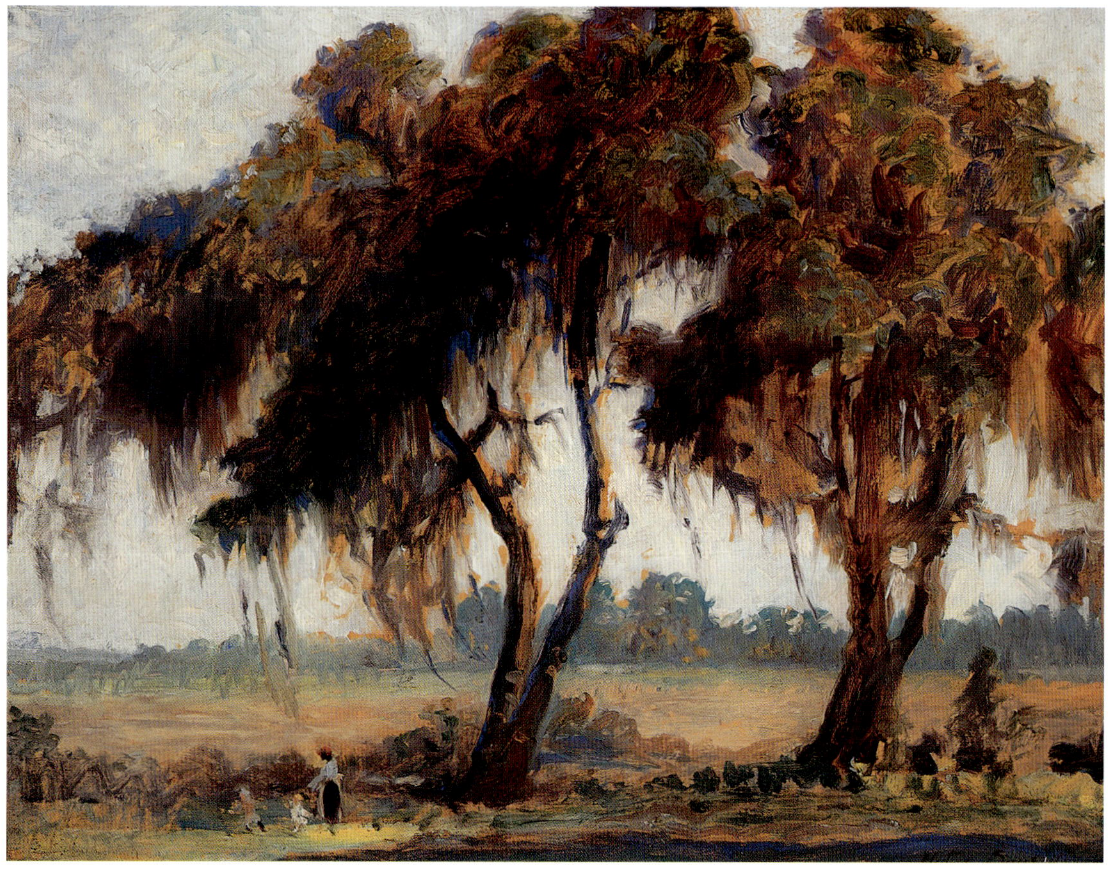

BONAVENTURE, n.d.
Oil on canvas
21 ½ x 27 ½ in. (sight) (55 x 70 cm)
Collection of H. Paul Blatner

BORN IN SAVANNAH ON ST. PATRICK'S DAY, 1890, Hattie Saussy grew up in a wealthy family. Her background in art began in the early 1900s in the Savannah public schools, where she studied under Lila Cabaniss. During her formative years Saussy frequented the Telfair Academy of Arts and Sciences, where she learned from an extensive collection of American Impressionist works.

Inspired by her widowed mother, Saussy continued her artistic endeavors after high school at the Mary Baldwin Seminary in Staunton, Virginia. An outstanding student, she exhibited her work at the Jamestown Tricentennial exposition in 1907. In 1908 she and her mother moved to New York, where Saussy studied at the New York School of Fine and Applied Arts (now the Parsons School of Design) under the tutelage of R. Sloan Bredin; at the National Academy of Design; and at the Art Students League, where her instructors were Eugene E. Speicher, Eliot O'Hara, Frank V. DuMond, and George Bridgman. In 1913 Saussy was invited to teach at the New York School of Fine and Applied Arts but chose instead to study in the Parisian studio of E. A. Taylor, a stained-glass designer.

During her stay in Europe, Saussy traveled and sketched in Luxembourg, Switzerland, Germany, Austria, and Italy. With the onset of World War I, she returned to the United States and, except for a brief stint as a government worker in Washington, continued to work in New York and Savannah.

In 1920–21 Saussy taught at the Chatham Episcopal Institute (now Chatham Hall) in Virginia and visited Europe again. Then settling in Savannah permanently, she became a full-time artist while continuing her studies under Adolphe W. Blondheim and Edward S. Shorter. Saussy was an active member of the Savannah Art Club and the Association of Georgia Artists and participated in several Georgia exhibits—at the Telfair Academy, the Columbus Museum, the Augusta-Richmond County Museum, and the High Museum of Art.

Saussy's style is a blend of Impressionism and realism. Her subject is the leisurely life of southern culture in the twentieth century, which she captured in landscapes, genre scenes, and portraits, in oils and in watercolors. With a characteristic delicate touch and using a limited palette, in *Woodboo* she depicts a massive oak drooping with moss and sheltering a meadow on a sunny day. In *Bonaventure* she continues to examine landscape composition, this time describing two massive trees whose tops consist of dense layers of paint in contrast to the light staccato brush strokes of the ground. In *Palm Trees at Woodboo* she concentrates on the nature of the marshes, applying muted tones with quick strokes of her brush.

Hattie Saussy devoted her life to painting. In oil and watercolor she captured a genteel world of peaceful landscapes, vases of flowers, and loving friends.

K.L.H.

Woodboo, 1950s
Oil on board
23 ½ x 31 ⅛ in. (sight) (60 x 79.1 cm)
Collection of Catharine and Gordon Varnedoe

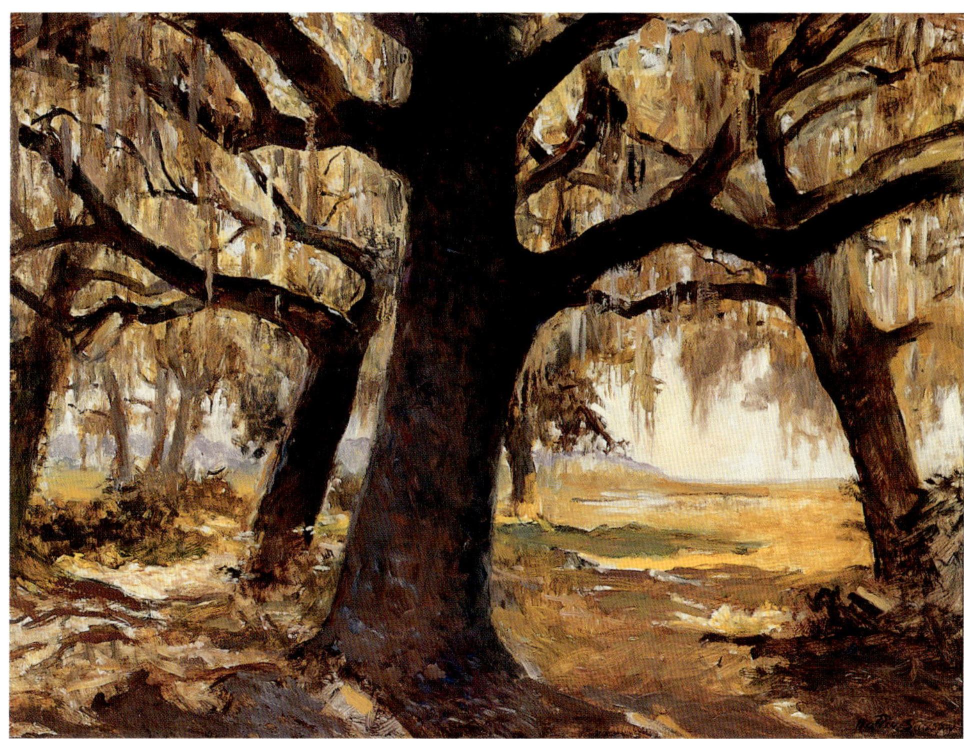

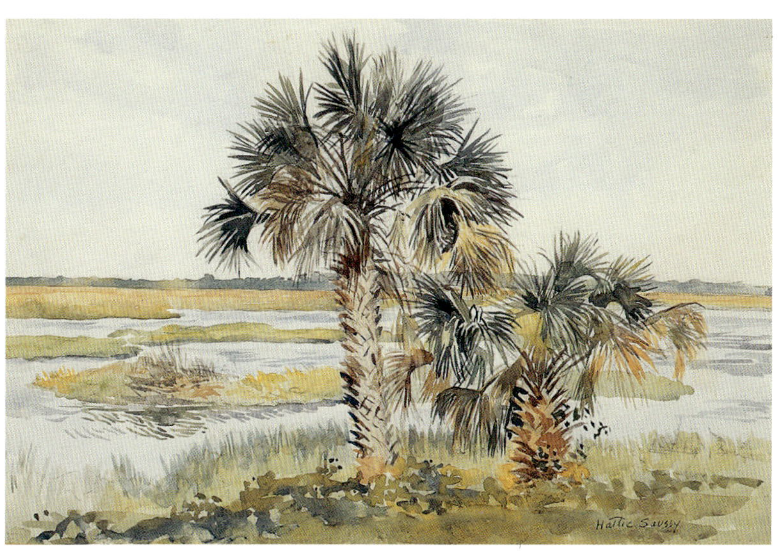

Palm Trees at Woodboo, n.d.
Watercolor on paper
14 ½ x 21 ½ in. (sight) (37 x 55 cm)
Collection of Catharine and Gordon Varnedoe

Mark Sheridan

(1884–?)

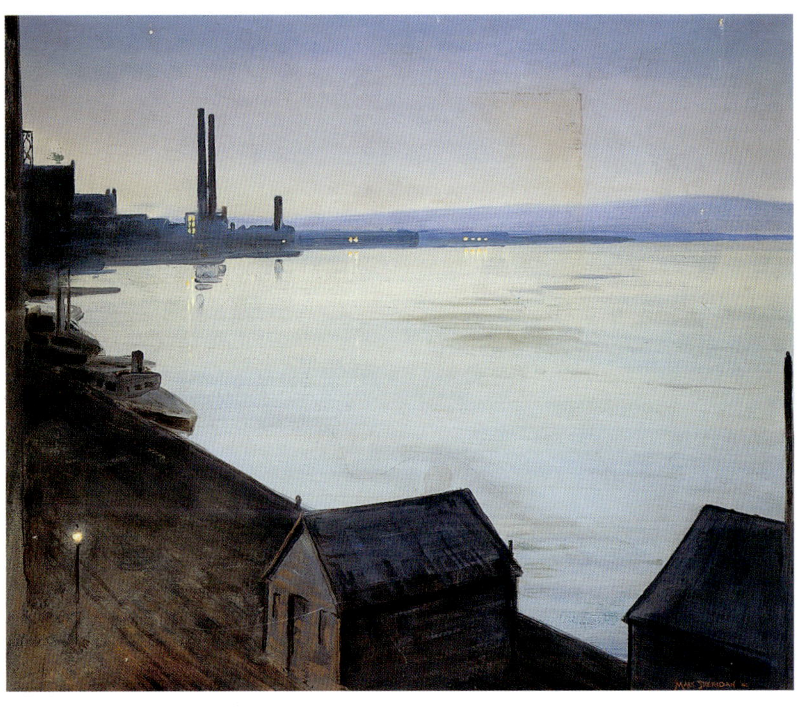

River Nocturne (On the River), 1941
Oil on canvas
31 ⅜ x 36 ¼ in. (80 x 92.1 cm)
Telfair Museum of Art, Museum Purchase, 1941

Mark Sheridan was born in Atlanta but lived and worked for many years in Savannah. He trained at the Georgia School of Technology and at the Pennsylvania Academy of the Fine Arts. He settled in Savannah until sometime after 1948, then moved to nearby Ridgeland, South Carolina.[1] An active member of the art community both locally and nationally, he exhibited with the National Arts Club, the Association of Georgia Artists, and the Savannah Art Club.

Sheridan executed murals and easel paintings, such as *River Nocturne (On the River)*, a work that was included in the *Thirteenth Annual Exhibition of the Association of Georgia Artists* at the Telfair Academy in 1941. The Telfair purchased the painting from the exhibition, awarding Sheridan the Third [place] Purchase Award.

River Nocturne depicts what appears to be the Savannah River at nighttime. Sheridan did not choose the typical Savannah riverfront scene with the picturesque historic buildings on River Street, but instead selected an area perhaps farther up the river showing the industrial landscape. Images of American industry were common from the 1920s through the 1940s, when many artists created views of the industrial landscape as a celebration—or critique—of modern American life. By contrast Sheridan created a romanticized panorama of the river at dusk in subtle tonal variations of the color blue, indicating a possible debt to J. A. M. Whistler. Whistler too had called his works nocturnes, asserting his belief that a painting is primarily an arrangement of colors and not necessarily a narrative. He used the musical title "Nocturne" for a series of nighttime views of the Thames River in which the color blue dominates. The similarity of Sheridan's *Nocturne* is evident; the difference is that Sheridan chose a modern American subject for his industrial scene.

C.L.B.

1. Who's Who in American Art *(1959) gives his address as Ridgeland. His name no longer appears in the Savannah city directory after 1948. Nothing is known of his activities after 1959.*

William Posey Silva

(1859–1948)

William Posey Silva, the son of a Confederate soldier and prominent local merchant, was born in Savannah. Although from early childhood painting was Silva's consuming passion, he did not initially pursue a career in art, choosing instead to continue his father's chinaware business in Savannah and Chattanooga, Tennessee. He continued to paint throughout his life, however, and during the summers of 1900 through 1905 he studied composition with Arthur Wesley Dow in Ipswich, Massachusetts.

It was not until 1906, at age forty-seven, that Silva finally decided to make a career of painting. He sold his business, and he and his wife, Caroline, traveled to France. He studied figure drawing at the Académie Julian in Paris under Jean Paul Laurens and Henri Royer, and landscape painting at Etaples under Chauncey Ryder.

Silva's work was greeted with immediate success. Less than two years after arriving in Paris, he was included in the Salon Grand Palais des Champs Élysée, and in 1909 he had his first solo exhibition at the Galeries Georges Petit.

In 1909, Silva returned home to Chattanooga and spent a year touring and painting in the southern states. He then moved to Washington, D.C., and served as president of the Society of Washington Artists. In 1913, Silva settled in Carmel, California, where he established the Carmelita Gallery. He remained in Carmel the rest of his life.

Georgia Pines at Sunset, *Misty Morning*, and *Fog on River, Savannah* are typical examples of Silva's southern paintings, which combine a loosely painted Impressionist style with the harmonious palette of the Tonalists. *Georgia Pines at Sunset*, in particular, shows the influence of George Inness. The tall pines in Silva's painting echo those in Inness's series from the 1890s, painted when Inness stayed in Tarpon Springs, Florida.

After moving to California, Silva continued his contact with the South. In 1921, he helped establish the Southern States Art League and regularly exhibited in Georgia and Tennessee. After his death in 1948, the Telfair Academy hosted a memorial exhibition of his paintings and drawings.

J.A.

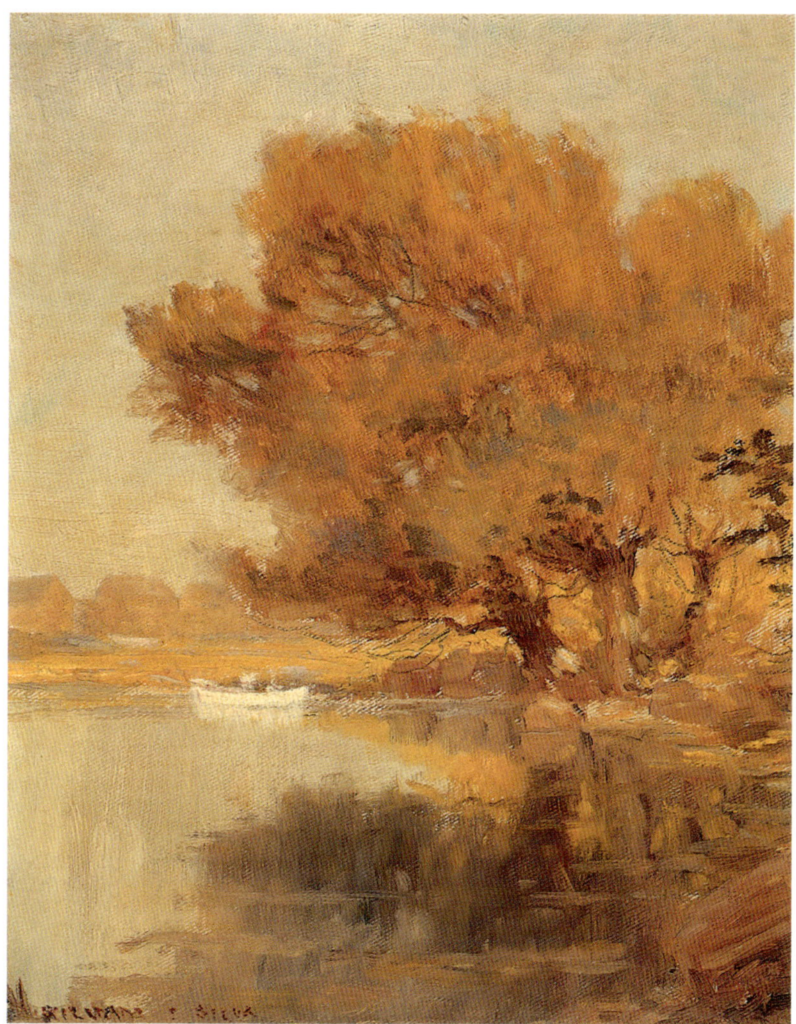

Misty Morning, n.d.
Oil on masonite
14 ½ x 11 ½ in. (37 x 29.2 cm)
Telfair Museum of Art, Gift of Abbot Silva, 1954

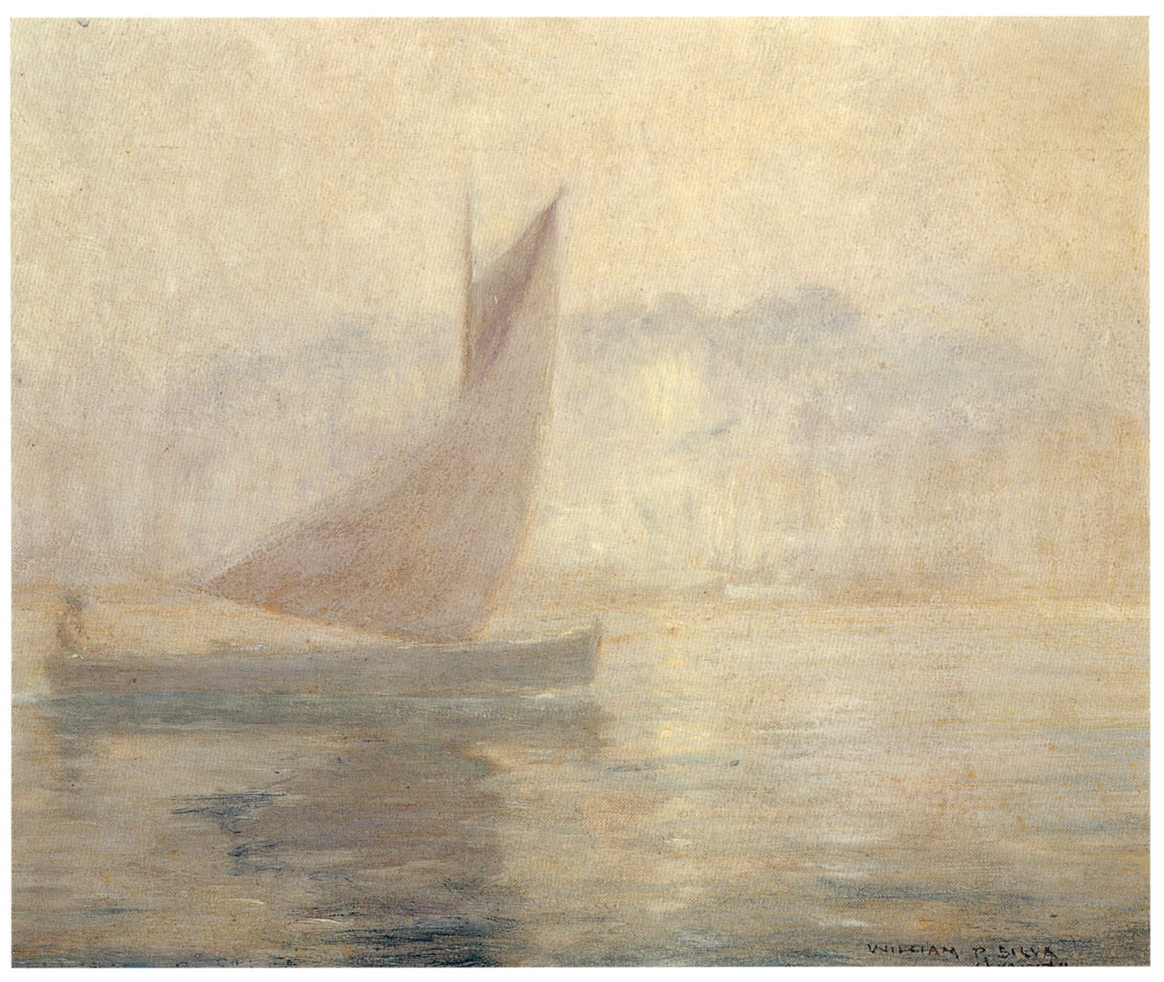

Fog on River, Savannah, n.d.
Oil on academy board
14 x 18 ½ in. (36 x 47 cm)
Collection of
Mrs. Grace Silva Cabaniss,
great-niece of the artist

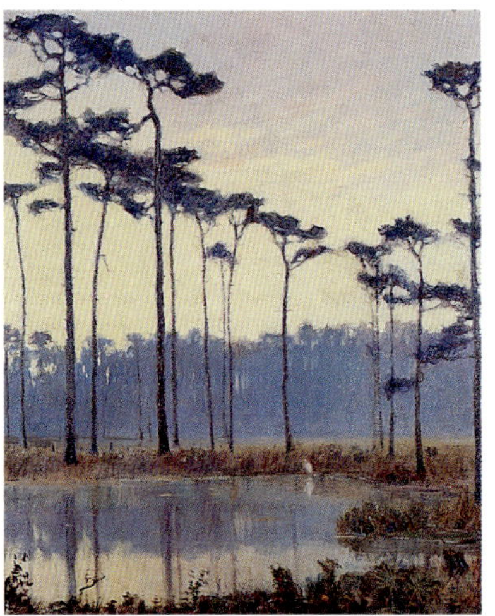

Georgia Pines at Sunset, c.1924
Oil on canvas
30 ⅛ x 25 ⅛ in. (77 x 64 cm)
Cheekwood Museum of Art,
Transfer from the Nashville
Museum of Art

Walter A. Simon

(b.1916)

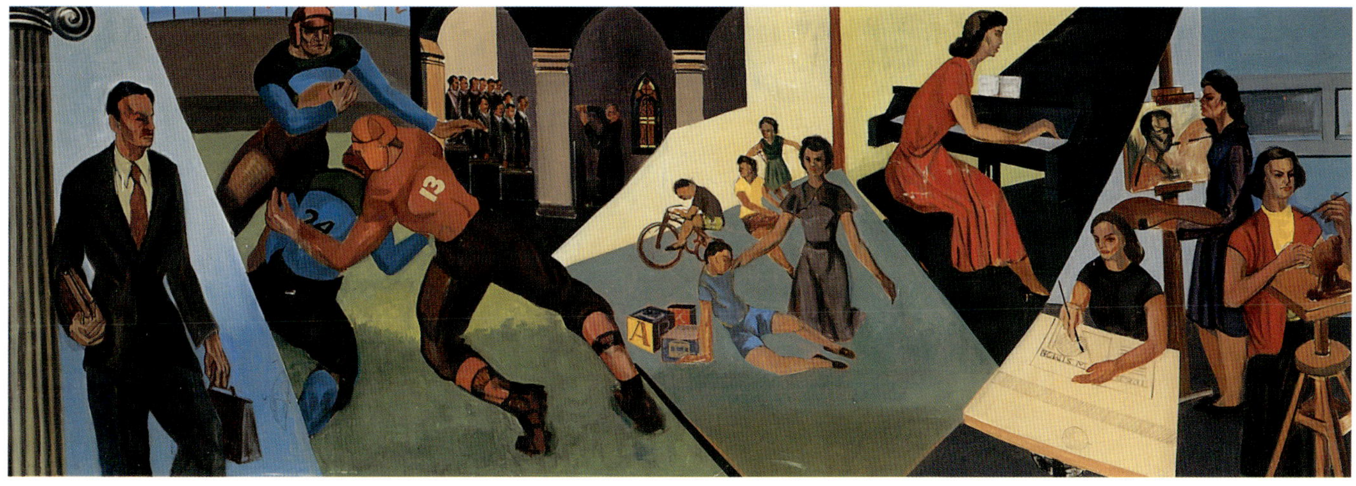

UNTITLED (one of a pair), 1949
Oil on canvas
50 x 142 in. (127 x 361 cm)
Collection of Savannah State College

WALTER SIMON WAS AN ADVOCATE FOR EDUCATION, especially that of African Americans. Commenting on an exhibition of junior school teachers' work which he organized, he said:

> Education in a democracy is not primarily concerned with developing 'great art' or artists. Rather, it should be concerned with helping the 'average' student further to develop his sensitivities which education in the past has tended to deaden and frustrate instead of broadening and enriching.[1]

As a teacher in several schools, including Savannah State College and later Atlanta University, Georgia State University, Virginia State University, and Bloomsburg State College, he was known to practice his convictions, not merely to espouse them.

Born in Brooklyn, Simon had a conventional art education, studying at Pratt Institute, New York University, and the National Academy of Design. His interest in art began at the age of ten, when he started making portraits.[2] His art would evolve to a kind of realism, often leaning toward abstraction to varying degrees.

Simon came to Savannah State in the 1940s, when the college's art department was in its infancy. He produced two large paintings for the school illustrating various careers, as well as campus activities. The work included in the current exhibition illustrates, among other things, art classes, musical performances, and a football game. The man in a business suit with a briefcase may indicate the hope that the future will bring a job requiring such accoutrements. The artist has combined these images into a single work by juxtaposing the various scenes on separate planes, each having a different vanishing point, and all separated by insistent diagonal boundaries. Through coloration the whole is made into a cohesive composition.

Savannah State College has contributed to the community in many ways since its founding in 1890 as the Georgia State Industrial College for Colored Youth.[3] Not the least of its contributions is its advancement of the arts through the work of dedicated teachers such as Walter Simon.

P.D.K.

1. *Cedric Dover,* American Negro Art *(Greenwich, Conn.: New York Graphic Society, 1960; reprinted, 1972), 50.*
2. *Ibid., 51.*
3. *The school became a part of the University System of Georgia in 1932; it was renamed Savannah State College in 1950. Donald L. Grant,* The Way It Was In The South: The Black Experience in Georgia *(New York: A Birch Lane Press Book, Carol Publishing Group, 1993), 246–47.*

Paul Goadby Stone

(1928–1976)

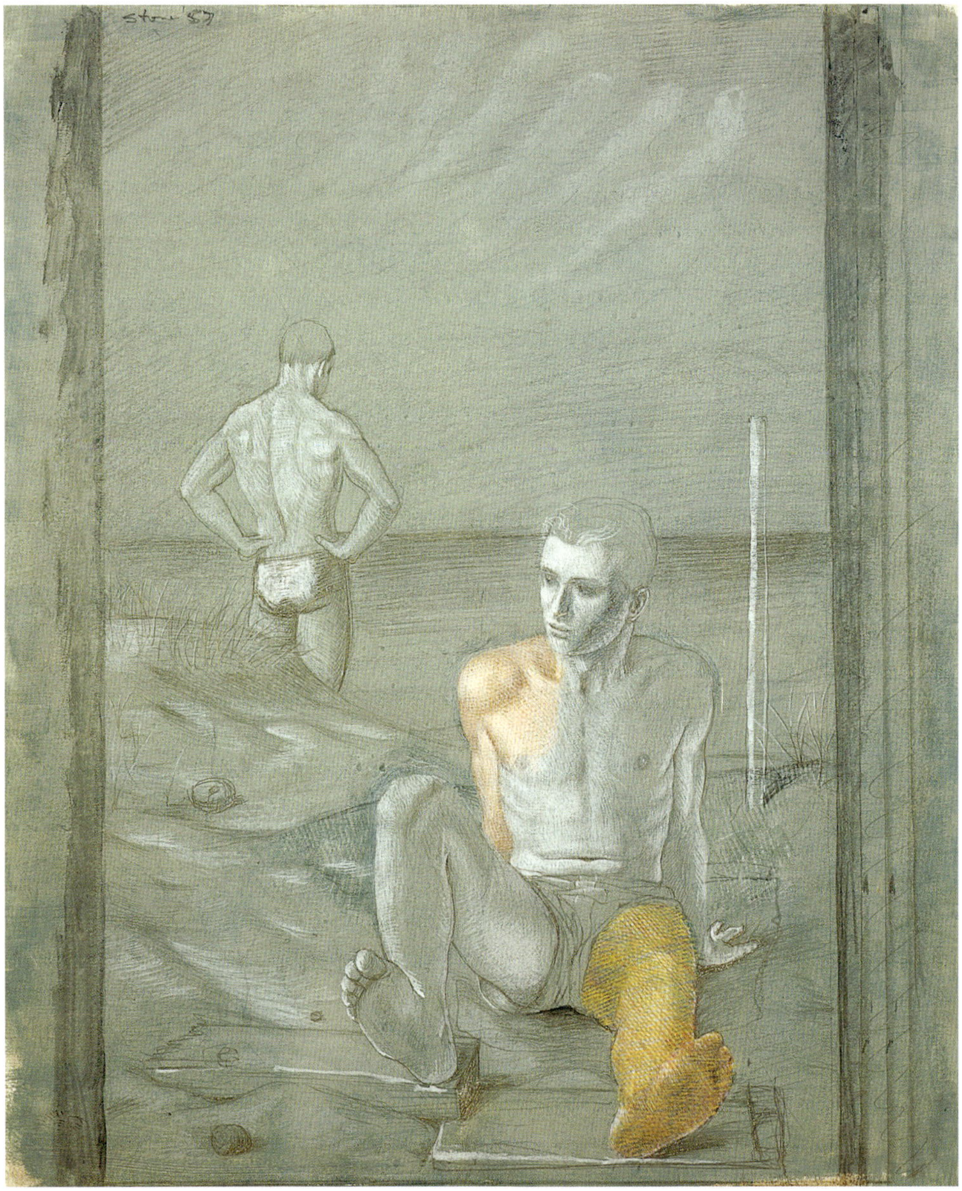

Untitled (Two Figures on a Beach), 1957
Mixed media
16 1/16 x 13 3/16 in. (32.7 x 25 cm)
The Comer House Collection

> I am really a religious artist. . . . My subject is not religious, my motivation is. . . . In my paintings what I am trying to do is to [recreate] razor-sharp poignancy which nature has created.[1]

PAUL STONE was born in Lumberton, North Carolina. During his youth Stone and his two brothers, the sons of a navy chaplain, traveled around the world. At Phillips Academy in Andover, Massachusetts, Stone studied art. In 1949 he graduated from Harvard University, where he had been president of the art association for two years. He also studied at the Boston Museum of Fine Arts. While living in Boston, he painted a number of portraits, one of which belongs to the Kennedy School of Government and another to the law school of Harvard. In Boston he had several one-artist shows and he was associated with the Margaret Brown Gallery. Although known for a number of fine portraits in oil, Stone favored tempera and watercolor, sometimes using a drybrush technique and embellishing areas with white or color.

After moving to Savannah in 1957—perhaps influenced by his parents' retirement to a small town near Beaufort, South Carolina—Stone continued to produce and exhibit, as well as teach, both privately and at Armstrong State College. A 1988 article, written in conjunction with a memorial exhibition at John Lee's New Southern Paintings gallery, relates that Stone also entered art shows and usually won.[2]

In 1960 Stone exhibited twenty-one paintings at the Atlanta Museum of Art (now the High Museum of Art). That same year he married Adeline Oxnard, whom he met when he was commissioned to paint an Oxnard family portrait. In 1963, at a one-artist show of thirty paintings at the Wellfleet Art Gallery on Cape Cod, he sold three works to trustees of the Boston Museum of Fine Arts.

Stone's life in Savannah, which began with such promise, ended in tragedy. By the 1970s, physically and emotionally ill, he exhibited increasingly irrational behavior. Divorced, alone, and impoverished, he depended on the care of friends and family. The events surrounding his death in 1976, when he was just forty-eight years old, remain a mystery. Stone burned to death, perhaps by his own hand, while siphoning gas from a truck parked near the driveway of his home.[3]

The two works in this exhibition reveal Stone's talent and foretell a possibly brilliant career.[4] Here the subject matter continues a tradition that began with the ancients and was reintroduced during the Renaissance: the celebration of the male form as the embodiment of physical and spiritual grace. These drawings, while related by subject, are quite different in presentation and emphasis. The composition of three figures stresses a powerful physicality and pays homage to countless studies of muscular nudes at rest or in motion. In the drawing of two figures on a beach, the subjects are separated by space and the turn of their bodies, which suggests a psychological separation and an underlying drama as well. Here, Stone's debt to the Renaissance, and specifically to linear perspective, is acknowledged: he has posed the seated figure provocatively with one leg bent and the other, heightened with color, perfectly foreshortened as it extends full-length into the foreground.[5]

D.L.

1. *Quoted in "Paul Stone, The Unusual Artist,"* Savannah Magazine, *April 1971.*

2. *Rosanne Howard, "Paul Stone: Artist's Life, Work Recalled,"* Savannah News-Press, *February 7, 1988, pp. 1F and 6F.*

3. *"Savannah Artist Burns to Death,"* Savannah Morning News, *September 30, 1976, p. 1D. According to Arthur B. Kouwenhoven, Jr., at the time of his death—which his brother, Albert Stone, and a friend, Lee Ullman, believe was accidental—his work was shown at New York's Leslie-Lohman Gallery.*

4. *Because Stone did not arrive in Savannah until 1957, works that fall within the time frame of this exhibition are extremely limited in number. In the Telfair collection there are five Stone drawings, all post-1960.*

5. *In his small, exquisite portraits from the early 1950s, the inspiration of Northern Renaissance artists is obvious. In works from the 1970s, the barns, solitary figures, and sharp-focus realism suggest the influence of Andrew Wyeth. In the two exhibited drawings, Stone's technique and subjects appear closest to the work of Paul Cadmus.*

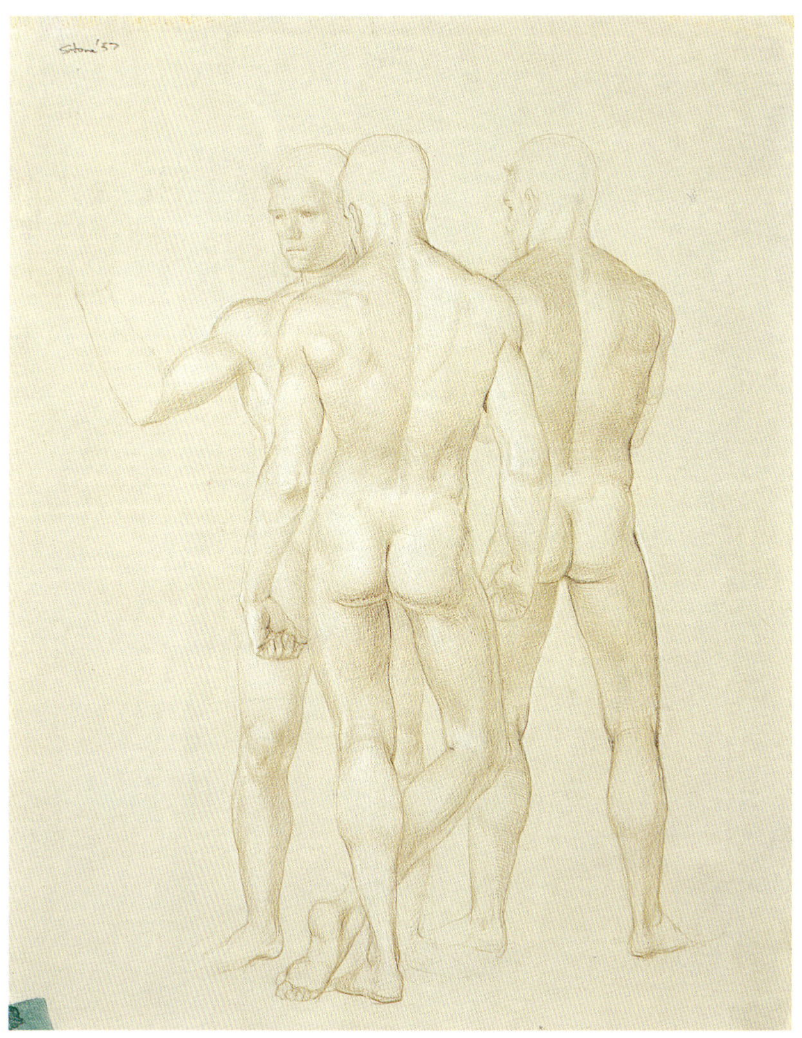

UNTITLED (THREE MALE NUDES), 1957
Pencil and gouache on paper
12 ⅞ x 9 ¾ in. (41 x 34.3 cm)
Collection of Arthur B. Kouwenhoven, Jr.

Hugh Tallant

(1869–1952)

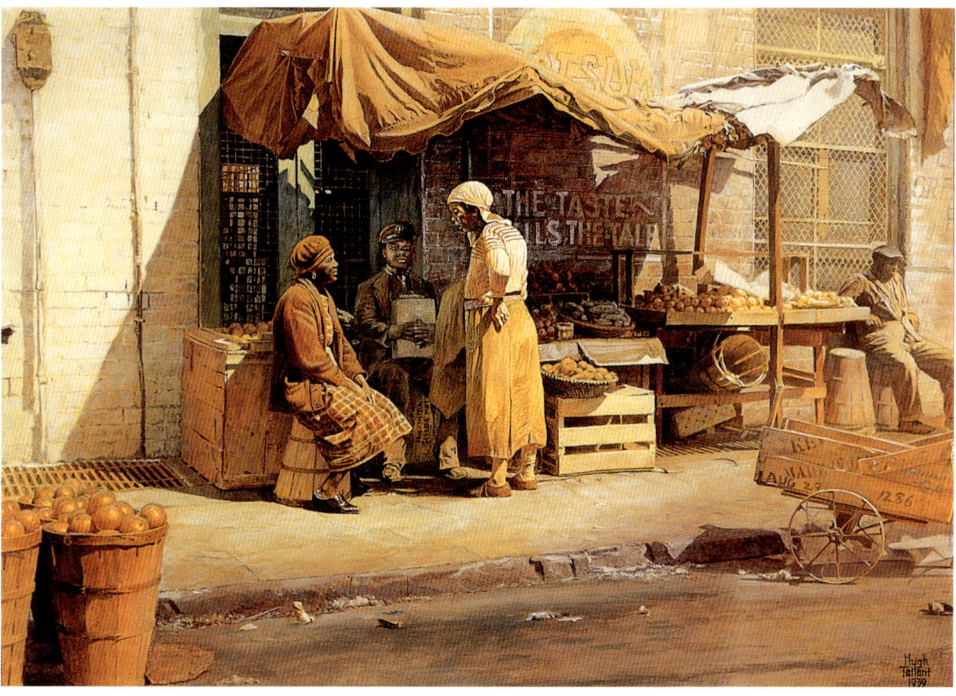

Noonday Gossip at the Market, 1939
Watercolor on paper
24 x 30 in. (61 x 76.2 cm)
Collection of Mr. and Mrs. Richard Meyer III

Hugh Tallant began his career as an architect after graduating in 1887 from Harvard with a master's degree. He furthered his education through a Harvard fellowship that allowed him to study at the Ecole des Beaux-Arts in Paris. In 1897 Tallant returned to the United States and worked in New York City for the next thirty-four years.

Upon his retirement in 1934 Tallant moved to Savannah. At the request of Charles Ellis, a leading business executive who sat on the board of education, he directed the Public Works Arts Project, a government-funded program that provided jobs for artists during the Depression. Tallant supervised the painting of two murals in Savannah, one for the Richard Arnold School and the other for the children's room at the main branch of the public library. Tallant's involvement with art in Savannah did not end with the completion of the murals. He was a member of the Board of Managers of the Telfair Academy of Arts and Sciences and an avid painter of Savannah scenes.

Noonday Gossip at the Market focuses the viewer's attention on the street and the day's produce—squash, citrus fruit, and potatoes. A sign painted on the wall behind a vending booth reads, "The taste tells the tale," perhaps a reference to the gossip that is also a very popular item at the market. While Tallant's figures are the focal point of his painting, he also provides details that give a sense of how busy the market has been: items like an abandoned cart, broken crates, and garbage strewn about the street inform the viewer of the day's hustle and bustle.

In the early years of the twentieth century, artists like Robert Henri and George Luks glorified such common scenes in their paintings of New York's Lower East Side. In the 1920s and 1930s views of the American scene became more popular and diverse. In *Noonday Gossip at the Market* Tallant has described a Savannah scene with the alluring appeal of good company and interesting conversation.

D.B.

John W. Taylor

(1897–1983)

A CHILDHOOD SPENT IN EASTERN TEXAS, near the Louisiana border, whetted Jack Taylor's appetite to explore a southern iconography. In the late 1930s he, along with his artist-wife Andrée Ruellan, made several trips to Charleston and Savannah, producing many canvases of the local scene.

Taylor's artistic career began in California in 1916 in the advertising department of the *Los Angeles Times*. His interests led him to other artists and night classes in drawing. An influential teacher of Taylor in the late 1910s was Stanton Macdonald-Wright, the cofounder of the movement called Synchronism; Taylor recalled in 1972, "I still set up my palette according to principles I learned from him."[1]

Taylor went to New York City in 1923 and supported himself painting scene backdrops for movies and, briefly, for the Schuberts in theaters on Broadway. Several years later Taylor studied at the Art Students League with Boardman Robinson and John Sloan. His association with the Woodstock Art Colony began in the early 1920s. In 1926 he purchased a house and farm in nearby Shady, New York.

The ultimate goal for artists at that time, however, was to go to Paris. In 1928 Taylor traveled to France with fellow artist and Woodstock resident Emil Ganso. There he met and married Andrée Ruellan, who described Taylor as "earthy and intellectual."[2]

Throughout their careers, Taylor and Ruellan influenced each other's painting. They shared a desire to record the world around them in a forthright manner. Taylor concentrated more on the landscape rather than its inhabitants, however. Using broad strokes of paint he built his scenes in planes, the elements of which work in concert to effect a fresh vision of a common subject. In *Creek Street, Savannah*, the artist has taken for his subject a dirt road and clapboard houses, recording an ordinary scene with few details.

Taylor and Ruellan made many trips to the South. Taylor taught at Tulane University in New Orleans and at the University of Florida in Gainesville. Although the couple maintained their home in Shady, they created pleasant memories and many brilliant canvases inspired by the South.

P.D.K.

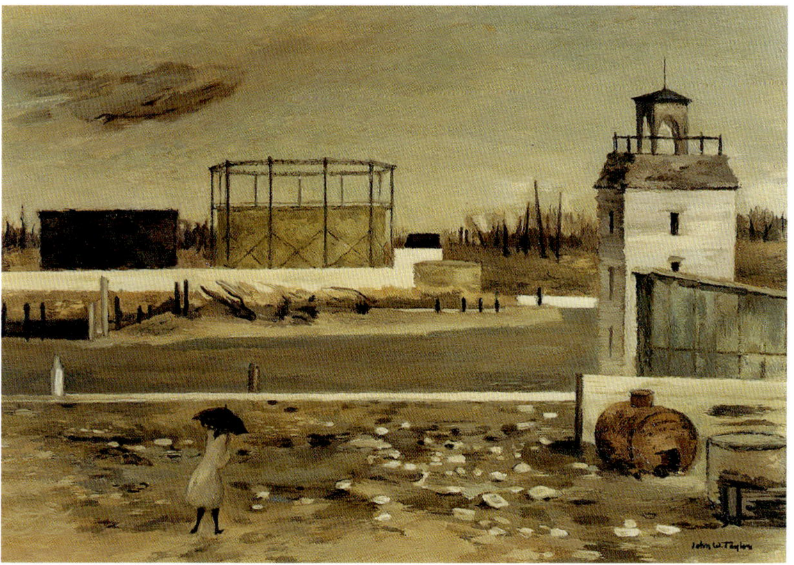

RIVER LANDSCAPE, c.1940
Oil on canvas
14 x 20 in. (36 x 51 cm)
Estate of the artist, Courtesy of Conner-Rosenkranz, New York

1. *Lillian Fortess, "John W. Taylor,"* Woodstock's Art Heritage *(Woodstock, N.Y.: Overlook Press, 1987), 134.*
2. *Conversation with Andrée Ruellan, May 7, 1996.*

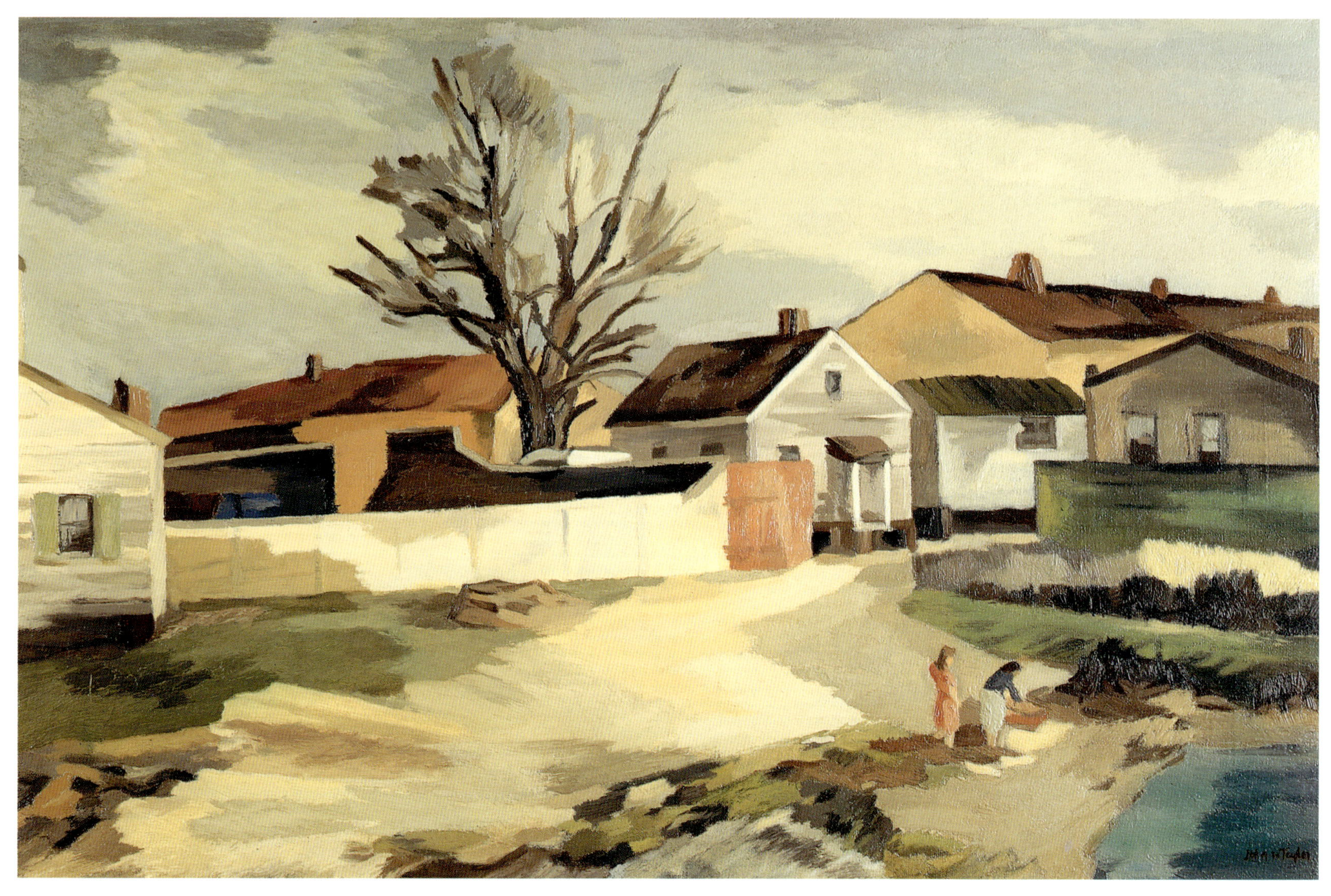

Creek Street, Savannah, 1941–43
Oil on canvas
20 ¹⁄₁₆ x 30 ¼ in. (51 x 77 cm)
Collection of Steven and Susan Hirsch, Courtesy of Conner-Rosenkranz, New York

Jon Paul Thomas

(active second half of the 1940s)

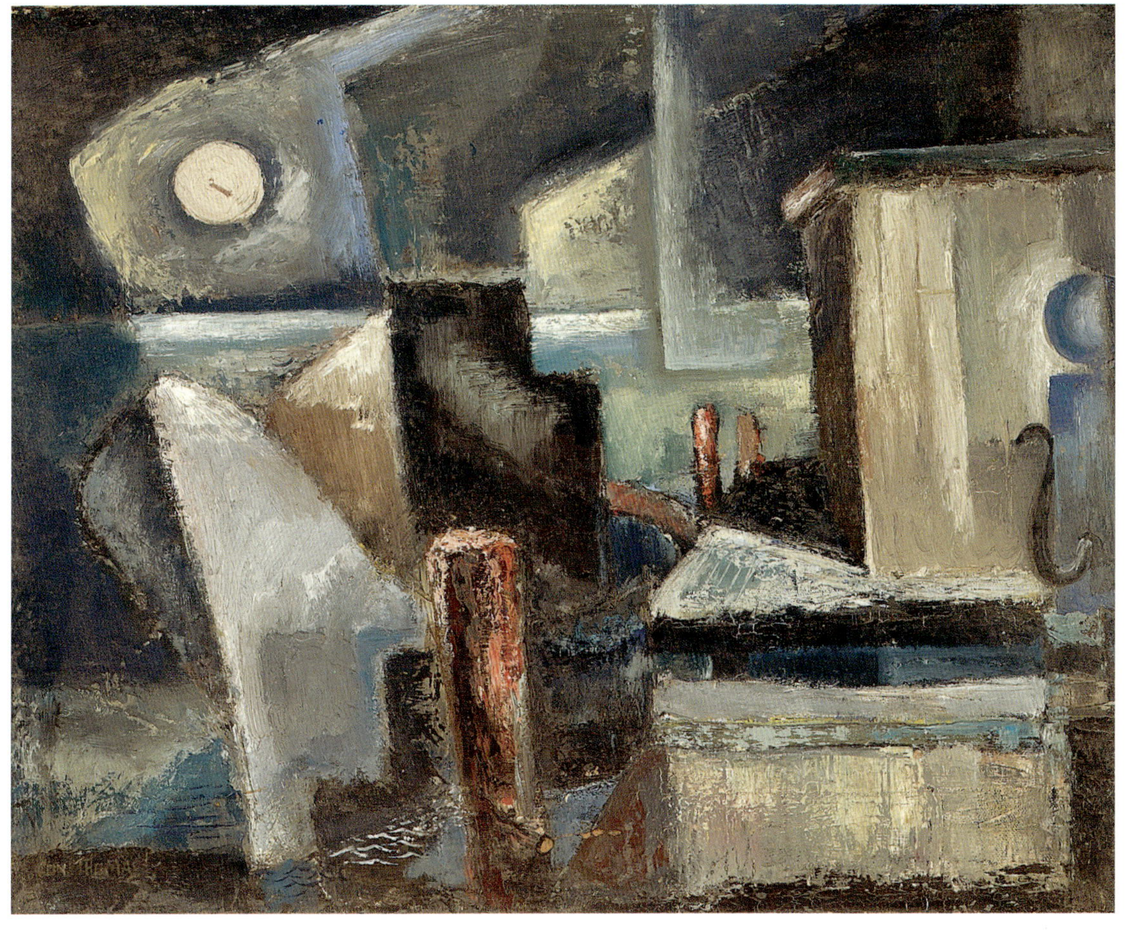

Dock Scene, #2, 1948
Oil on canvas
20 ½ x 16 ½ in. (52.1 x 42 cm)
Telfair Museum of Art, Gift of the Savannah Art Club, 1948

Dock Scene, #2 IS ONE OF THE FEW MODERNIST PAINTINGS in the current exhibition. Intersecting planes activate the composition but do not obscure the recognition of the subject matter, a local scene.

Jon Paul Thomas was a student of Reuben Gambrell at the University of Georgia Savannah campus in 1947 and 1948. He served as president of the art students' campus organization and was an active member of the Savannah Art Association. He won prizes from both in exhibitions; *Dead End* (location unknown) was the top prize winner in the university's student exhibition in May 1947, and *Dock Scene, #2* was the purchase prize of the Savannah Art Association's annual spring exhibition of 1948.

P.D.K.

Walter Whitcomb Thompson

(1882–1948)

MARSH AND MOONLIGHT, c.1931
Oil on canvas
20 x 24 in. (51 x 61 cm)
Collection of Mr. Vince Sikorski

WALTER WHITCOMB THOMPSON, a native of South Carolina, studied art at the University of Florida. He exhibited at the Telfair Academy and became director of the Beaufort, South Carolina, art colony. He was a member of the Association of Georgia Artists and the Savannah Art Club.

Thompson's *Marsh and Moonlight* continues the long tradition of American landscape painting that began in the early nineteenth century with the painters of the Hudson River School and their large expansive paintings of the wilderness. In the mid- to late-nineteenth century, artists like George Inness incorporated the approach of the French Barbizon School. Landscape was still the favored subject, but now the focus was on the expressive use of oil paints, not only to record an image, but also to evoke a mood. In the late nineteenth to early twentieth centuries, painters such as Inness carried Barbizon a step further, preferring poetry over factual representation. This stylistic trend is often called Tonalism.

Marsh and Moonlight is an expansive, ethereal view that shows Thompson's interest in light effects and his use of loose brushwork. Light unifies the composition that is otherwise bisected by the emphatic horizon line. The moonlight, shimmering through the sky and reflecting on the water, creates a kind of visual tone poem, which Thompson describes in lavenders and blues. Marshes, painted in dark tones, frame the water, almost engulfing the lone rowboat—a suggestion, perhaps, that nature is more powerful than man.

D.B.

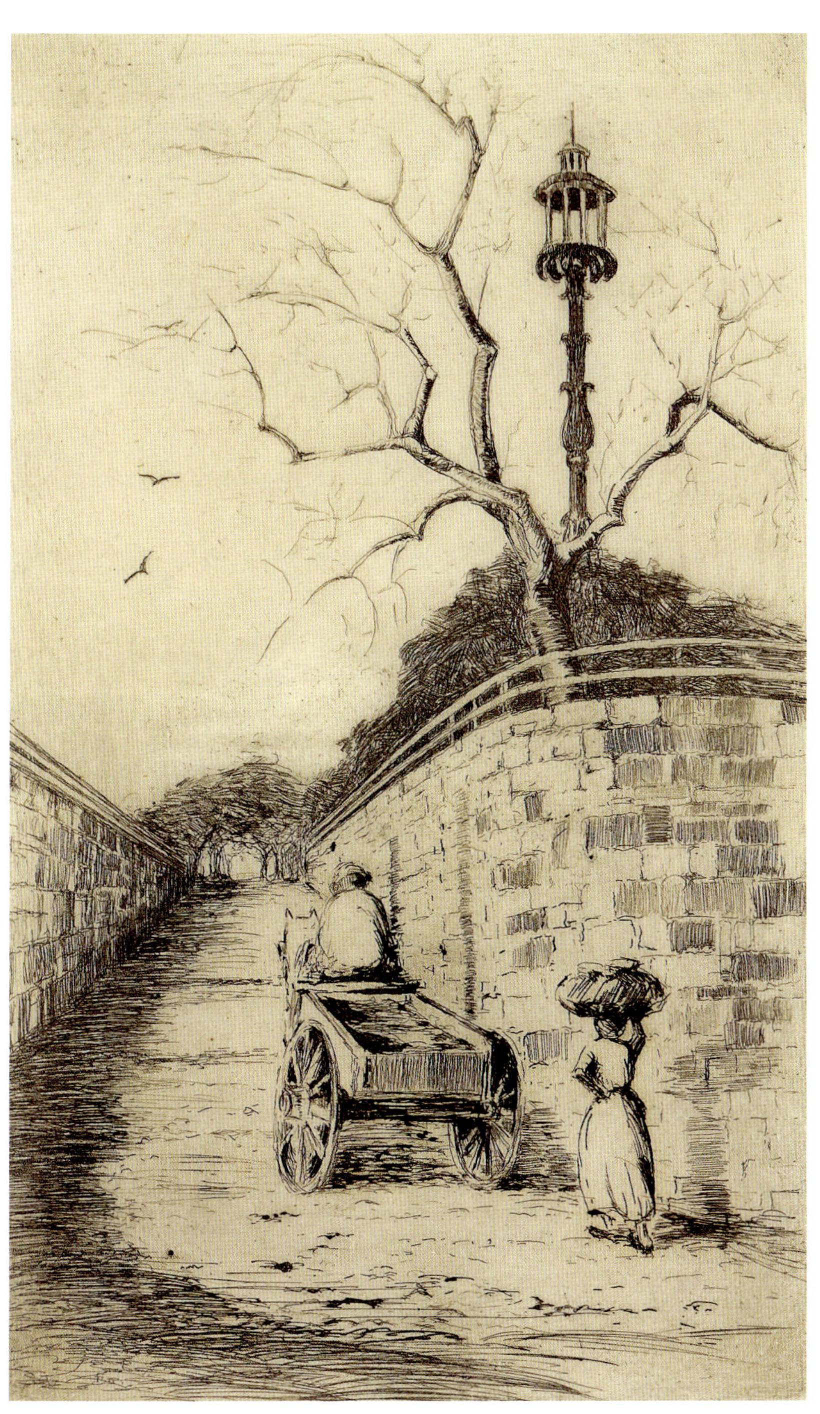

Elizabeth O'Neill Verner

(1883–1979)

ELIZABETH O'NEILL VERNER was an artist, a teacher, and an advocate for historic preservation. Her training as an artist began in her hometown of Charleston, where she studied with Alice Smith; she continued her studies at the Pennsylvania Academy of the Fine Arts under Thomas Anshutz.

Verner considered her art work a hobby until the death of her husband in 1925, when of necessity she turned to printmaking as a source of income. One of her first commissions came from Walter Hartridge of Savannah. Hartridge, who was concerned about preserving Savannah's unique beauty, asked Verner to produce etchings of the city's architecture. *River Street*, *River Slip*, and *Harbor Light* are part of this series.

Verner's passion for historic preservation is almost palpable in her Savannah etchings. The three compositions shown here exhibit strong verticality, which is characteristic of her work. As in many of her etchings, architecture is the subject and the human presence is deemphasized. All three works reflect the rich quality of Savannah's unique ambiance and the artist's devotion to preserving the city's irreplaceable beauty.

D.B.

THE HARBOR LIGHT, SAVANNAH, c.1926
Etching on paper
8 ⅜ x 5 in. (plate) (21.3 x 13 cm)
Telfair Museum of Art, Gift of Mrs. John Andrew Hamilton, 1976

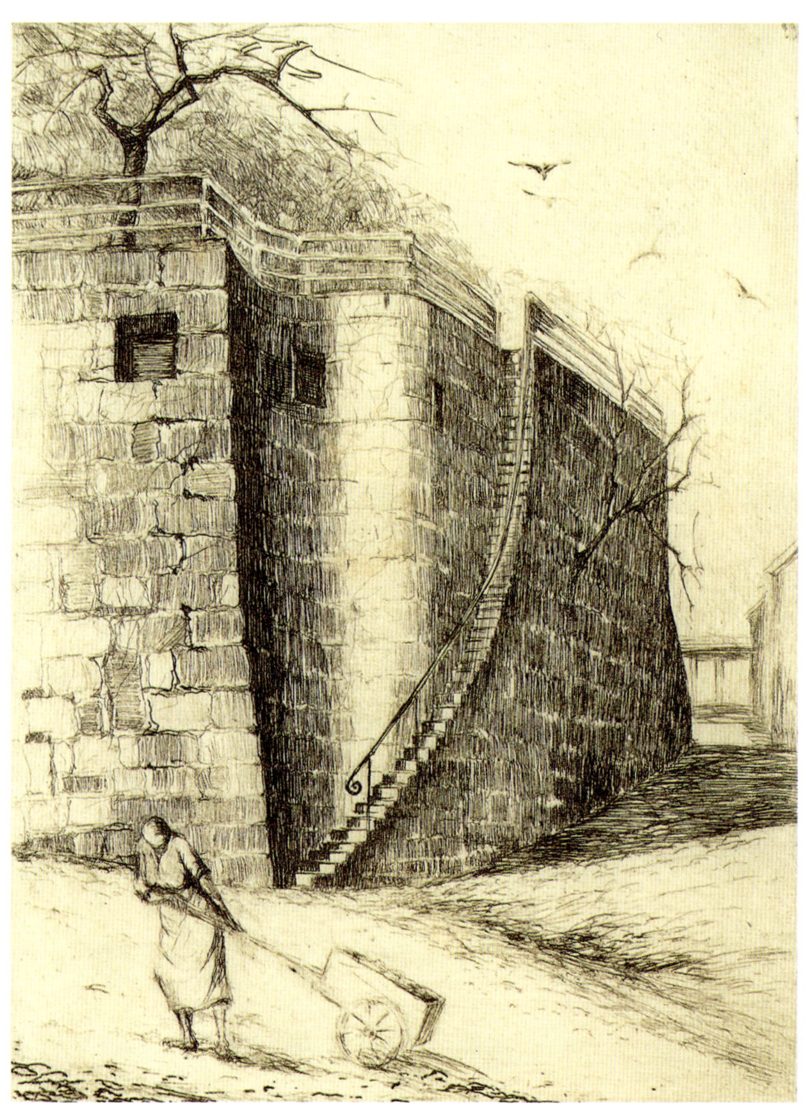

River Slip, Savannah, c.1926
Etching on paper
6 ¾ x 5 in. (17.1 x 13 cm)
Telfair Museum of Art, Gift of Mrs. John Andrew Hamilton, 1976

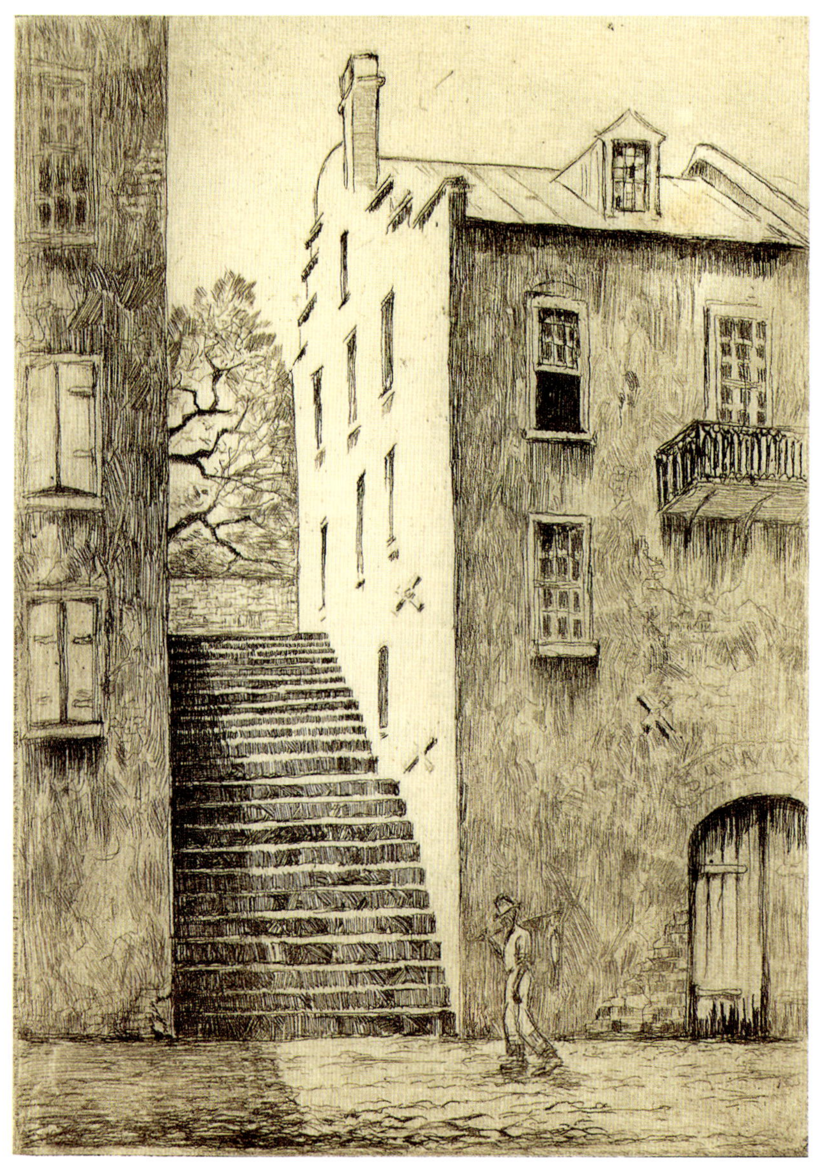

River Street, Savannah, c.1926
Etching on paper
6 ⅜ x 4 ½ in. (16.2 x 11.4 cm)
Telfair Museum of Art, Gift of Mrs. John Andrew Hamilton, 1976

Edward Weston

(1886–1956)

WHILE THERE ARE MANY PHOTOGRAPHERS whose work takes them all over the world, there are also many whose best work is made in their immediate environs—quite literally, in their own back yard. Edward Weston was at his best when close to home, in Carmel, California. But so great was his ability to extract the absolute essence of a visual image that one could say he saw the cosmos wherever he was—in shells, fruits and vegetables, human figures, and other natural forms, as well as in immense vistas. In his *Daybooks*[1] Weston pairs on facing pages his image of the Occano Dunes and two nude studies to illustrate the obvious formal similarities between the landscape of nature and the landscape of the human form. Weston felt that concentrating on good composition was the best possible way of seeing, no matter what the subject. For him this meant a photograph so densely composed that it seems to be bursting at the seams. The net result is the sometimes contradictory notion of the image being physically proximate yet emotionally aloof.

Perhaps Weston's greatest accomplishment within the genre of the landscape was the body of work he produced at Point Lobos near his home in Carmel. Life on the road did not present the same opportunity for reflection that he had at Point Lobos. As Ben Maddow put it so well in his appreciation of Weston, "when one arrives, stops, and looks, one is presented with an entire horizon, a sweep of vision as much as 360 degrees; having been seduced by air and distance, one now has to stop, reduce and compose."[2]

In his image of Bonaventure Cemetery in Savannah, made in December 1941 for an illustrated version of Walt Whitman's *Leaves of Grass*,[3] Weston focused on several grave markers under a canopy of Spanish moss-draped trees, utilizing the components of light, space, and time to achieve an image of atmospheric integrity. Reflecting on the *Leaves of Grass* project, over which he had free rein, Weston said on April 28, 1941,

> There will be no attempt to "illustrate," no symbolism except perhaps in a very broad sense. . . . The reproductions . . . will have no titles, no captions. This leaves me great freedom—I can use anything from an airplane to a longshoreman. I do believe . . . I can and will do the best work of my life. Of course I will never please everyone with *my* America—wouldn't try to.[4]

C.S.

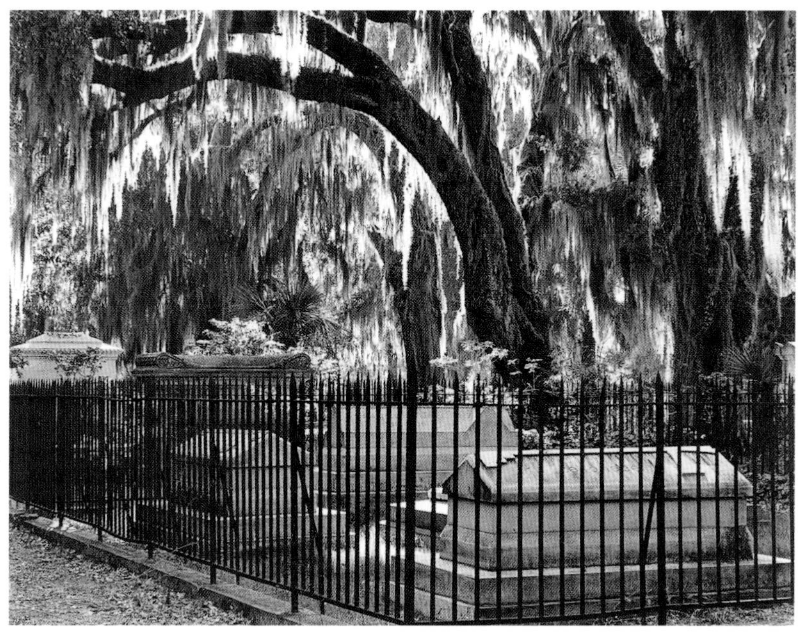

BONAVENTURE CEMETERY, SAVANNAH, 1941
Gelatin silver print
8 x 10 in. (20.3 x 25.4 cm)
Center for Creative Photography, The University of Arizona

1. *Nancy Newhall, ed.,* The Daybooks of Edward Weston, *2 vols. (Millerton, N.Y.: Aperture, 1961 and 1973).*
2. *Ben Maddow, "An American Hero,"* American Photographer *(September 1986): 53.*
3. *Walt Whitman,* Leaves of Grass *(New York: Limited Editions Club, 1942).*
4. *Quoted in Nancy Newhall, ed.,* Edward Weston: The Flame of Recognition *(New York: Grossman Publishers, 1971): 70.*

Emma Cheves Wilkins

(1870–1956)

Playing with Reds (Camellias) c.1930–31
Oil on canvas
25 ⅛ x 32 ⅞ in. (64 x 84 cm)
Telfair Museum of Art, Museum purchase, 1931

Savannah native Emma Cheves Wilkins was one of many women who played a pivotal role in the development of the arts in Savannah in the early years of the twentieth century. She was fortunate to have more professional training in art than most women of her generation. Wilkins began her studies at the Telfair Academy under director Carl Brandt, and then traveled to Paris, where she studied with Gustave Courtois and Louis-Auguste Girardot at the Académie Colarossi, one of the leading private ateliers of the time. After her return to Savannah she taught art to other local women, including Hattie Saussy and Augusta Oelschig.

In her oil still life, *Playing with Reds (Camellias)*, Wilkins shows her command of the dark palette and bravura brushwork of the Munich School and the aesthetics of contemporary Parisian art, both of which dominated the American art world after the turn of the twentieth century, perhaps most notably in the work of the influential American painter and teacher, William Merritt Chase. Wilkins's still lifes bear a close resemblance to those of Chase. *Playing with Reds*, as the title may indicate, also shows the influence of the Aesthetic Movement, or "Art for Art's Sake," which was championed by James Abbott McNeill Whistler in the second half of the nineteenth century and became particularly fashionable around the turn of the century in the work of artists such as Chase. Many works of this period stressed the primacy of color, composition, and brushwork over subject matter and content. In *Playing with Reds*, Wilkins explores the aesthetic issues created by the repeated use of the color red, in the camellias, the ceramics, and the reflections on the polished tabletop and brass coffee urn.

In addition to still lifes, Wilkins painted interiors, landscapes, and portraits, examples of which are

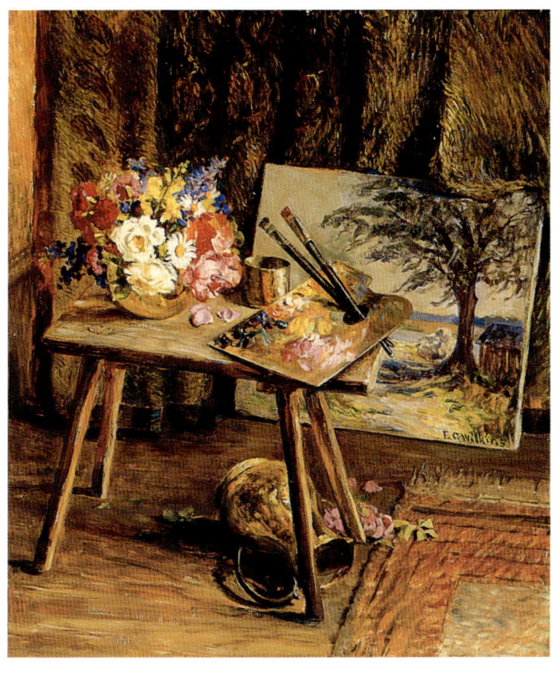

Corner of a Studio, late 1930s to 1940s
Oil on canvas
33 ¼ x 27 in.
(85 x 69 cm)
Collection of Ben N. Adams

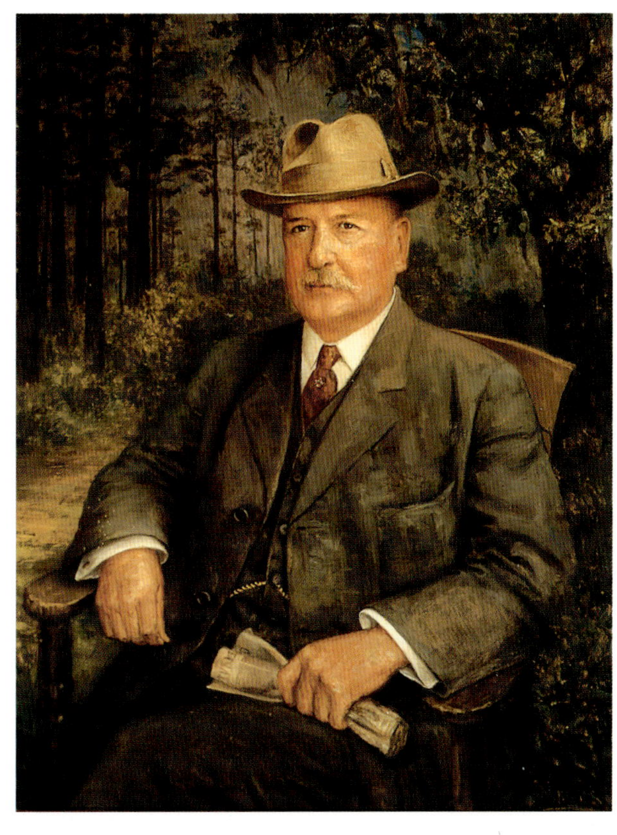

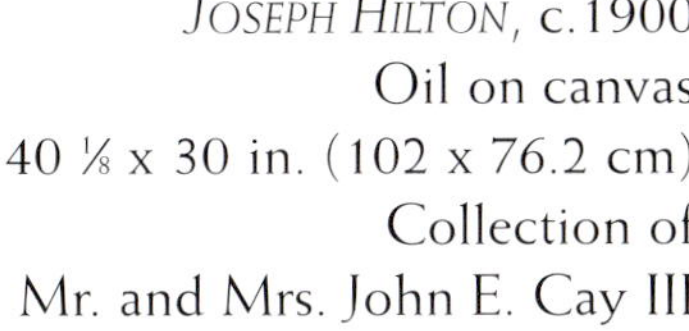

Joseph Hilton, c.1900
Oil on canvas
40 ⅛ x 30 in. (102 x 76.2 cm)
Collection of
Mr. and Mrs. John E. Cay III

included in this exhibition. *Bonaventure Cemetery* and other landscapes were created on site in the painterly style of the Impressionists. The same loosely brushed style is evident in the casually composed *Corner of a Studio*, which can be read as emblematic of Wilkins herself and her profession as a painter: the palette and vase of flowers on the table represent, respectively, her medium and one of her favorite subjects, and the painting in the background shows her interest in landscape.

Wilkins was well known in Savannah for her portraits of prominent citizens, including Savannah mayor Thomas Gamble. Her commissioned portraits are more traditional, with a somewhat tighter but still painterly style, as in her *Portrait of Joseph Hilton*. Hilton (1843–1920) was a prominent businessman who owned the Hilton Dodge Lumber Company of Darien, Georgia, and Long Island, New York. Wilkins represents him seated in front of a forest background, an attribute, or symbol, of the sitter's profession.

C.L.B.

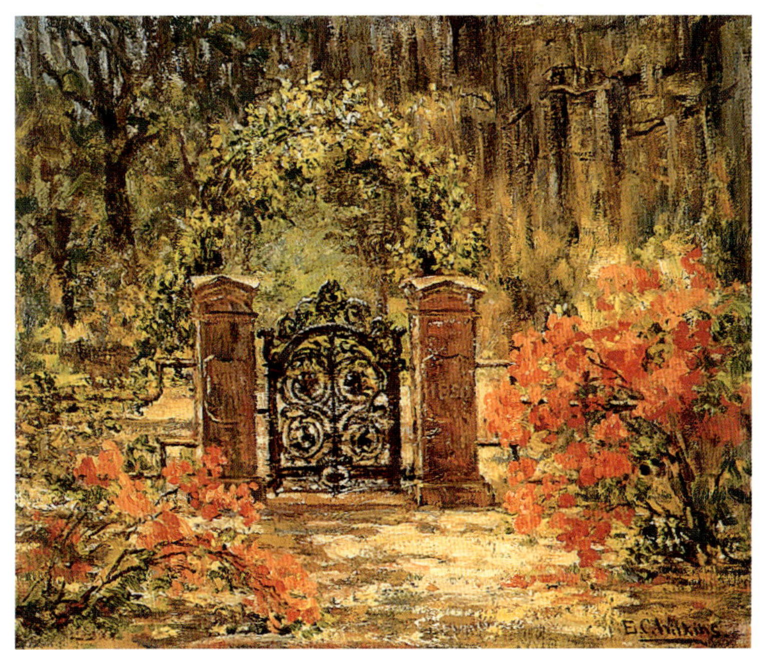

Bonaventure Cemetery, n.d.
Oil on canvas
16 x 19 in. (41 x 48.3 cm)
Collection of Mr. and Mrs. Richard Meyer III

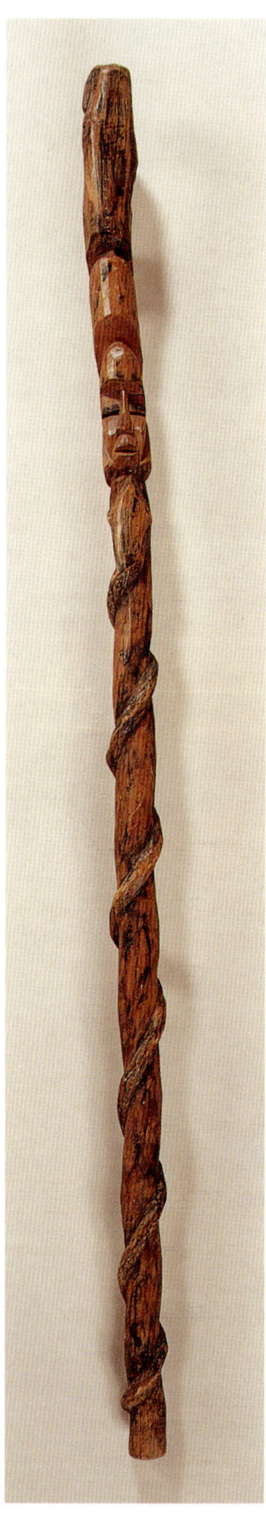

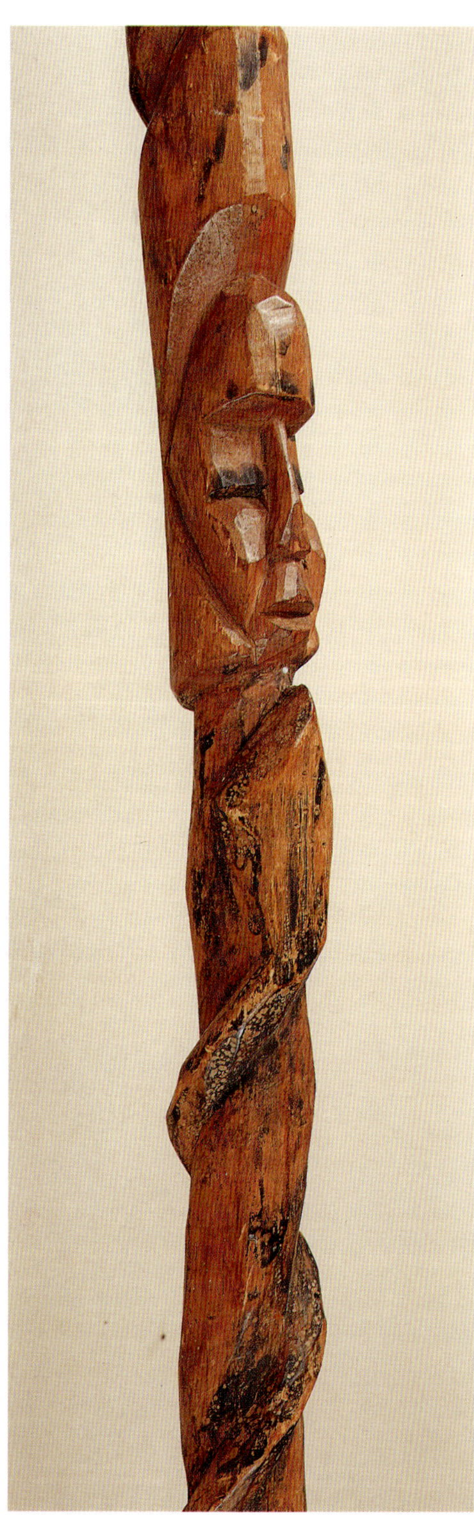

Unidentified Artist

ALTHOUGH NUMEROUS WOODEN CANES by African American carvers were documented in Savannah in the 1940 *Drums and Shadows*[1] project, few extant examples have been located. The cane shown here was said to have been owned by an African American man in Savannah in the late 1930s. The wear on the piece is commensurate with such a date, and the iconography of the cane relates to other work documented in the city at that time. Like William Rogers of Darien, the unknown maker of this cane has used the motif of a frontal human figure surmounting an aerially viewed reptile. A link is therefore suggested between this cane and others in the African American carving tradition. This example differs from other documented Savannah works in its ruggedly crude carving; and the figure, unlike that in other canes, does not serve as the actual handle. A series of tiny holes punched into the flat head of the serpent form the letter "E" (perhaps the owner's or maker's initial); at one time these holes may have been studded with beads or nail heads for emphasis. A faint, painted "E" is also discernible in the well-worn handle.

H.H.D.

1. *Georgia Writers' Project,* Drums and Shadows: Survival Studies Among the Georgia Coastal Negroes *(Athens, Ga.: The University of Georgia Press, 1940; reprinted, Brown Thrasher Books, The University of Georgia Press, 1986).*

CANE (full view and detail), c.1930s or 1940s
Carved wood
L. 37 ⅞ in. (96 cm)
Collection of H. Paul Blatner

Unidentified Artist

INSCRIBED "SAVANNAH 1919," this small but powerful piece does not fall within other known sculptural activity in the city during this period. Reportedly purchased from an African American source by a dealer in North Carolina, this portrait of an African American man displays a greater tendency toward naturalism than the African American figurative wood sculpture documented in the 1940 *Drums and Shadows* publication.[1] This book included photographs of small, abstracted figurative busts, as well as a naturalistic stone sculpture of a fig, which had been carried as a charm by the owner's grandfather, a man originally from Santo Domingo.[2]

Although the size of the portrait head could indicate an intended portability, the original setting or use of the work is not known; it is flat on the bottom, but balances precariously at best. Skillfully carved from soft black stone, the portrait is specific enough to suggest that the maker was working from life or from the memory of a particular person. It is unknown whether the color of the stone was chosen to relate to the subject, or whether the maker was reacting to the possibilities of shape and color inherent in the stone. The maker did not attempt to burnish out small scratches and tool marks, which are noticeable in the smoother surfaces of the neck and back. Until similar examples come to light, the question will remain as to whether this work represents a creolized sculptural mode or whether it is an individual, idiosyncratic expression.

H.H.D.

1. *Georgia Writers' Project,* Drums and Shadows: Survival Studies Among the Georgia Coastal Negroes *(Athens, Ga.: The University of Georgia Press, 1940; reprinted, Brown Thrasher Books, The University of Georgia Press, 1986).*
2. *Ibid., 54.*

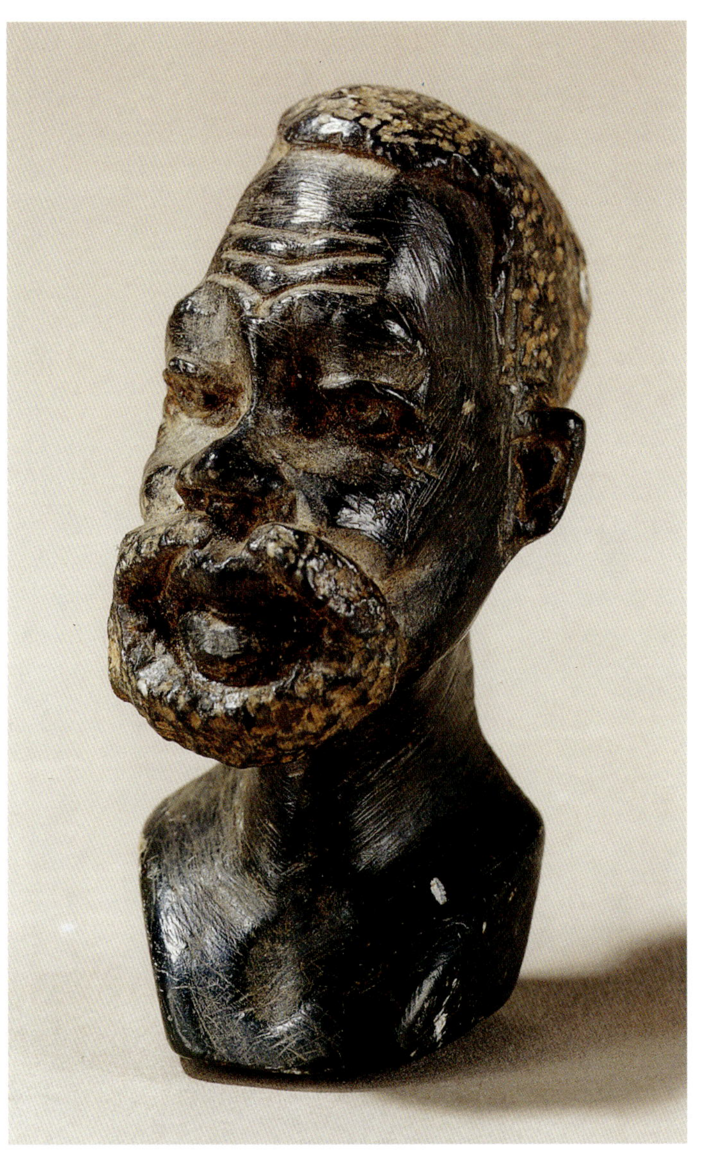

SMALL PORTRAIT HEAD, 1919
Carved soapstone(?)
3 x 2 ¼ x 1 7/16 in. (8 x 6 x 4 cm)
The Acacia Collection of African-Americana

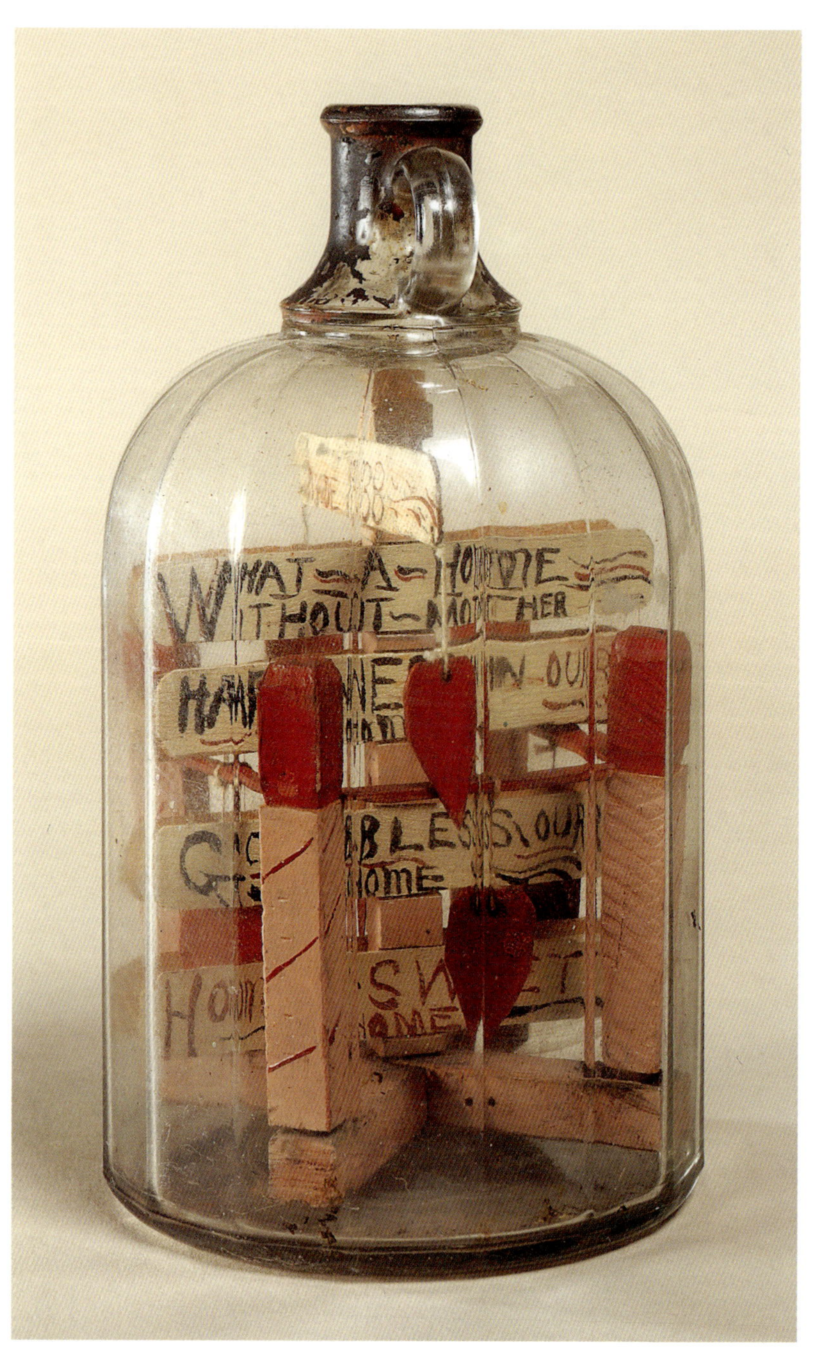

Unidentified Artist

DECORATIVE CONSTRUCTIONS UNDER GLASS, known as "whimsies," were a popular part of the Victorian interior in Europe and the United States. Although mass-produced examples and homemade copies survive, few resemble these two intricate bottles made by African Americans in Savannah. Purchased in the 1970s from different sources in Savannah, the two objects consist of inscribed and decorated wood constructions sealed inside gallon glass jars. The inscriptions on both seem to point to a commemorative, perhaps spiritual, intention in their making. Although they bear no nautical motifs, both works may be related to the puzzle bottles often associated with sailors.[1]

Both bottles feature religious inscriptions. In *Puzzle Bottle*, the entire Lord's Prayer is lettered across a series of horizontal bands of wood attached to a central element in the manner of a signpost. On the reverse of these elements is the inscription, "What a home without mother/ happiness in our home/ God bless our home/ home sweet home." In each of these bands the word "home" is singled out on a separate line, creating the effect of a visual chant or song. The signpost is crisscrossed by another band at the top, inscribed "made 1938." There is little carving in the wooden elements, which are painted in red and white. Around the signpost are four additional posts linked by horizontal elements suggesting a fence or enclosure.

Castle in the Sky contains an overtly architectural structure con-

PUZZLE BOTTLE, 1938
Wood construction with white and red paint, string, glass bottle
H. 12, Dia. 6 ¼ in. (H. 30.5, Dia. 16 cm)
Collection of H. Paul Blatner

sisting of individual chip-carved elements. This work has a distinct front and rear with elaborately arched entryways. Attached to a central treelike form are X-shaped panels inscribed on one side with the names "Thomas Murray/Eliza Nix" and "Savannah, Georgia"; on the reverse X shape are the inscriptions "Asleep in Jesus" and "Oh how sweet." The individual elements are painted predominantly in gold and white, with delicate stripes and polka dots of gold, blue, and green. The chip-carving technique may suggest a relationship to what has been inaccurately called "tramp art."[2] The inscriptions, as well as the object's name may indicate a memorial or funerary purpose. The term "castle in the sky"—used by a descendant of the maker—may refer to the biblical quotation, "In my father's house are many mansions" (John 14:2).

H.H.D.

1. *Puzzle bottles, possibly by sailors, are illustrated in Lynda Roscoe Hartigan et al.,* Made with Passion: The Hemphill Folk Art Collection in the National Museum of American Art *(Washington, D.C.: Smithsonian Institution Press, 1990), 182.*
2. *Tramp art objects are usually made of wood and ornamented by the carving of notches or gouges into surface texture or details. See Visual Arts Center, North Carolina State University,* This is Not Tramp Art *(Raleigh, N.C., 1993).*

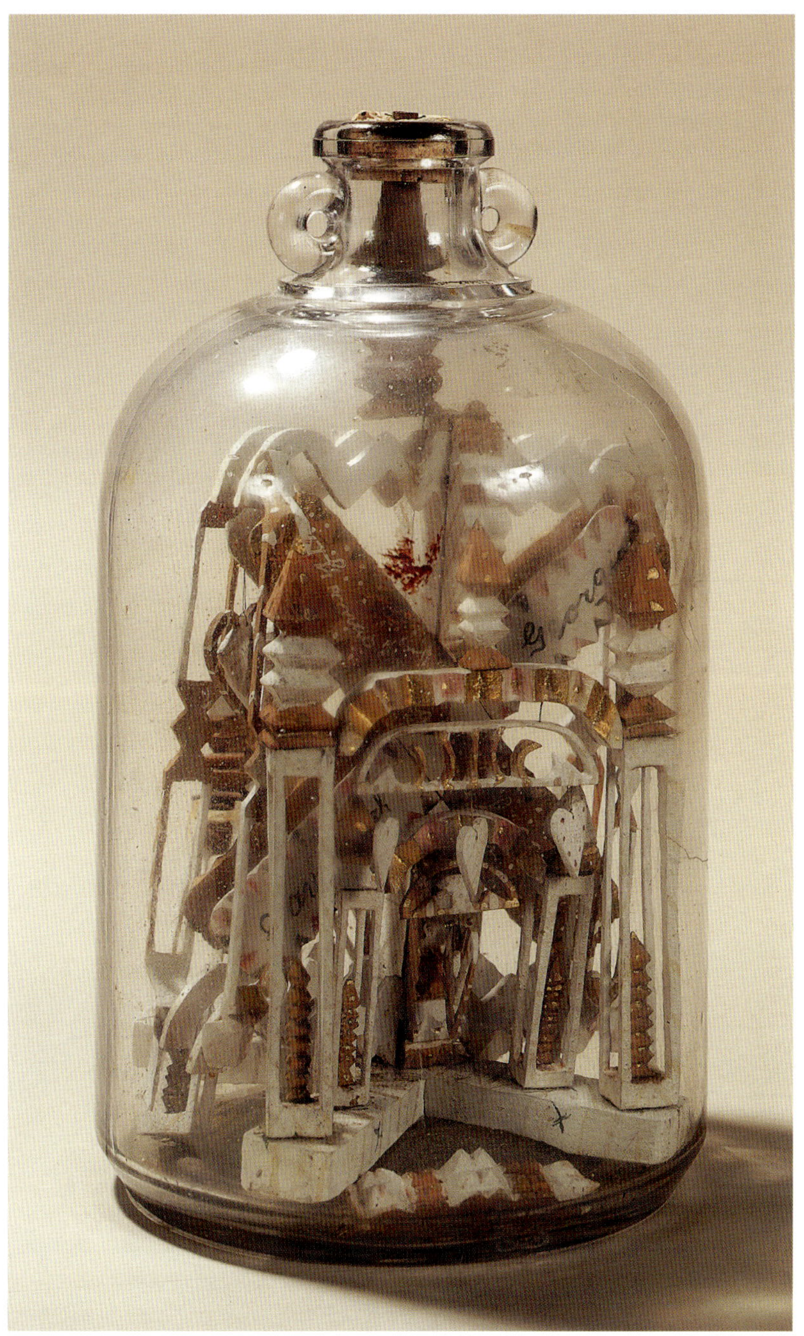

Castle in the Sky, c.1930s
Chip-carved wood construction
with white and gold paint, glass bottle
H. 11 ½, Dia. 5 ¾ in. (H. 30.5, Dia. 16 cm)
Collection of H. Paul Blatner

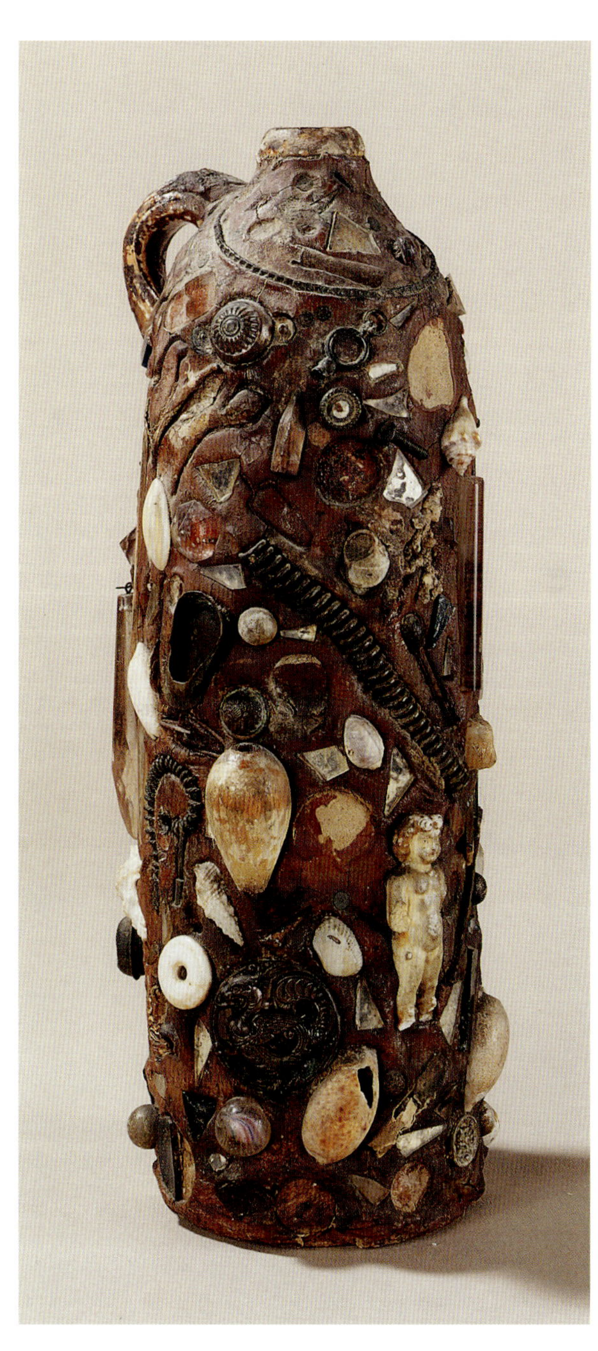

Unidentified Artist

MEMORY JUGS ARE DECORATIVE SCULPTURAL OBJECTS that date from the late nineteenth century onward. Typically, a memory jug is a ceramic bottle or jug, covered in clay or concrete, which is imbedded with a variety of objects. Whereas parallels exist in European and Victorian popular arts, African American memory jugs have been linked to the African American practice of decorating graves with broken pottery and shells and the last items used by the deceased; this is believed to ensure that the dead spirit will not return. Robert Farris Thompson and others cite the use of similar objects on Kongo graves to represent the boundary between the worlds of the living and the dead.[1] The purpose of these pieces, whether spiritual or decorative, appears to vary widely. Examples have been found throughout the United States, and memory jug-like objects have been found in both Europe and Africa. These intriguing objects may well represent a form that incorporates traditions of different origins.

According to the current owner, the Savannah *Memory Vessel* was removed by family members of the deceased from a grave at the Woodville cemetery, in an African American neighborhood in west Savannah.[2] The support is a Holland ceramic gin bottle covered in clay, into which the maker has embedded a richly significant array of objects: cowrie shells (once used as currency by Yoruba and other African peoples), broken glass of various colors, bits of mirror, springs, brass buttons, glass lamp prisms, peanut shells, animal bone fragments, figurative items (including a porcelain cameo of a woman's head in profile and a "frozen Charlotte," a popular turn-of-the-century toy), nails of various sizes, a small metal chain, coral, a baby conch, an auger shell, olive shells, a piece of reflective stone, glass and clay marbles and a bell.

H.H.D.

1. *Robert Farris Thompson,* Flash of the Spirit: African and Afro-American Art and Philosophy *(New York: Random House, 1983), 132–35.*
2. *Telephone interview with H. Paul Blatner, May 7, 1996.*

MEMORY VESSEL
Probably Savannah, c.1915
Metal, glass and porcelain objects,
bone, peanuts, and shells on clay-covered ceramic bottle
H. 12 ½, Dia. 4 ¼ in. (H. 32, Dia. 11 cm)
Collection of H. Paul Blatner

Additional Reading

For additional information on many of the artists included in the exhibition, please see the following sources:

BELCHER, HILDA

Jacqueline Calder, *The Paintings of Martha Wood Belcher and Hilda Belcher* (Montpelier: Vermont Historical Society Museum, 1993).

Hattie Saussy, "Hilda Belcher and Her Work. An Appreciation," *Savannah Morning News*, research files of the Georgia Historical Society, Savannah.

BOURKE-WHITE, MARGARET

Marianne Fulton, *Eyes of Time: Photojournalism in America* (Boston: New York Graphic Society, 1988).

Vicki Goldberg, *Margaret Bourke-White* (New York: Harper & Row, 1986).

BROOK, ALEXANDER

Dorothea Greenbaum, "Alexander Brook," *Proceedings of the American Academy and Institute of Arts and Letters* (New York: American Academy and Institute of Arts and Letters, 1981), 65–67.

Edward Alden Jewell, *Alexander Brook* (New York: Whitney Museum of American Art, 1931).

Alma S. King, *Alexander Brook (1898–1980): Looking Back* (Santa Fe, N.M.: Santa Fe East, 1981).

CABANISS, LILA

William Gerdts, *Art Across America* v. 2 (New York: Abbeville Press, 1990).

Savannah Evening Press, April 30, 1969.

CHADWICK, WILLIAM

Connecticut and American Impressionism (Storrs, Conn.: William Benton Museum of Art, 1980).

An Exhibition of Paintings by William Chadwick (Wilmington, Del.: Society of Fine Arts, 1927).

Richard H. Love, *William Chadwick, 1879–1962: An American Impressionist* (Chicago: R. H. Love Galleries, 1978).

CLARK, ELIOT

Donald D. Keyes, *Impressionism and the South* (Greenville, S.C.: Greenville County Museum of Art, 1988.)

DAVIS, ULYSSES

Virginia Kiah, "Ulysses Davis: Savannah Folk Sculptor," *Southern Folklore Quarterly* 42 (1978): 271–85.

Jane Livingston and John Beardsley, *Black Folk Art in America, 1930–1980* (Jackson: University Press of Missisippi; Washington, D.C.: Corcoran Gallery of Art, 1982).

DODD, LAMAR

Lamar Dodd, A Retrospective Exhibition (Athens: University of Georgia Press, 1970).

Lamar Dodd, Monhegan Watercolors (Atlanta: David S. Ramus, Ltd., 1987).

Gudmund Vigtel, *100 Years of Painting in Georgia* (Atlanta: Alston and Bird, 1992).

DODGE, WILLIAM DE LEFTWICH

Marjorie Balge, "William de Leftwich Dodge: American Renaissance Artist," *Art & Antiques* (January/February 1982): 96–103.

Donald D. Keyes, *Impressionism and the South* (Greenville, S.C.: Greenville County Museum of Art, 1988).

Frederick Platt, "A Brief Autobiography of William de Leftwich Dodge," *American Art Journal* 14 (spring 1982): 55–63.

EVANS, WALKER

John Szarkowski, *Walker Evans* (New York: The Museum of Modern Art, 1971).

FRENCH, DANIEL CHESTER

Michael Richman, *Daniel Chester French: An American Sculptor* (Washington, D.C.: The Preservation Press, 1976).

GARVIN, EDGERTON CHESTER

Bart St. Lawrence, "Lingering Impressions: Augusta through the Eyes of Photographer Edgerton Chester Garvin," *Augusta Magazine* 22, no. 1 (August–September 1995): 44–51.

Louise E. Shaw, *A Century of American Landscape Photography: Selections from the High Museum of Art* (Atlanta: The High Museum of Art, 1981).

Halsey, William
Jack A. Morris, Jr., *William Halsey: Retrospective* (Greenville, S.C.: Greenville County Museum of Art, 1972).

Hoffman, Harry L.
Jeffrey Andersen, *Harry L. Hoffman: A World of Color* (Old Lyme, Conn.: The Lyme Historical Society, Florence Griswold Museum, 1988).

Holzhauer, Emil
Robert Henri, *The Art Spirit* (New York: J.B. Lippincott Company, 1960).
Gudmund Vigtel, *100 Years of Painting in Georgia* (Atlanta: Alston and Bird, 1992).

Hunter, Anna
Ann Marshall, "Savannah Artist Faces Milestone," *Savannah Evening Press*. June 23, 1973, pp. 9, 12.
Margaret Minis, "Artist's Portrait," *Georgia Gazette and Journal Record*. February 12, 1979, pp. 7, 14.
"Savannah Artists to be Guest Exhibitors at Gertrude Herbert Institute Today," *Augusta (Georgia) Chronicle*, December 6, 1953.

Jones, Myrtle
Joy Gallagher, "She Captures a Certain Mood," *Savannah Morning News*, February 24, 1963.

Lane, Mary Comer
Louis T. Cheney, *Mary Comer Lane: A Retrospective Exhibition* (Savannah: Telfair Academy of Arts and Sciences, 1948).

Low, Juliette Gordon
Gladys Denny Shultz and Daisy Gordon Lawrence, *Lady from Savannah* (New York: J.B. Lippincott Company, 1958).

Murphy, Christopher A. D.
Christopher Murphy, Jr., and Walter C. Hartridge, *Savannah* (Columbia, S.C.: Bostick and Thornley, 1947).

Rogers, William
John Michael Vlach, *The Afro-American Tradition in Decorative Arts* (Athens, Ga.: Brown Thrasher Books, The University of Georgia Press, 1986).

Saussy, Hattie
Bruce Chambers, *Art and Artists of the South: The Robert P. Coggins Collection* (Columbia, S.C.: University of South Carolina Press, 1984), 34.
James C. Kelly, *The South on Paper: Line, Color, and Light* (Spartanburg, S.C.: Robert M. Hicklin, Jr., Inc., 1985), 56.
Gudmund Vigtel, *100 Years of Painting in Georgia* (Atlanta: Alston and Bird, 1992), 24.

Silva, William Posey
Donald D. Keyes, *Impressionism and the South* (Greenville, S.C.: Greenville County Museum of Art, 1988).

Simon, Walter A.
Richard A. Long et al., *Highlights from the Atlanta University Collection of Afro-American Art* (Atlanta: High Museum of Art, 1973).

Tallant, Hugh
"Services for Hugh Tallant Slated Today," *Savannah News-Press*, December 9, 1952.

Thomas, Jon Paul
"Jon Paul Thomas' Painting Wins Top Prize at Telfair," *Savannah Morning News*, May 25, 1947.
"Prizes Awarded to UGS Students for Telfair Exhibit," *Savannah Morning News*, May 27, 1947.
"Savannah Art Club Exhibit Will Open at Telfair Today," *Savannah Morning News*, May 2, 1948.

Verner, Elizabeth O'Neill
James C. Kelly, *The South on Paper: Line Color and Light* (Spartanburg, S.C.: Robert M. Hicklin, Jr. Inc., 1985), 64–65.

Wilkins, Emma Cheves
William H. Gerdts, *Art Across America: Two Centuries of Regional Painting, 1710–1920*, v. 2 (New York: Abbeville Press, 1990).
Gudmund Vigtel, *100 Years of Painting in Georgia* (Atlanta: Alston and Bird, 1992).

Telfair Museum of Art Staff

Olivia E. Alison, Curator of Decorative Arts and Owens-Thomas House

Sarah Cabaniss, Head Docent, Owens-Thomas House

Harry H. DeLorme, Jr., Curator of Education

Jane F. Espy, Financial Officer

Sandra S. Hadaway, Administrator

Joan Harwood, Shop Assistant

Eleanor S. Haynes, Housekeeper

Colleen Hodge, Assistant Curator of Education

Harry Johnquest, Gardener/Caretaker, Owens-Thomas House

Eddie Jones, Custodian, Telfair Academy

Pamela D. King, Curator of Fine Arts and Exhibitions

Diane Lesko, Director

Jennifer Marsik, Media Specialist/Administrative Assistant

Elizabeth A. Moore, Assistant Curator

Roz Neuhauser, Administrative Assistant, Owens-Thomas House

Milutin Pavlovic, Designer/Preparator

Joan Peterson, Head Gardener, Owens-Thomas House

Tania Sammons, Registrar

Kim Sams, Housekeeper, Owens-Thomas House

Letty A. Shearer, Development Officer

Thomas Strickland, Security Guard, Telfair Academy

Dee Sutlive, Museum Shop Manager, Owens-Thomas House

Agnes M. Tison, Curator Emerita

Nancy C. Warth, Front Desk Manager, Telfair Academy

Photography Credits

Every effort has been made to appropriately credit the owner or copyright holder of each image.

Most of the works in the exhibition were either photographed by Van Jones Martin for the Telfair Museum of Art or supplied by the lenders. Additional acknowledgment is due to the following:

Jeff Barnes: 83, center
Bill Burt, Old Lyme, Connecticut: cover; frontispiece; 36
Margaret Bourke-White, *Life* Magazine © Time, Inc.: 31–32, all
Camerarts, New York: 99, 100
Chromatics, Nashville: 37
Comer House Collection: 11, right
Mike Culpepper, Columbus, Georgia: 86, right
Harry H. DeLorme, Jr., Savannah: 20
Erwin Gaspin, Savannah: 64, right
Daniel L. Grantham, Jr., Graphic Communication, Savannah: 30; 34, center and top; 38; 47; 79, bottom; 106
Collection of Robert M. Hicklin, Jr.: 12
Dwight Howard, Atlanta: 40; 41, bottom left and right; 52, bottom
Peter Jacobs: 41
Joslyn Art Museum: 70
Greg Kinney, Nashville: 94, bottom
Jerry LeBlond, Rutland, Vermont: 26; 27, top
Library of Congress: 17, both; 18; 19
Melville McLean, Nelson-Atkins Museum of Art: 71
Blake Praytor, Greenville, South Carolina: 44
Keith Schreiber, Center for Creative Photography: 105
Dimitris Skliris, Wichita Art Museum: 89
William H. Struhs, Charleston: 54; 69
Brian Thena, Rudd's Camera and Video: 57

Index of Artists